# WOLF'S TALE

## MEMOIR OF A MAN NAMED WOLF

John York

# Acknowledgements

My parents, my brothers, and my sisters have always been a source of inspiration to me. I was lucky enough to come from a wonderful, loving family. My mother taught me manners and grace and how to embrace life as it's doled out to us. My father was an inspiration to me in many ways and my model of what a good man should be. My positive, enthusiastic outlook on life is a reflection of being raised in a wonderful family.

I want to thank Paula and Bruce for helping me edit this book. Any errors in punctuation or grammar are despite of their persistent efforts to keep my work free of these distracting errors. Thanks to Joyce Strand, who helped me figure out how to get a book published and with many important connections in marketing this work. Thanks also to Rachelle Ayala for getting the words in all the correct formats for publishing.

Thanks to all of the people over the years who told me, "You ought to write a book." Okay, here it is.

This book is dedicated to my best friend and my wife, Paula. Putting up with the likes of me over the years was not easy. She kept me grounded, at least as best anybody could hope for.

# Introduction

Someone once said that the world is not full of people, it is full of individuals, each with his or her own story, full of unique hopes and dreams, triumphs and failures. Demographic researchers estimate that there have been approximately 100.8 billion people who have lived and died on our planet before us. That is a lot of stories.

It's hard to think of a story that is not predicated on a particular time and place, as well as in the context of a specific backdrop of human affairs during that time and place. Even "Once Upon a Time" stories are, in fact, based on a specific time and the events that occurred or might have occurred during that time. When I think of life, my own and the lives of those around me, I can't help but think about it philosophically.

On the occasions when we need to, or really want to know an individual more intimately, it's pretty common to evaluate that person based on our personal, preconceived notion of who we think they should be, based largely on whatever social, racial, political, economic, or sexual group or groups we consider them to be part of. Furthermore, it's fairly obvious that we all project ourselves, our personal beliefs, our interests, and our emotions onto those closest to us. This is why intimate relationships with family members and close friends are so challenging. Since we are all individuals, no one can possibly live up to the other's expectations. These complicated experiences, combined with the complex world in which we live, are the stuff that make the stories of individuals so interesting.

This is the story of one man's life in the context of the world he lives in, as told from his unique perspective. His story takes place over a specific period of modern time that reflects many changes in world events, cultural norms, styles, politics, and all of the things that had the potential to color and influence all of our lives. It is a story of how this man evolves, revealing all his personal dreams and motivations, as well as his shortcomings and flaws. In other words, this is a story of a relatively typical person, not a storybook hero or a tragic figure. It's a collection of the stories that developed as he lived his life.

What may be unique about this man is that he tried his hand at so many things during his life, things that he thought were worth doing. Unlike Thurber's Walter Mitty, the man in this story did not live his life vicariously through fantastic daydreams. While our main character certainly daydreamed frequently, and big daydreams at that, he dove into his daydreams like jumping off a cliff with an impulsive enthusiasm that many would call reckless. He seemed to subconsciously rely on the proverbial wings of fate, which he trusted would take him to wherever his destiny awaited.

The poet, Mary Oliver, concludes her beautiful poem, *The Summer Day*, with this question: "Tell me what it is you plan to do with your one wild and precious life?" In fact, our main character didn't really analyze his life's choices all that much. He just lived each day enthusiastically, and that makes his story interesting.

# Part I

## The Boy

*I once was a young boy*
*I had some toys*
*Like all little boys*
*I played at make believe*

# Chapter 1

The old man was sitting at his desk, preparing to write the story of his life. He was struggling with his memory though, having difficulty distinguishing between fact and fantasy – unsure about the embellishments of all the stories he had told over his life, where they began and where they ended. As his mind drifted, he reflected on this feeling that had been nagging him lately, that in the autumn of his life, things seemed so anti-climactic. Yet, he felt at peace, and he was certainly not unhappy. There was, however, a persistent notion that there was still more to be done, more to come. He guessed that writing this story must be that "next thing".

Thinking back through the years, some parts of his life now seemed more like a movie, maybe one he might have watched, or a book he might have read. His time at the Catholic seminary in Santa Fe, the combat tours in Viet Nam and Thailand, the year he spent in Alaska trying to get work on the pipeline, the "pirate period" of his life in South Florida. Those events, and the people involved, were increasingly difficult to bring into focus. Then there was his time in the restaurant business, the bodybuilding competitions, his college degree, the "real job" career in computer science, the music, the fire department, the ranch and the winery. He had been married four times, and had a daughter. There was a lot to remember.

Yes, his life had been full of significant events and adventure, likely more than the average person, he thought. He felt compelled to write about his life. After all, people had often told him "You should write a book about your life," didn't they?

So, here he was trying to recall if there was actually anything worth writing about. Perhaps it was best he could not recall all of the details after all. He would just add a little embellishment here, an exaggeration there, just like he had done in the past when telling his stories to friends. It would make the story that much more interesting he thought.

# Chapter 2

I recall an observation that somebody famous once made regarding adventure. Maybe it was Sir Edmond Hillary. Adventure usually involved doing something unpleasant that you didn't really want to be doing at the time, but was jolly good fun to recall to your friends when it was over.

I have never purposely pursued adventure for the sake of adventure. On the contrary, I consider myself to be a risk adverse, generally cautious person. I am, however, somewhat impulsive, which I suppose could lead to unexpected experiences that one might later call an adventure. I would like to think the goals that I set in my life were inspired, but then that would probably be an exaggeration. In fact, most of my experiences have been the result of spontaneous, impulsive ideas that quickly evolved into a vague notion of something I thought was worth doing. Before I took the time to think through the idea, I was typically well on my way toward just doing it.

When I was quite young, I once heard my mother tell one of my teachers that I was "flighty". I mulled that assessment over and over in my head, but I honestly couldn't figure out what she meant by that at the time. In retrospect, however, I suppose that this trait might have contributed to the relatively large number of things that I've tried to do in my life.

I suppose I have to admit that I am a bit of a ham. I also must confess that I crave attention, acceptance, and recognition. Perhaps it has something to do with growing up in a large family, where one has to compete for attention, or that I was the first-born and felt compelled to be the center of attention. Whatever the reason, I've often made decisions in my life simply to attract attention and gain admiration. Not particularly admirable, I know, but this candid introspection helps to unravel and explain some of the amazing twists and turns of my life.

My parents named me Wolf, Wolf O'Brian. I never thought to ask them why they decided to give me such an unusual name, perhaps because my brothers and sisters were also given rather uncommon names. Well, more so for me and my brothers. Our parents apparently thought that impressive, powerful animals would be a good source of names for the boys. My brothers were named Bear and Tiger. I guess I should be thankful they didn't decide to name us Ichabod or Ebenezer. When my sisters were born, my parents thought flowers would be a more suitable source for feminine names, and so my sisters were named Violet and Daisy.

Our names just seemed normal to us as we grew up. At various stages of our lives we all suffered some level of ridicule because of these names, especially the boys, but I like to think that this helped us to build a strong personal character. Going through life with the name Wolf compels one to behave in a manner that lives up to the potential expectations that others have in a person with such a name. At least that's what I chose to think.

Aristotle said, "Some kinds of animals burrow in the ground; others do not. Some animals are nocturnal, as the owl and the bat; others use the hours of daylight. There are tame animals and wild animals. Man and the mule are always tame; the leopard and the wolf are invariably wild." I think perhaps I was destined to live what many might think of as a relatively wild life.

Being the first born in my family, I considered it to be my God-given role to provide leadership to my siblings. Of course one has to rule with a firm hand in a large family, and I honed my leadership skills to a fine point with my brothers and sisters at a very young age. I felt that my mother encouraged this trait since she always exhorted me to watch over them and protect them, especially my sisters. I also imposed this leadership role on any cousins and neighborhood children who came within my reach. As a result of this early, mostly successful experience, I always assumed a leadership attitude in most of the things I have attempted to do in my life. I discovered very early that most people want to be led. Well, perhaps it's just that most people allow themselves to be led.

# Chapter 3

While I did not seek adventure for adventure's sake, there was plenty of opportunity for a young boy to find adventure in the mid-west Ohio farm country where I grew up. Exploring the woods in the back of the family farm, building elaborate tunnels and forts from bales of hay in the old barn's hay mow, or hunting for crawdads in the creek were all typical boyhood activities that filled our days back in the fifties. Building forts was one of the more alluring pursuits in those days. I recall getting a pretty good beating when a neighbor's tractor fell into a hole that I and "the gang" had dug and then covered up to serve as an underground fort.

Starting a zoo was also a favorite pastime. Somebody would find an animal such as a salamander or a baby rabbit, and that would be the catalyst for getting the gang to go collect other specimens. The menagerie would always include creatures such as frogs, tadpoles, crawdads, garter snakes, and turtles. These were not hard to find where we lived. These would be augmented with a duck and a chicken borrowed from the farm, a cat or two, and Weezer, our beagle. We would set up all our exhibits, and then cajole our parents to come visit the zoo, trying to exact a small entrance fee of five cents. The parents were usually good natured about the game, but it would always end with them ordering us to "let the poor creatures go". Life was simple. Life was good.

In those days, parents didn't shuttle their children around to organized sports or swimming lessons or all those sorts of things that today's parents are consumed with. In those days, you were shuttled out the back door after breakfast and told not to come in the house unless you had to use the bathroom or were called in for lunch. Kids made up their own games and entertainment.

Television started to become fairly common in American households when I was very young. I clearly remember my dad bringing home our first TV. It was a really big deal. We weren't allowed to watch TV unless my mother or dad specifically allowed it to be turned on, which was usually in the evening when my parents wanted to watch Jack Paar or the Honeymooners. We kids were allowed to watch an hour or so of TV on Saturday morning. There were cartoons, which my dad happened to enjoy, but my favorite show of all was Tarzan Theater, Saturday morning at 7:00 am.

I loved Tarzan and wanted to be like him. After watching one of those movies, I would often make my way to the woods behind our house and pretend I was Tarzan. I would take off my shirt and pants, and run around the woods in my underwear, climbing trees and calling out, "Simba, bundalo. Where Cheeta?" Two days later, I would be covered from head to toe with blisters from Poison Ivy. My mother could not fathom how I could become so thoroughly stricken with this rash, and accused me of purposely rolling around in the plant. I learned quickly how to avoid the awful stuff.

My neighborhood "gang" consisted of my brother, my sister, occasional cousins, some neighbor girls, and Francesco. Francesco was the oldest son of Italian immigrants who lived about a half mile down the country road we lived on. I was probably 4 or 5 when Francesco and I first met.

Francesco didn't speak much English then. His mother didn't speak any English. His father, Vito, was a bartender who worked at night in a tavern down in Columbus. Vito was always sleeping during the day, so we had to play outside to ensure that it was quiet in their house. Francesco also had a bunch of sisters, who I would entertain by eating dog food out of giant sack, they kept for their equally giant Great Dane. Over time I learned to speak a tiny bit of Italian and Francesco learned English.

Francesco was the only boy in the immediate vicinity who was not a relative, so we developed a close friendship and spent a lot of time together. When we were 10 years old or so, he introduced me to another, older boy, Bobby, who lived another half mile further down the road from Francesco's house. Bobby was a transplant from the city and he was cut from an entirely different mold from us. I think in those days he would have been considered a "greaser", as opposed to a jock or a nerd. Francesco and I definitely fit into the nerd class, but even worse, we weren't teenagers yet, and still worse, we were country hicks. That's what Bobby said we were. He was probably 14, whereas Francesco and I were still just kids. From Bobby's perspective we were at the lowest level in the social order.

Nevertheless, he would occasionally lower himself to socialize with us. After all, out there in farm country we were his only option. I am pretty sure that Francesco and I were looked upon as mere minions by the cool and domineering Bobby.

One summer night, when I was spending the night at Francesco's house, Bobby showed up at the bedroom window. He tapped lightly on the window pane, scaring the shit out of us both. Francesco got out of bed and opened the window.

"Get up and get dressed," Bobby whispered. "I've got my old man's car and we're going to go cruising."

"What's that mean?" I asked.

"Don't be a dork," Bobby hissed. "Get your asses dressed and hurry up."

Not stopping, even for a moment, to consider the consequences of leaving the house in the middle of the night, through a bedroom window, we obediently complied. We quietly snuck through the yard and out through a back gate. There on the side of the road, as promised, was Bobby's father's brand new 1958 Ford Thunderbird, with a turquoise body and a white convertible top. Even 10-year-old kids knew that this was a very cool car. This cruising thing might be pretty cool.

We all got into the car. I was relegated to the back seat. Bobby manipulated some controls on the dashboard and the top of the car began to lift up and back into a forward compartment of the trunk. It was amazing! Bobby turned on the radio to the Wolfman Jack show. I knew Wolfman Jack was famous, but my parents never listened to him. With a name like Wolfman, I figured he had to be great. This was going to be a fun experience, I thought.

"We've got to get some gas," Bobby said. "My old man can't know that we used any gas, so we'll have to get some."

At age 10, I was not familiar with such matters, but I was sure that Bobby would know how and where to get gas. I wasn't sure what he meant by his "old man" either. I wondered why he would have an old man and why this person would care about the gas. Neither Francesco nor I said anything. He drove off into the night. There was a moon high above providing a soft, pale light across the surrounding countryside. Although this was my very first experience with taking a cruise, I was sure that this was the perfect night for such a thing.

About a mile or so down the road, Bobby pulled over to the side of the road, turned off the headlights, and turned the ignition off. There was a driveway barely visible just ahead.

"Come on, get out," Bobby called in a low voice as he opened the car door and headed toward the trunk.

Francesco immediately got out of the car. I sat there a moment, suddenly feeling a bit uneasy.

"Hurry up, dork," Bobby hissed back at me, "and keep quiet."

As I approached the back of the car, Bobby was handing Francesco a small gas can and a hose he had extracted from the trunk.

"This guy's got a truck that he keeps by the barn in back of the house. Fill this can up from that truck. If the house lights come on, head for the woods. I'll have to take off."

I stood there in total confusion. I had been to the gas station with my dad. I knew how you got gas, so this didn't compute. Was there a gas pump in the truck? What did he mean he would have to take off if the lights came on? Head for the woods? Suddenly our midnight cruise didn't seem as attractive.

"I don't know what to do," I whined.

"Francesco does. Just do what he tells you to do," Bobby replied impatiently.

I looked at Francesco, but he was already heading toward the driveway. He still hadn't said anything since leaving his house. He was apparently just doing the master's bidding. Maybe he had done this before.

We walked slowly up the drive, past the house and toward the silhouette of a barn that was beginning to emerge in the shadowed light of the moon. We found the truck, just as Bobby had predicted. So far, no lights. Francesco stopped next to the truck, put the can on the ground, and removed the truck's external gas cap. He stuck the hose down into the gas tank and looked over to me. I was still confused and disoriented, and now I was beginning to feel a growing sense of foreboding. I had pretty much figured out what was about to happen.

He handed the hose to me, and whispered, "You suck on the hose until gas comes out and then you stick the hose into the can."

What else could I do? I was merely a minion. I put the end of the hose in my mouth and sucked. It was just a moment later that I discovered what a bad idea this method of obtaining gas really was. I violently spit gasoline from my mouth, certain that I had just initiated my own death. I totally forgot the part where I was supposed to put the hose into the gas can. Francesco grabbed the hose from my hand and completed the clandestine process. I continued to spit and gasp for clean air, tears now streaming from my eyes. He pulled the hose from the truck, calmly replaced the truck's gas cap, drained all the contents from the hose into the can, and replaced the can's lid.

"Let's go," he whispered, and ran back toward the car.

I reflexively ran to join him, wondering if I would live long enough to make it back to the car. We reached the Thunderbird where Bobby took charge of the gas can and the rest of the fueling operation. I stood there in a wretched state of combined terror and misery, trying not to let Francesco, and especially Bobby, see that I was a cry baby, dorky, ten-year-old. Once the gas was in the car, the can and hose were returned to the trunk and we resumed our midnight cruise. They sat in the front laughing and punching each other's arm in a conspiratorial manner. I sat quietly in the back seat wondering if I would ever have feeling in my mouth again.

Fortunately, the car was a convertible and the top was down. I'm certain that I would not have survived the closed space of a back seat given my gasoline saturated circumstance. As it was, the fresh night air helped me slowly recover my sensibilities and realize that I might not die after all, at least not imminently. I eventually also recovered my composure.

My mother would say, "That which does not kill us, makes us stronger." Based on this experience, I felt that I was destined to become nearly superhuman over the years. She might also ask, "If everyone else jumped off the Empire State Building, would you?" Although at that young age, I wasn't sure what an Empire State Building was, but I was pretty sure that it was probably not a good idea to jump off of it. My mother was the queen of cliché. She had one for every occasion. One of her most repeated sayings was "live for today, for tomorrow you may die". I took that suggestion to heart throughout my life.

After hearing of this, however, Mother would simply advise me that Bobby was too old for me to associate with and a "bad influence". She would probably be right. I could see the wisdom of that advice now. I decided right then and there that my midnight cruising days were over.

# Chapter 4

I started taking piano lessons when I was around that same age. My dad played the piano, as did my Uncle Jim. When they played, we all listened and my mother would say complimentary things about their music. I wanted some of that admiration. I knew that our neighbor's daughter, Marsha, was taking piano lessons. I convinced my mother to retain Marsha's piano teacher so that I could begin receiving formal lessons.

I hated piano lessons. I soon discovered that the process is very structured and very boring, but even worse, the songs were stupid. My dad and my uncle played very exciting stuff and that's what I wanted to do. As it turned out, I was lousy at learning how to read music, but I had a strong, inherent ability to play songs "by ear". So I could mimic the assigned lessons after hearing my piano teacher, Cecil, play them. I struggled through the music exercises, but played the assigned songs perfectly.

Since getting attention and praise from my parents was my primary motivation, I decided that I would use my newly discovered skill to play something that I had heard my dad or uncle play. I arbitrarily chose a number that I had heard my uncle play many times, called "Meditation". I asked Cecil if he could obtain the sheet music for this composition and he good naturedly brought it to me one afternoon. It was like the *War and Peace* of sheet music, consisting of five pages of notes that were several magnitudes of complexity above my piano lesson book. After the initial shock, I was not really that intimidated because I couldn't read music anyway.

The day came when all of Cecil's students were to perform in a recital. That was a very big deal to me because it provided an opportunity to get the attention of lots of people. I had never done anything like that in front of a whole room full of people. The song I was assigned to perform was called "The Donkey Trail", or something dumb like that. Cecil made me practice and practice until I thought I would die of boredom. Secretly, I had been rehearsing "Meditation", and on the "big day", I thought I was ready to play this piece as an encore.

There was, in fact. no provision for doing encores in the kid recital. But I had seen Liberace do it on TV, so I knew how it was done. As it turned out, I was the last kid scheduled to play on the recital program. The big day came and we were all assembled in a school auditorium with what seemed like hundreds of families out in the audience sitting on folding chairs. Each kid performed his little, dumb kid number to polite applause. Then, it was my turn.

When I walked out on stage and saw all the people, I became instantly terrified. I hadn't really considered the impact of so many people focused on me, expecting me to do something entertaining. I was more of a spontaneous performer. Okay, I was a show-off. No backing out now though. I sat at the piano and dutifully played my donkey song without any actual recollection of what I was doing. At the end I stood up and faced the audience, who were dutifully applauding, and beginning to make slight movements toward the table of cookies and drinks at the back of the room. From the corner of my eye, I saw Cecil coming out on the stage for some parting comments.

I turned around and sat back down on the piano bench, and put my hands in the ready position on the keyboard. I saw Cecil stop dead in his tracks, hands in mid-clap. The room had gone dead silent. My heart was beating as if it would burst from my chest, but I was determined to play the damn song. I started to play.

With Herculean effort, beyond the capabilities of any mortal nine-and-a-half-year-old boy, I focused my whole being on playing "Meditation" without making any mistakes. It takes about 10 minutes to complete this piece, and the ending includes a whole sheet of thirty-second notes played an octave apart. Did I mention that at age nine I had hands the size of dinner plates? Despite the odds, I completed the piece flawlessly. Well, let's say I didn't make any obvious mistakes that this audience would detect. I sat there on the bench. The room was still silent. Cecil was still standing on the stage as if he had become a statue. I had a moment of panic. Perhaps an encore at a kid recital was something that one just didn't do.

Suddenly, the room erupted into loud applause of genuine admiration and, no doubt, amazement. Cecil ran up to me and grabbed my shoulder, bubbling over with agitated praise. I was in my glory. I turned around to take my bow and saw my mother and father moving toward the stage, big smiles on their faces. I jumped down off the stage to greet them and my mother hugged me. Then one of the most memorable moments of my life occurred. My father took my hand and shook it, saying, "good job, Son." It was the first time he had ever shaken my hand and I could tell he was genuinely proud of me. The day had exceeded every expectation I had dared to daydream about.

Looking back, I'm sure that my parents thought they had a child prodigy on their hands. As it turned out, however, I didn't play the piano again until I was in my fifties. I couldn't face the prospect of more lessons. Perhaps that's what my mother meant about being my being flighty. I'm pretty sure that this was among the first of many disappointments my parents experienced over me.

# Chapter 5

I tell people that I grew up in a *Leave It To Beaver* family environment. If you are a Baby Boomer, you know that this refers to an iconic TV family known as the Cleavers who exemplified the idealized suburban family of the mid-20$^{th}$ century. Although my family lived in a rural setting, there were many aspects of the Cleavers that mirrored my memories of our family life. Dad went to work every day, Monday through Friday. Mother stayed home to keep the house and raise our large family. We all sat down to dinner as a family every evening. We all went to church every Sunday. On most summer days, my brothers and sisters and I joined the few kids who lived close by to play outdoors the entire day. As I got older, I had to work during the summer, often on the family farm. There were rules to be followed, manners to be minded, and lots of love. It was a good, wholesome life.

In a time when there were no computers, restricted TV, no cell phones, not much money for toys, and no such thing as parents ferrying their children to organized sports every day, kids were expected to entertain themselves. We were instructed to stay outside until called in for lunch or dinner. If a summer storm blew up, we were expected to play in the nearest garage or barn.

In the afternoon, on most hot summer days my mother would bring out a milk bottle full of Kool-Aid and a stack of Dixie Cups. We would all share this sugary treat with gratitude and delight. On some occasions, Mother would freeze the Kool-Aid in ice trays and serve the frozen cubes in colored aluminum cups. It was a big deal. Each kid had claim to their own color, which had been worked out in kid fashion over the years. God help the kid who grabbed a cup that was not their assigned color. My youngest brother had to use the yellow cup. Once, when we were on a family trip, he had to pee, but my dad didn't want to stop, so my mother had him do it in the yellow cup. Need I say more?

While this kind of arrangement might sound like cruel and unusual punishment to future generations, the lifestyle was idyllic to those of us who lived it. We had freedom that would probably be considered close to neglect in present times. We all had bicycles which were necessary to travel the expansive distances to friends' homes or to get to the little country store.

The country store was a good two miles from our home and was the only vestige of civilization in what seemed like a thousand miles. On the very rare occasion when somebody came into the possession of dime, a selected few would be chosen to accompany that person to the store to participate in the ritual consumption of candy and soda pop. With a dime, one could purchase a 16 ounce bottle of RC Cola, and a candy bar. Since candy bars were difficult to divide into suitable portions, something like Necco Wafers was usually selected because it consisted of lots of individual pieces of candy. This combination resulted in the ingestion of a substantial amount of glorious sugar. For us, it was not about quality. It was all about quantity.

Since having any money at all was quite rare, most of the daily wandering involved getting to somebody's house, or exploring the country roads, or visiting the creek. The creek had a special allure that was irresistible to kids, but highly suspect to mothers. The creek was a place where you could hunt for crawdads, or fish for Bluegill, or catch tadpoles and frogs. There were hidden bends where little pools had formed that were quite suitable for swimming. The creek was a mysterious place, shrouded by trees and other vegetation. Wild animals of all kinds could be found along the creek, including raccoon, possum, muskrat, mink, and deer. It was easy to find turtles sunning themselves on logs in and along the creek.

The creek was also a place of potential danger, as our mothers would often warn us. They would tell us that there were snapping turtles that could bite a kid's hand or foot off. There might be wild dogs with rabies, leaches in the water, snakes, and worst of all, hobos and bums. The definition of hobos and bums was a little vague to us kids, but our mothers described them as something akin to trolls. They might live under bridges, and God only knows what would happen if they caught you.

The default rule was, you could not go to the creek unless you told your mother that you wanted to go, that somebody was going to go with you, and you actually got permission to go. Permission came with an obligatory litany of warnings and prohibitions, including instructions not to park your bike along the road where it might get stolen.

# Chapter 6

I woke up one summer morning to a blue sky filled with puffy white clouds, the kind that you can look at and imagine you see all kinds of shapes that remind you of other things. It was the day I had planned to go to the creek with Francesco to see an old metal boat that had washed up on the bank near the bridge where we always accessed the creek. He called me the night before to tell me that he and Bobby had discovered it. It sounded quite intriguing and I felt it demanded my personal inspection.

That night I asked my mother if I could go to the creek the next day and she gave a hesitant "we'll see" response. I took that as a "yes", but the final permission might require some cleaver manipulation. I told Francesco that it was a go and we set a time of around 10:00 am. I would ride my bike to his house and we would head for the creek from there.

When I got out of bed the next morning and got dressed, I made sure to be particularly polite and attentive to my mother. I asked if there was anything I could help her with. I did little helpful things around the kitchen like getting cereal for my youngest brother, helping to feed my baby sister, wiping her food encrusted face, and just generally being my most charming self.

At the appropriate moment, when I felt sure that Mother was in a good mood I asked, "Oh by the way, can I go to the creek this morning with Francesco. We wanted to go fishing."

I could have won an Oscar for my affected nonchalance. She didn't say anything for several moments, obviously weighing the options that only a mother can think of.

Finally she said, "Yes, but you have to take your brother, Bear."

*What?* I thought, but had the good sense not to say it out loud. Good Grief! This could ruin everything, but this condition had caught me off guard and I couldn't think of any convincing reason to object. My brother, Bear, and I were normally on good terms. He could be quite rebellious of my big brother authority at times, but all in all he was okay to play with. He could actually be useful at times for fetching things for me or doing other small favors.

"OK," I said with as much cheer as I could muster, staring at him with a "you better appreciate this" look.

We went out to the garage to collect fishing gear and our bikes. We had to make a detour to the septic system's leach field out behind the house to dig up some earthworms for bait. This was easy work since the ground was always soft and full of worms. The worms were secured in a glass jar.

We peddled down the country road to Francesco's house. He was nowhere in sight so that meant we had to go through the front gate and across the yard, fending off the gauntlet of dogs that always roamed their property. The German Shepard was the scariest, with all his ferocious snarling and snapping. You couldn't turn your back on him or you'd lose a piece of your ass. Ironically, the dog that did the most damage was the very friendly Great Dane. While you backed up toward the house, keeping your eye on the Shepard, the Great Dane would come up behind you in eager greeting, simulating a good hard spanking with his whipping tail. Joining in the mayhem were various smaller dogs, all barking furiously and nipping at your heels. While all of this chaos was common when visiting Francesco, it was no less terrifying.

Before we reached the house, Francesco came out and yelled at the dogs, which immediately retreated to the back yard. Close call, but we were no worse for the wear. Francesco grabbed his bike and we were off to the creek.

At 9:30 in the morning, the air was already warm, but there was a pleasant breeze blowing. The sounds and smells of the countryside were abundant. The loud drumming song of the cicadas came from all directions. In those days there were flocks of birds everywhere and they filled the air with songs and cheeps and chirps. The scent of grasses and wild flowers mingled with the faint smell of barnyards. Even at my young age, I was acutely aware of these things and I felt sure it was going to be a glorious day.

The creek was about two miles down the road and we arrived there soon after we left Francesco's house. We pushed our bikes off the road, down toward the creek and hid them in some brush, away from the bridge. This was the same spot we always went to when we visited the creek.

This was Blacklick Creek, named by Native Americans who noticed the animals that frequented the creek licked its black-colored salt stones. It is a rock and slate-bed creek, which made it a good place to find crawdads, which resemble tiny lobsters. It was fun just to find and catch crawdads for no other reason than the thrill of the hunt, but they were also very good to use as bait. The creek was a good source of fish, including catfish, bluegill, and bass.

Today, however, our mission was to recover the old metal boat that Francesco and Bobby had discovered. I wanted to see if we could get it to float. Francesco led us to where this treasure lay half hidden. We stood there looking at it for a few moments. To call it a boat seemed a bit of a stretch. It was about 10 feet long, made of very thin, very rusty metal. It sported a number of well distributed holes in the hull, pretty much guaranteeing it was unseaworthy.

"Is that it?" Bear asked incredulously.

"Yeah," Francesco replied.

"I don't think it's going to float," I said, investing a few more moments of critical appraisal. "Well, let's drag it out where we can get a closer look at it."

With all the energy that only kids full of unreasonable optimism are capable of mustering, we laboriously dragged the hulk out of the tangle of weeds and water-logged deadfall and onto the edge of the creek. Despite its flimsy appearance it was surprisingly heavy. We studied it carefully and opined about the potential to patch it up before giving up the project as hopeless.

We distracted ourselves from our disappointment with a half-hearted hunt for crawdads, traveling up the creek in search of the ideal crawdad habitat. I noticed a distinctive looking log wedged along the opposite shore just a little farther upstream. It looked like it had been cut from a large tree as it was clean cut at one end with a kind of natural point at the other end. It might have been a tree that had been struck by lightning, splitting it down the middle. The tree must have been hollow because there was a cavity most of the way down the split. As I stood there studying this curious marvel, I realized that this was essentially a natural canoe. Okay, well that might be a bit of a stretch, but it warranted closer inspection, and, after all, we were in a nautical frame of mind.

I pointed out my observation to Francesco and Bear. They quickly recognized its potential and we set about getting this thing free of its natural moorings. We took off our shoes and waded across the creek. The water was not deep where it was lodged and it was not long before we had it floating toward a spot clear of brush and other entanglements.

It was a pure wonderment! It had to be at least twelve feet long and over three feet wide. There were four or five short branches that stuck out from its sides to form crude outriggers. The front of the log was slightly narrowed and pointed upward. There were only about six inches of hollow space inside the log boat, but we quickly surmised that it would be adequate for our fishing gear and shoes. It was heavy, but not so heavy that the three of us couldn't handle it as long as it was floating. The creek was swollen with summer rains, so there was plenty of water to support this ungainly craft.

I suggested that we try it out and the others readily agreed. We pushed it out into the creek and set to the task of figuring out how to get ourselves up on the thing. It took some effort and cooperative coordination, but eventually the three of us sat astride the log and it began to float lazily down the creek.

After a few moments of basking in the glory of our accomplishment, I had the foresight to realize we needed to stop and make a plan. I said as much, and we paddled toward the shore, using our hands as oars.

"We're going to need some kind of paddles or poles to steer this thing where we want it to go," I said. "Look around for something we could use. Let's also put our fishing stuff in the hollow."

The others set about this task, while I collected our fishing gear. Three stout sticks were found that would serve nicely as our poles. We stashed our shoes close to the bikes and re-boarded our yacht. We knew all too well that losing or ruining your shoes was right up there among the worst things a kid could do.

"Let's not go too far. We can float down past the bridge to see what's down there. We can find a place where we can get out of the creek and walk back here," I said.

# Chapter 7

Neither Francesco nor my brother had any objection to my plan, nor did they have any better plan for that matter, so off we went. In the past, we had always kept our exploration of the creek to the north of the bridge. There was no particular reason for this that I can recall, that was just the way it was. Now, however, we were contemplating an unprecedented venture to the south. At the time, that didn't seem like a consequential decision. I don't think we were even conscious of the possibilities of exploring new, unfamiliar territory. We just needed someplace to float our boat, and downstream was the only realistic option.

As we glided under the bridge, we fell quiet. I don't know about Francesco and my brother, but I admit was looking for trolls. Fortunately, none were forthcoming and we floated past the bridge unscathed. We all got caught up in the excitement of navigating our crude boat into this new territory. Since the creek was seasonally swollen with summer rain, the current was sufficient to propel us at a speed that relieved us from any strenuous poling. We only had to occasionally fend off of snags and shallow points around bends in the creek.

Before long we came upon an idyllic pool, carved out of a bank at a bend in the creek. Large trees surrounded the pool and shaded the water with their abundant canopy. A couple of large fallen trees lay at one edge of the pool, half submerged in the water. Along the exposed surface of the logs, several turtles were sunning themselves. They all dove into the creek at our approach. We noticed signs of fish breaking the surface of the glassy pool and decided this would be a good place to try our luck at fishing.

We steered our boat to the shallow edge of the pool at the point bar of the creek's bend and began getting our fishing gear ready. Our tackle was simply bamboo poles with line tied to the skinny end of the pole. A hook, a lead sinker, and a bobber completed the rig. Simple, but effective in these waters. Sitting there on our log boat, we cast our lines toward the deep end of the pool. I had the foresight to grab a package of graham crackers as I left the house that morning. I thought this was a good time to break out the snacks and offered them to my shipmates. Ah, this was indeed the good life.

Sitting there focused on our bobbers, I caught a movement out of the corner of my eye. On closer inspection I realized that a duck had swum into view from downstream and was heading toward the deep end of the pool. The others now noticed it as well. I was thinking this intruder might scare away our chances for catching a fish when suddenly, with a brief but furious commotion and a desperate sound that you don't normally hear from a duck, it disappeared violently from sight, into the depths.

"Whoa! Did you see that?" we all exclaimed together.

We immediately withdrew our feet from the water and sat there expectantly, waiting to see something further that might explain what just happened, but the calm, smooth surface of the pool eventually recovered itself and there was no evidence that a duck had ever been there.

Well, it was quite disconcerting to be sure, and we decided we should move on down to less inhospitable territory. We considered abandoning the adventure then and there, but there was no obvious way out of the creek from this area. Both sides of the steep creek embankment were covered in thick underbrush. Since we had left our shoes by our bikes, the prospect of exiting the creek in these conditions didn't seem practical.

We pushed our craft back into the creek, carefully keeping our feet up out of this now, very suspicious water. The "pool of death", as we started calling it, was soon left behind. We all agreed that we needed to look for a place to get out of the creek. The natural barricade along the shore, however, continued to foil us. The banks seemed to be getting higher and up ahead we could see that there were some rapids. Rapids! Now that was pretty cool.

We temporarily lost interest in escape and began building up enthusiasm for traveling down some actual rapids. It was a relatively small creek, so the rapids were quite tame and fairly shallow. After sizing things up, we all agreed that this was doable and prepared to enjoy the thrill of the ride. Unfortunately, we did not anticipate the limitations of a heavy log as an appropriate vehicle for shooting rapids. The log beached itself in the middle of the whitewater. Try as we might, we could not get the log to budge from its new berth. We were forced to abandon ship.

Now we were faced with a dilemma. Nobody wanted to go back upstream because that would mean having to go through the "the pool of death". My little brother flatly refused to go back to that place. As we looked downstream, we could see the banks of the creek grew ever higher preventing any obvious exit. We decided to continue in that direction since there seemed to be no other viable alternative.

We spent most of the time wading in the water. What there was of a shore provided little room to walk on dry land. After some considerable distance, navigating several bends in the creek, we came upon an amazing sight. A small waterfall blocked our path. It was probably only four or five feet from top to bottom and the water was not particularly deep at the top of the falls. It was, in fact, an interesting distraction from our plight. After some closer inspection, it appeared that a person could climb down one side of the falls using exposed flat rocks as foot and hand holds. The rocks were slippery wet and potentially dangerous, so I sent my little brother down to determine their viability. He survived without mishap so I followed. Francesco came down after me.

It had become an uncomfortably hot day, but the mist generated by the falls was very cool and refreshing. There was a small pool at the bottom of the falls and we decided that this was an ideal spot for a swim. We removed our T-shirts, but left our jeans on and jumped in. It was glorious.

Refreshed, we pulled our shirts back on and trudged onward. The geography around the creek abruptly changed from smooth, flat rocks to small, crumbly shale. It crumbled to the touch and made our footing more precarious. The banks on either side of the creek rose steeply into shale cliffs of 25 or 30 feet. Now there was no shore at all other than the cliffs.

Just then, we heard a loud clap of thunder, so loud it made all three of us flinch. A summer storm was coming up. As country boys, we all new instinctively that this could be a big problem. If the storm brought heavy rain, we could be swept up in a torrent with no apparent way to get out of the creek. We redoubled our effort at moving downstream.

The rain came and with it our anxiety soared. Now we were wet, soaked to the bone, and the air temperature had dropped precipitously. The rainfall intensified. I noticed a small, scrubby tree trying to grow from a muddy spot where the creek made a slight bend.

"Let's get to that little tree and wait this out," I cried over the noise of the rain. "We might be able to use it to hold on if the creek suddenly rises."

"Yeah, that's a good idea," Francesco agreed. My brother looked stricken. If he was crying, I couldn't tell considering his face was wet from rain.

# Chapter 8

The rain began to let up, but it was apparent the creek was indeed beginning to rise. It got up to our knees when a wonderful thing happened. Upstream, maybe a couple hundred feet away, I saw our log boat floating toward us.

"Look," I yelled. "It's our boat!"

There was no telling how deep the water was away from our little tree sanctuary, but, since we were just at the point bar of the creek bend, the log was headed right for us. When it came near us we lunged and grabbed hold of it with one arm, tossing our fishing poles into the hollow with the other. We may have been scared out of our wits, but kids knew better than to lose stuff like your dad's fishing poles.

We hung on for dear life, occasionally hitting the bottom of the creek with our feet. The rain driven current was moving us along at an impressive speed. As suddenly as it had started the rain stopped. Within fifteen or twenty minutes the creek level began to lower and the current slowed. Eventually, we came to a tangle of deadfall that lay nearly all the way across the creek. It was clear that our boat would not make it through, so we grabbed our fishing gear and headed for the nearest shore.

The shoreline had become much less imposing along this portion of the creek, but it was thickly wooded. Since we had no shoes, we needed to find a farmer's field that was adjacent to the creek, or a bridge. We continued down the creek in search of a way out and eventually came to another idyllic looking pool. Recalling the earlier event in the "pool of death", we were reluctant to wade or swim through this pool, but, due to the confinement of the banks at this spot, there seemed no choice.

Pools are almost always at a bend in the creek and therefore usually had a deep side, the cut bank, and a shallow side, the point bar. We crossed the creek toward the point bar and began a cautious route around the pool. There was practically no shore leading up to the point, so we had to wade in the creek much of the way. The bottom was slimy mud, quite a departure from the rocky bottom that we had encountered up to this point. The mud felt soothing on my feet, which by now were cut in many places from the sharp rocks and shale. We passed by the pool without being eaten alive, and rounded the bend where we spotted a bridge.

"Look!" my brother cried, "It's a bridge. Let's hurry!" My thoughts flashed to *The Wizard of Oz*.

The bottom beyond the pool was still muddy and that made walking through the water more difficult. Our spirits soared, but I quickly became anxious about our situation. It was late. We should have been back home a long time ago. Since it was summer, the days were long and it was hard to tell what time of day it really was, but I knew we had been gone for a long time. Also, I had no idea where this bridge was, so we would have to figure out where we were and find a way back to the bridge we had started from that morning.

As we neared the bridge, sloshing our way out of the water and onto a patch of solid ground, I heard a voice.

"Well, looky here," a high-pitched, creepy male voice arose from the direction of the bridge.

"Hey, where you boys been?" another, deep male voice called. The acoustics of the bridge gave both voices an echo as if coming from a cave, giving them a disembodied quality.

Startled, we all jerked our heads toward the direction of the voices. Two large figures were coming out from under the bridge. Oh no, I thought. Trolls! I mean hobos! A cold, unfettered fear rose from the pit of my stomach and caught in my throat. Two tattered, bearded men appeared from under the bridge, directly in front of us. One was wearing the remains of what must have once been a hat; the other had long bushy hair that was sticking out in every direction. They were a frightening sight, and I realized that we were cut off from the road above.

"You boys have any money?" one asked.

"No," I answered meekly. He had to be kidding, I thought, despite my fear. Kids never had money longer than it took to get to a store and spend it.

"How 'bout them fishing poles," the other said pointing to the one in Francesco's hand? "You don't need them anymore, do ya?"

We stood there paralyzed with fear. Nobody said a word. Then the one with the wild hair pointed down to our bare legs and feet.

"Looks like you boys got a problem with leaches," he sneered with a phlegmy laugh.

We reflexively looked down at our feet. We shrieked with sudden horror at the sight of more than a dozen fat, slimy leaches attached to our bodies below our rolled-up jeans. This drew more laughter from both hobos, or trolls, or whatever they were, as if it was the funniest thing on earth rather than the reality that all of our blood was being sucked out by these gross denizens of the deep. My brother started screaming hysterically. I couldn't blame him. The trolls started to look alarmed.

Just then we heard a car pull off the road, just past the bridge. I looked up. It was a Sheriff's car. I heard the car door slam and a deputy appeared in front of the cruiser. He looked down at where we were standing. My brother was still screaming hysterically, snot running from his nose. The two trolls scampered back under the bridge. I grabbed my brother's arms and tried to calm him down.

"We're going to be okay," I said. "The Sheriff is here." Bear looked up at the deputy working his way down the steep embankment.

"What's going on down here," the deputy asked.

We all spoke at once. "Hobos, trolls," "Tried to take our poles. Leaches," accompanied with more screaming from my brother. "Lost, trapped in the creek, pool of death, the duck." It all came out amid tears of relief and leftover fright.

"You boys are in a heap of trouble," the deputy said. I guess they actually say that. "Your parents have been looking for you and are worried sick. We need to get you back home."

Oh no. I realized we were about to go from the frying pan, into the fire, as my mother might say. No matter how dangerous and difficult our travails had been this day, they were nothing compared to the prospect of facing my mother and father after this little episode. Was there no end to our miseries?

No matter though. I would face a dozen beatings to be back in the bosom of my family, getting rid of these blood-sucking leaches, and having some dry clothes. Still, it was hard to relish our rescue with the certainty of incurring the parental wrath that loomed before us.

"Your mothers found your bikes and shoes up at the bridge north of here," said the deputy. "They called the Sheriff's department because it was getting late and you were nowhere to be found. We figured you were downstream somewhere, so I've been stopping at this bridge as part of my rounds this afternoon. Those old boys under the bridge were supposed to make sure you stayed put if you showed up."

"They tried to take our fishing poles," Francesco protested, "and they asked if we had any money."

"I think they're harmless enough," the deputy replied. "They knew I was coming back. Still, you boys should stay away from under the bridges. You never know who or what might be lurking there."

My mother was right, I thought. Well, our bikes and shoes had been recovered. I still had my eye glasses and we didn't lose our fishing poles. These redeeming facts might save us from some of the impending fury awaiting the return of the prodigal sons.

# Chapter 9

The deputy drove up to Francesco's house. He got out of the cruiser to fetch Francesco. Francesco's mother was already out the door and heading toward the driveway gate, dog pack in tow.

"Bye Francesco," I said. "I hope I get to see you again someday."

"Bye," he replied, and with a look of trepidation in his eyes he exited the car.

There was a brief exchange of words that we couldn't hear. I wondered if the deputy spoke Italian. He got back into the car, scratching his head, and we headed for our house. Now the reality of facing Mother and Dad hit my brother and me like a ton of bricks. My anxiety kicked into high gear, and I began to breathe fast and hard. My brother began to cry again.

As the cruiser pulled into our driveway, the deputy must have sensed our deep apprehension. "I think your parents will be very glad to see that you're safe," he said. He stopped the car and got out to open our door. The dimming light outside told me that it was late in the day. We had been gone for hours. This was going to be bad.

My mother came out the front door. My father was not in sight yet. The deputy gave my mother a short version of how he found us and that we seemed to be alright, save for the leaches. At this news, Mother looked down at our legs and feet, which were now dripping with blood from the leach wounds and cuts from the shale, and she gasped. She thanked the deputy profusely and then turned her attention to us.

"Let's get you into the house and get those nasty leaches off of you," she said.

She latched onto our shoulders and marched us toward the house. Once inside, I saw my father standing there in the middle of the living room, hands on his hips and a scowl on his face. My brother began wailing, and I began to swallow great gulps of air in a paroxysm of remorse. A sort of animal–like moan escaped my lips. I had let my parents down. I had upset them. In retrospect, I knew I had made bad decisions that day. As my mother would say, hindsight is always 20-20. I was so glad to be safe at home, yet dreading the penance that must come.

My mother said nothing, but pointed to the leaches on our legs. My father said, "Good Grief!" He was a man of few words. We all headed for the bathroom. We were made to strip off our clothes, exposing the fact that we had more leaches than were visible below our pants. Some of the leaches were already beginning to drop off on their own. Mother and Dad expertly removed those that remained attached. They treated each wound with my dad's styptic pencil to help stop the bleeding and then applied a bandage.

Looking back, this process of removing leaches may have saved our lives. By the time we were leach free and bandaged up, the worst of the storm seemed to have passed. We were told to go put on our pajamas and come out to the kitchen. Once seated, with both my mother and father sitting there at the table with us, my mother asked us what had happened.

My brother immediately threw me under the bus. "It was Wolf's idea," he whined.

That was true enough, I thought begrudgingly. I explained how we only intended to float a little way, and that we were careful about our bikes and shoes. I told them about how things just started to happen, and the "pool of death", and how the log got stuck, and the rain storm, and the canyon, and then the trolls.

"The trolls?" my mother queried, eyebrows rising. My father's attention was suddenly peaked.

"I mean hobos or bums, I guess," I replied a little embarrassed. "They came out from under the bridge and they looked really scary. They laughed at the leaches on our legs."

"They tried to take our fishing poles," my brother finally contributed.

My parents exchanged looks.

"Did the Sheriff see them?" asked Mother.

"Yes," I replied. "He said he knew they were there and he told them to keep an eye out for us, and if they saw us, to keep us there so that he could pick us up. They went back under the bridge when the Sheriff came down to the creek. He said that they were alright, but we should stay out from under bridges. They were awful looking men or trolls or whatever they were. They scared me."

I had tears rolling down my cheeks at this point. My brother was vigorously nodding his head in affirmation.

My father got up from the table and went into the living room without another word. Then the most amazing thing happened. My mother made us a sandwich and poured a glass of milk for each of us. She explained how worried both she and our father were, and how she hoped we had learned a lesson. My brother and I looked at each other in the sudden realization that we were not going to get the beating of our lives. We assured Mother that we had learned our lesson and we were sorry for making her worry. Before we went to our bedroom, at Mother's suggestion, we went into the living room to tell Dad the same thing. He simply said "OK". Life is a wonder.

Lying there in my bed, I recalled the adventure of that day. As I started to drift off to sleep, I thought about how cool it was going to be to tell this story to the neighbor girl, Marsha. She was going to be very impressed.

# Chapter 10

I was raised Catholic in a very Irish Catholic family. My parents sent me to a Catholic school where the Catechism of the Catholic Church was a prominent focus of instruction. As a young boy, I received my first Holy Communion and the sacrament of Confirmation. My family all went to Catholic mass every Sunday and we went to confession every other Friday. My father led the family in prayer every night, all of us kneeling together next to one of the beds in the boys' bedroom. We said grace before dinner.

I didn't know until much later in my life that in those days many people harbored negative feelings for Catholics, especially Irish Catholics. Perhaps the propensity to assign disparaging names to categories of people was more prevalent in the 50's, but growing up in an insular country environment I had never heard names like Mackerel Snapper, Papist or Mick. I once heard the term "Wop" from one of the neighbor kids, and when I asked what it meant I was told to ask Francesco. I did ask Francesco, and he told me it meant an Italian. He didn't tell me this with any apparent rancor, so I didn't think more about it. It was years later that I finally figured out it was a pejorative slur. Francesco's family was also Catholic, so I guess he would have been a mackerel snapping Wop, whereas I was a mackerel snapping Mick.

Catholic school was strict. The nuns who taught us did not tolerate any nonsense, and I knew that if I got into any trouble at school I would be in even more trouble when I got home. So, I towed the line. I guess I was kind of a sissy when I first started school. My wolf personality had not yet kicked in. I cried and cried as my mother left me that first day. The nun assured my mother that I would be just fine after a little while. As soon as my mother was out of sight, Sister Carmelita told me in a stern voice to stop acting like a baby and take my seat.

Of course, I dutifully took my seat and tried to stifle my tears. A couple of the other kids talked to me and I eventually settled down to learning the first day's lessons. These lessons were about discipline and how Jesus expected all little children to be good at learning everything they were taught. Okay, I thought. If Jesus wanted me to be good and learn, then that's what I would do.

At lunch time, I went to the back of the room to fetch my brand-new Robin Hood lunchbox. I knew that my mother had made chocolate milk for my little thermos. I was very excited about this because I loved chocolate milk. Unfortunately, when I grabbed my lunchbox the lid popped open and the thermos came tumbling out and onto the floor. When I got back to my desk and opened the thermos I discovered that the glass bottle inside the metal exterior had shattered. I knew I shouldn't try to drink the chocolate milk, but I wanted it so badly. I was crushed and started to cry again.

Sister Carmelita noticed me crying and came back to scold me for being a baby again. I tried to explain why I was upset, but she would not suffer any nonsense, so I pushed my disappointment aside and ate my peanut butter and jelly sandwich, sans chocolate milk.

Later that afternoon, I raised my hand to tell Sister Carmelita that I had to go to the bathroom. She told me in no uncertain terms that I would have to exercise more self-control and I should have gone when we had all taken a bathroom break earlier. I was afraid to contradict her so I just sat there trying desperately to have more self-control. Turned out I didn't have enough control and I crapped my pants there in my little desk chair.

I guess the good news was I was wearing brown corduroy pants. The bad news was that I smelled like crap. I was supposed to ride the school bus home that first day. I found my bus and sat down in one of the seats. I heard kids around me asking each other what that awful smell was. I assumed they were referring to me, but I was pretty sure they didn't know for sure that it was me, so I kept my mouth shut.

When I got home, I went into the house and told my mother what had happened. She was horrified. I had never seen her so angry, and I thought she was going to give me a good spanking for not exercising self-control, but as she stripped off my pants and underwear, and began the disgusting process of cleaning me up, it became clear that she was pissed off at Sister Carmelita. I had mixed emotions about that. I was very grateful that my mother was sticking up for me, but dreaded what it might mean to my status in Sister Carmelita's classroom.

The next day my mother drove me to school. After the morning prayers and the Pledge of Allegiance to the wall, Sister Carmelita was summoned to Mother Superior Agatha's office. A feeling of dread came over me. My mother didn't realize that this little incident was probably going to mark me as a prime candidate for knuckle rapping for the entire school year. I had heard the stories from the older kids about what angry nuns could do to you.

About twenty minutes later, Sister Carmelita came back to our room. She looked the picture of serenity and calm. She didn't look at me, but just sat down and commenced the day's lessons. I never heard any more about it, and never experienced any hideous nun-inflicted injuries, at least no more than anybody else received as a normal consequence of being in a Catholic school taught by nuns. In my prayers each nightI silently thanked Jesus in my prayers each night for sparing me. I always wondered what my mother must have said to those nuns.

# Chapter 11

One late summer day, my father came home and announced we were all moving to New Mexico. His company was transferring him to Albuquerque and it would mean more money. New Mexico. Where the heck was that, I thought? We kids were all excited about the prospect of going someplace exotic, but we didn't have a clue where New Mexico was. I noticed that my mother looked more anxious than excited.

My dad brought out a map of the United States and unrolled it on the dining room table and as we all gathered around. He pointed his finger to where we lived currently, and pointed another finger to where Albuquerque was. "Wow!" everybody exclaimed in unison. My dad was obviously psyched about the move. He was all smiles.

Things moved quickly after that day. My mother organized a yard sale and all of us kids had to get rid of as much stuff as possible, things like old clothes, toys we didn't play with anymore, and our bikes. Understand that our bikes were a really big deal in our lives. Our bikes were, like, sacred. The news that we could not take them with us went down hard, but in the spirit of all pulling together for the "big adventure", we eventually reconciled ourselves to the loss.

The day we left, my parents and five kids piled into the family station wagon. The back of the car was crammed with luggage and road essentials. Behind the car was a large U-Haul trailer, equally crammed with everything we hadn't sold or stored at the family farm. Our house had been sold so there was no turning back. We pulled out of our driveway for the last time. I heard my youngest sister, Daisy, say, "Goodbye house", and a quiet resolve settled into all of us as we headed for New Mexico.

Five long days later we pulled into Albuquerque and into the Western Motel. None of us kids had ever been out of Ohio, so the trip across the United States had been a sequence of wondrous sights. At the time of our trip there were no freeways, so we saw the country as it looked from Route 40 and Route 66. It was memorable to be sure, and as we progressed into the American Southwest, seeing the transformation in the landscape, with all its mountains, plateaus, rock formations, pine forests, and deserts, we became mesmerized and charmed by what looked to us like exotic beauty.

There was a change in the family dynamics over those first few weeks in our new home. To begin with, our family had gotten to know each other much better after spending five days on the road. My dad, who was always a kind of mystery to us kids, was in great spirits and more talkative than we had ever seen him. Mother was focused on setting up a new home and we all tried to lend a hand. After just two weeks in Albuquerque, my dad came home one day with a pair of cowboy boots for all of us. This seemed particularly extravagant since we had always been told how expensive shoes were and that we had to make one pair of play shoes and one pair of good shoes last, seemingly, forever.

My dad traded the old station wagon in on a brand-new Volkswagen bus. This was viewed as quite a novelty by us kids. My mother made curtains for all the windows so we could use it as a camper, and my dad started taking the family on weekend camping trips so we could discover New Mexico.

One of our trips was to Santa Fe, the capital of New Mexico. Dad was mostly interested in scoping out the nearby Pecos River for potential fishing spots. We spent the night in a little camping area on the eastern outskirts of the city limits so we could get an early start exploring the town the next day.

Santa Fe is an old town with an impressive array of historic sites and buildings. My mother and father were interested in visiting those places, probably thinking it would be educational for their children. We saw the Cathedral Basilica of Saint Francis, bordering the town square. We visited the Loretto Chapel with its famous miraculous staircase and the San Miguel Mission, considered the oldest church in the United States. Perhaps it was the age of these buildings, the history, or the profound sense of being in consecrated spaces, but I became totally absorbed into the experience of visiting these beautiful places.

My mother must have sensed something different about my demeanor during our tour. She came over to me at the San Miguel Mission and put her hand on my shoulder.

"It's quite inspiring, isn't it?" she said.

I looked up at her and just smiled. She gave my shoulder a squeeze.

# Chapter 12

I had made a new friend after moving to Albuquerque. He was part Native-American, and his name was Michael. We teased each other about him being a Native-American and named Mike, while I was a white-as-you-can-get Anglo, named Wolf.

He told me that his brother was attending the seminary in Santa Fe. He confided that he was thinking of attending himself the following year, that they had a program for high school age boys. I was 14 and would be entering the ninth grade the next school year, and, while it had never before entered my mind to become a priest, being there, seeing those places, I suddenly felt the need to take a closer look at the possibility.

I asked my mother, "Do you think we could visit the Immaculate Heart of Mary Seminary today? It's here in Santa Fe somewhere."

My father had heard my request, and both he and my mother were now looking at me with a most peculiar expression. My mother looked over at Dad. He walked over to the Mission's visitor reception desk and asked where the seminary was located. The receptionist told him it was just down the Old Santa Fe Trail about a half mile from the Mission.

He walked back to where we all stood. My brothers and sisters were already getting restless and my mother was trying to keep order.

"Let's go visit the seminary," Dad said, and off we went.

Driving up the entrance to the seminary campus we passed a Carmelite Monastery on the right. A cloistered order of nuns lived there. I did not know much about them at the time, but the building and grounds were beautiful. Just ahead was a new chapel, flanked by several older buildings, all designed in the pueblo style that was typical in the Santa Fe area. The chapel was tall, topped with a simple adobe arch from which hung a large bell. The front of the chapel included an odd shaped mound that did not seem to serve any practical purpose. The campus was set in the pinon-covered foothills below a mountain called Sangre de Cristos.

I was completely entranced by it all. It was quiet, with only a few seminarians walking about. The seminary was not a tourist destination, so there wasn't a visitor's center. I asked if I could get out of the car to look at it all more closely. My parents were reluctant, but seemed to understand that something was happening with me and told me it should be okay. I got out and looked at an older building on the right. It was meticulously landscaped with a religious grotto off to one side. Across the way was a building that looked like classrooms. I was drawn to the chapel and moved slowly toward the steps leading up to the massive front doors. The area around the doors was decorated in mosaic depictions of religious figures. I tried the doors, but they were locked.

As I turned and started down the steps, heading back to the car, a priest appeared around the odd shaped dome at the corner of the chapel. He wore a cassock with a black sash, tight around the waist, the long ends of the sash hanging down to mid-thigh. I had never seen a priest dressed like that. Frankly, I thought it made for a dashing look, if that term could be applied to a priest.

"May I help you son?" he asked, then glanced over to our car to see my whole family staring back at us.

"I have a friend who said he was thinking about coming here and I wanted to see what it looked like," I replied.

"I see," he said. How old are you?"

"I will be 14 in October," I replied.

"And you think that you have the calling to become a priest?" he asked.

"I don't know," I replied, "but I feel something different since moving here from Ohio."

"Is that your family waiting in the car?" he asked.

"Yes," I replied. "I asked them to bring me here so that I could see this place."

"Let's go over and I'll introduce myself," he suggested.

He put his hand on my shoulder the way my mother had done at the Mission and led me toward the car. "You know this is a very serious and important decision," he said as we approached the car. "Not something to be done lightly."

As we drew near the car, my mother and father got out. My mother looked back to tell the others to stay in the car, incurring a great deal of whining complaint.

"Hello, my name is Father Baer," the priest said and held out his hand.

Introductions were made and pleasantries exchanged. Father Baer was a tall, thin man in his thirties. He had close cropped blond hair and ice blue eyes. He was friendly and gracious, but it was clear that he was a man who tolerated no nonsense. He gave my parents a brief history of the seminary, which had been created specifically to produce Native-American and Hispanic priests who would serve those large ethnic populations in the Archdiocese of Santa Fe.

"Oh," my mother exclaimed. "I guess Wolf wouldn't be what you're looking for then." With my blond hair and blue eyes, I was clearly not a Native-American or Hispanic.

"On the contrary," Father Baer said. "We welcome all young men who have the calling."

There it was again. That word, the "calling". That sounded much more serious than "I'm thinking about studying to be a priest." My mother and father looked at me with an expression I'm sure I had not seen before. You see, being from an Irish

Catholic family, having a priest in the family was like winning the lottery. I suddenly realized that this was a big deal and my parents were now thinking about me in a whole new, very positive way.

Father Baer gave my father his card, and we said our goodbyes. As I got into the car, he put his hand on my shoulder and said he hoped he would hear from me again, and then he turned and walked back toward the chapel. I got into the car and shut the door. I sat there for a moment deep in thought, until I suddenly realized everyone had become quiet and they were all looking at me, Mother, Dad, brothers and sisters. I looked down at my hands sheepishly, not sure what to say, or do, or think. What was happening?

Ultimately, I decided that I definitely wanted to attend the seminary. The mere consideration of attending seemed to change how my parents and even my brothers and sisters treated me. I learned that there was a general murmur of approval throughout our extended family back east when they heard the news. As the family enthusiasm grew, I basked in the attention. I know now that I was too young to distinguish between my fervor for this vocation and the resulting attention I was receiving as the primary motivator in making my decision.

The next few months were a whirl of reflection, emotion, and preparation. My parents arranged a meeting with the local parish priest to discuss the possibility of me attending the seminary. To be admitted, several requirements had to be met, including a recommendation from the pastor of our parish and a recommendation from my current public school. Transcripts, certificates, and medical records had to be collected. A list of specific clothing had to be acquired and labeled with my name, everything from clothing, bed sheets, and even napkins. A cassock, a Roman collar, and a white surplice, a tunic worn over the cassock, had to be purchased from the seminary. Each seminarian was required to wear this priestly garb, which I found an immensely attractive prospect, as this appealed to my inherent desire to stand out. In the Catholic world, priests were like rock stars.

# Chapter 13

The opening day for the class of 1962 was set as September third. Parents were to have their young sons at the seminary between 4:00 pm and 8:00 pm that day. The whole family made the drive from Albuquerque to Santa Fe for the occasion. We arrived to find a crowd of anxious boys and their families saying goodbyes. We were to live at the seminary in a dormitory. Families could visit only on the last Sunday of each month. There were three vacations a year, Thanksgiving, Christmas, and Easter, when seminarians could go home for a few days.

Families helped their sons get established in the dorm as each boy found his assigned bed and locker. As parents left, the reality of separation fell on many of the first-year students with an uneasy finality. Resident priests and senior students helped the new students get settled. Many boys introduced themselves to each other, but a general air of awkwardness permeated the dorm. I was perhaps luckier than most because my friend, Mike, also entered the seminary that year and we were placed in the same dorm bay.

Beginning at 5:30 the next morning, we were all soon to discover just how structured our lives were to become. Seminarians were expected to follow the carefully regulated life of an ecclesiastical institution. We would be monitored and supervised by the rector in charge of the seminary and the dean of discipline. In addition to scholastic studies, we were required to attend daily Mass, periods of private prayer and spiritual reading, and regular periods of consultation with a priest-director assigned to us. Meals were to be consumed in silence, while senior seminarians read from a book about Father Jacques Marquette. We were required to make our bed, keep our area clean, take turns cleaning the restrooms, serve as waiters to upper classmen, and do our own laundry.

We spent a lot of time in the chapel focused on various religious endeavors, which included learning about Gregorian chant. We not only had to learn a specific repertory of chants considered appropriate for the Mass and the Office, but also the historic development of plainchant, the musical form of Gregorian chant, including the musical idiom and notation of the chant.

We were required to have a *Catholic Missal*, *A Guide to Meditation*, and a book called the *Young Seminarian*. The use of these books was also structured daily. Religious reading was required, but each of us could select what we wanted to read from a special library of such works. I decided to read an encyclopedic set of books, called *The Lives of the Saints*.

This new life took some getting used to, but after a month or so, I really got into the spirit of it all. I was comfortable with the regimen and structure. I liked being read to during meals and I really enjoyed reading the accounts of the saints, most of which were quite inspiring. I came to enjoy the chanting, which made me fall into a kind of trance-like state. Unlike many of my classmates, I didn't mind the cleaning, since that wasn't much different from what my mother expected of me at home.

The Sacrament of Penance, what we Catholics call Confession, is the process of confessing your sins to a priest in order to have them absolved. This is usually done at a church inside a confessional, which is essentially a dark little phone booth sized space. The priest is in an adjacent space and there is a little sliding door that, when opened by the priest, is the signal to start confessing your sins. You can't see the priest because there is a cloth covering the opening, so it's all private, which makes it easier to confess really bad sins.

At the seminary, we were assigned a specific confessor and we were required to kneel in front of that priest in an open room, so he knew exactly who you were. Our family typically went to Confession about twice a month. At the seminary we were required to go once a week. In the beginning, I found this arrangement to be quite uncomfortable, but as time went on, and given the very limited opportunity to commit sins in that environment, the real problem became trying to figure out just what sins I might have committed.

Early on, just before I went to see my confessor, I would go through the Ten Commandments to see if I had failed to obey any one of them. I hadn't worshiped any false gods. Lord knows I kept the Sabbath, not to mention every other day in the week. I couldn't dishonor my parents since they weren't there. I didn't cuss, murder anybody, steal, or lie. I wasn't really clear about what coveting actually entailed, but was pretty sure I wasn't guilty of wanting anybody's wife or ox. So, what was I to confess?

After the first few weeks, I told my confessor that I wasn't sure that I had committed any sins. Oh contraire! My confessor assured me that we were all sinners and I had surely sinned. I quickly agreed that I must be sinning, but just wasn't sure how to confess them. He instructed me to say something that essentially amounted to admitting to generic sin if I didn't have any specific sin to confess. That was good enough for me.

I did quite well in my scholastic studies, earning frequent praise from the instructors. There was, however, one subject that I struggled with. Latin was very difficult for me, and the instructor was Father Baer. He was a hard taskmaster and expected every student to excel at the daily assignments. Ecclesiastical Latin, or Liturgical Latin, is the official language of the Holy See, and if you were going to be a priest you had to know Latin.

Father Baer had a unique method for instilling the importance of learning your lessons. He would stand in the back of the classroom and call on specific individuals to read from our textbook, translating from English to Latin, or from Latin to English. When it was your turn, he would come up to you from behind and place the knuckle of his middle finger in your trapezius, between the neck and shoulder. If you faltered, he would encourage you by tapping his knuckle on your trapezius. The more you faltered the harder he tapped. I was brought from my chair to my knees on numerous occasions. The process eventually caused me so much fear that it was almost impossible to concentrate on an adequate translation in his class. I was eventually sent to the rector to explain my poor study habits.

Monsignor Tournier was the rector of Immaculate Heart of Mary Seminary, and he was an affable priest whom I liked a lot. I didn't want to complain, so it took some coaxing before I finally explained my problem of being so afraid that I couldn't concentrate. I told him I had memorized the entire Mass in Latin, but I admitted I had a difficult time learning Latin. I assured him that I was sincerely trying. He reminded me about the importance of Latin and told me he would speak to Father Baer to see if there was something that might be done to help me through this difficulty.

The next day, Father Baer did not stand behind me when I was called upon to stand and deliver. I still struggled, but managed to get through the exercise. After class he told me to come back to see him during a time normally set aside during the school day for study. I sheepishly reported as commanded, expecting a beating or a tongue lashing, or both. He told me to sit down and asked about my study habits. I explained how all my other subjects came easily to me but that I just couldn't seem to get Latin. I also told him I could memorize just about anything, but reading ad hoc was very difficult.

Later in life I came to discover that I had an inherent problem with other languages. During my travels and adventures, I earnestly tried to learn Japanese, Vietnamese, Thai, German, Spanish, Dutch and French, alas with no success. Once, I tried to impress a group of customers, visiting the U.S. from France, with my French language skills. They begged me to just speak English. I realized I did not have the natural skill for learning foreign languages, much like my inability to read music. I could memorize, but I could not fluently read and translate.

To Father Baer's credit, he decided he would take on the challenge of helping me learn Latin, so he had me come to him twice a week for private tutoring. While this definitely helped, it was hard to determine who became more frustrated, him or me.

Other than Latin, my life at the seminary was sublime, and I began to feel that I had an honest calling to the priesthood. My spiritual life blossomed and I was often transformed into a state of enlightenment, or at least what I perceived to be enlightenment. When my parents came to visit on the last Sunday of the month, they could see that I was different and they talked to me as an adult. I reveled in these visits and their attention.

When I went home for the Thanksgiving holiday, the parish priest had asked my parents to bring me to the Catholic school to speak to the seventh and eighth grade boys about the prospects of becoming a priest. Everybody treated me differently. It was difficult to keep my pride and ego under control. I now understood about such things as humility and vanity, and I struggled with myself and my motives, but it sure was hard not to bask in the attention.

Easter at the seminary turned out to be one of the most memorable events of my life. Easter Sunday is the biggest deal in the Catholic hierarchy of Holy Days, and in Santa Fe it was a major event. I had attended several Easter Sundays in my young life, and I knew there was a lot of ceremony that was part of the ritual, but in Santa Fe, New Mexico, Easter is taken to a whole other level.

The seminarians were to participate in the midnight Mass at the Cathedral Basilica of Saint Francis of Assisi, down in the town square. We would be in the procession, headed by the Archbishop, that traveled through the square and into the Cathedral. We would be chanting. I was definitely looking forward to the ceremony.

When we arrived at the assembly area near the square I could hardly concentrate. The girls from Our Lady of Lourdes Catholic School were gathered near where we assembled. They were in their school uniforms and wore beautiful, lace mantilla head coverings. Also assembling were the Knights of Columbus in their red capes, plumed hats and swords at their waists, and the Knights of Saint Patrick, decked out in green. At least two hundred priests were gathered just beyond our group. Their vestments were a riot of color and style. They were clustering around the Archbishop who was under a lavish canopy held by alter boys clad in scarlet cassocks and white surplices.

A thousand or more people crowded the square. The procession began to move toward the Cathedral. The Archbishop held a large, ornamental Monstrance, a vessel used to hold the consecrated Host representing the Body of Christ. On Good Friday, this vessel is covered until midnight on Easter. There were also to be no bells or music until midnight.

Upon reaching the doors of the Cathedral, everyone waited until the stroke of midnight, when the cathedral bells began to ring, and the Archbishop faced the people and uncovered the Monstrance to expose the sacred Host. The pipe organ in the cathedral boomed out its sacred music and everybody started singing the Gloria. The pageantry of it all brought goosebumps to my flesh and tears to my eyes. It was perhaps the most moving and memorable moment of my young life at that point.

# Chapter 14

A few months later, when my parents were visiting me at the seminary, I was informed that my father was being transferred back to Ohio. The program he was working with in Albuquerque was wrapping up. I was told that I had to make a decision about staying in New Mexico until the end of the school year, or transfer to another seminary back in Ohio. I had never been homesick or suffered from "separation anxiety" while at the Immaculate Heart of Mary Seminary. After all, my family was only an hour away in Albuquerque. The prospect of being left alone in Santa Fe, however, while they returned to Ohio instantly struck me with trepidation.

Since there were only about six weeks left in the school year, it was ultimately decided that I would finish out the year there in Santa Fe. On the last day, I packed up my things and was driven to the Greyhound Bus station for the long trip back to Ohio.

Upon my return, my parents and I looked for a seminary that included a high school program. We came up empty handed. If I was to continue to pursue my ecclesiastical studies, I would need to return to Santa Fe. Alas, my rapturous experience at Immaculate Heart of Mary and my sense of spiritual calling began to fade as I became absorbed in summer activities at the family farm.

By the beginning of the next school year, I was enrolled in a local public high school. In the years that followed, many people assumed that it was "girls" that distracted me from becoming a priest, but I knew that is was Latin. Ironically, many years later, after the company I work for eliminated my position, I was given a career assessment test as part of an executive exit package. The assessment indicated that I was best suited for a career as a clergyman.

# Chapter 15

During my public high school years I struggled to find myself. I was not athletically gifted. In fact, I did not make any of the teams I tried to join, and I tried them all. I was tall, but lanky, and my hand-eye coordination was pathetically lacking. I eventually discovered that I did have other talents. I was smart and I had artistic abilities. Instead of earning a letter in some sport, which I dearly coveted, I found myself the only boy on the school newspaper staff. I suppose some would consider this an advantageous opportunity, but I was too geeky to be of interest to the cheerleaders, majorettes and queens to whom I was attracted. And, despite all the assumptions that "girls" distracted me from pursuing the cloth, I really hadn't figured out the whole boy-girl thing yet. I was a "late bloomer".

I put a lot of energy into experimenting with my growing interest in art. In addition to my contributions to the school paper, I started painting. I did a series of oil paintings that included a single human eye floating in the upper right quarter of each painting. Many people found it disturbing, but I was trying to express how the "seeing eye of God" is watching over everything. I didn't think it was so weird. After all, there is an "All-Seeing Eye" on the American dollar bill. My temporary preoccupation with this subject probably stemmed from my latent regret for abandoning the priesthood.

Once I got past the eye paintings, I tried my hand at portraits. This effort was much more popular and I began to get many requests to do specific people. For these portraits I used pastels. My mother, especially, thought I had a talent that should be encouraged and nurtured. Although I never took any formal art training, I did engage in training myself, using "how to" books that I obtained.

In my senior year of high school, my friend Brian and I decided to do a comic strip for the local newspaper. Brian came up with a story for each strip and I drew them. The general theme was the misadventures of a Sad Sack sort of military guy. We called the comic "Therman Thrasher" and the local newspaper decided to publish them.

As I neared graduation from high school, my mother was determined to get me into Ohio State University to study fine arts, although I didn't see how we were going to afford it. I worked at a gas station to help my parents raise enough money for me to attend college. My father bought a car for me from a friend for $200. It was a 1953 Chrysler Crown Imperial. Not my first choice as a cool car, but I was very grateful to have transportation. In the fall of 1966 I started classes. Unfortunately, I was not destined to finish even that first quarter.

Although my car was specifically intended for use in getting to classes at the university, I was in a rock-and-roll band in those days and needed to get to and from practice and gigs. My parents were not enthusiastic about the band, but tolerated my musical inclinations. I'm sure they were dismayed that I played the drums in the band rather than a piano or organ.

In the middle of the first quarter at the university, I was returning from playing with the band at a dance, when I suddenly noticed the car was not performing well and I smelled something odd. I saw that my temperature gauge was showing the engine was quite hot. In fact, the needle was pegged to the hot side of the gauge. I was out in the middle of the countryside with no service station anywhere in sight. I tried to push on a little further. If I could just get to a service station I could resolve the problem. After a few more minutes, however, the car simply stopped running.

As it turned out, the car's engine was ruined with a cracked block from the extreme heat. There was no money to replace or repair that kind of problem. As a result, I could not get to my classes. My college days were over.

# Chapter 16

My parents were very disappointed in me once again, and I felt humiliated. I was always trying to impress my parents and make them proud of me, but I seemed to have a special talent for falling short of meeting their expectations. There seemed to be only one choice for me at this point, join the Foreign Legion. Well, okay perhaps the U.S. Air Force would do. It was the middle of the Viet Nam war and the draft had been reinstated. Lots of guys I knew were going into the Service. It would be a way to redeem myself, I thought.

My father had been in the Army Air Corp and my mother was a nurse in the U.S. Cadet Nurse Corps during World War II. I think they generally approved of my new plan, although my mother obviously worried about the possibility of me being in combat. I had been right. The prospect of joining the Air Force had distracted them from the bitter disappointment of my aborted attempt to go to college.

Unfortunately, during my physical it was discovered that I had an inguinal hernia, and I was told they could not enlist me until it had been successfully repaired. Since I was still a dependent of my parents at that time, and therefore still on my father's insurance plan, my hernia surgery was scheduled. I was to check back with the recruiter in eight months.

I was unprepared for the debilitating after effects of this procedure. It was painful. I lay around the house for a couple of weeks, growing progressively bored, when I decided that perhaps it would be a good idea to spend my convalescence in Florida with my grandparents. I'm not sure why I thought that was a good idea. It was yet another impulsive idea, but once I latched on to the possibility of it, I became focused on figuring out how to make it happen. To my surprise nobody objected, but the catch was digging up enough money to get me down there.

Finally, by hook and crook, enough money was pulled together to purchase a Greyhound bus ticket. Having already completed one bus journey, I considered myself a seasoned traveler on this conveyance. I got the impression that my parents were a bit relieved to have me gone. My mother, especially, made multiple, seemingly light-hearted comments about saving the money it cost to feed a teenage boy. I didn't give it too much thought though, and ultimately waved goodbye to everybody at the bus station, setting off on my next adventure.

Life in Florida at my grandparents' little house in New Port Richey was great. I was the center of their attention, which of course pleased me to no end. As I healed from my operation, I started helping my grandpa with little projects around their house. I also started drawing sketches of Florida scenes in a large sketchpad that my grandma purchased for me.

Grandma had always thought I was talented and encouraged me to do something creative. I started a portfolio of relatively simple scenes, such as a tropical garden with a large heron in the foreground, a sailfish jumping out of the water, and palm trees with parrots flying by. Before long she was bragging to all her friends about these sketches and people would ask to see them. Eventually, one of these people asked me if I could paint one of these scenes on their garage door.

In those days, it was popular to purchase a stencil kit that facilitated the transfer of a specific picture onto a wall. Some of the retired people, who made up a large percent of the local population, had tried to do this on their garage doors, but the stencil material did not hold up to the subtropical sun and weather. The person interested in having me do one of my sketches wondered if using outdoor paint would be more durable.

I thought it made sense, although I had no experience with such a thing, and I agreed to do it.

After the garage door painting was completed, it became a local sensation. Friends and neighbors came to look at the art. They were all impressed and I started getting more orders. I worked up some additional scenes so that these unexpected clients would have more options to choose from. I didn't charge the couple who ordered the first painting, not only because they were friends of my grandparents, but because they were becoming my best reference. I decided to charge twenty-five dollars per garage door. That was big money in those days, especially to me, who had zero income.

The fervor eventually died down, but I had garage door scenes all over New Port Richie before it ran its course. I was healing very quickly by this time, so I decided to try to find a job to earn more money. My brief celebrity as a garage door artist made me realize that money was a very useful thing. I had given much of what I had earned from painting to my grandparents, remembering my mother's comments about how expensive it was to feed me. I didn't want to be a burden.

## Chapter 17

I had made a friend in Florida, Robert, whose father was the sales manager at a local Ford dealer. Robert told me that he thought his father might have a job for me. I agreed to look into it. Within a week I was working as the guy who washes all the cars in the lot. When a new car was sold, I was the guy who detailed the car for the new owner. It was not a prestige job, but it was a job. I had purchased a used bicycle several weeks before, so I rode my bike to work each day. Robert's father knew that I was convalescing and agreed to not have me do any lifting as part of the work.

One day, Robert's father advised me that he had just sold a station wagon to his parents and he wanted me to get it cleaned up and attach the license plate, which he handed to me. I knew that would be a special deal to him since the new owners were his parents, so I dropped everything and headed for the car. It was parked off to the side of the main lot, in front of the mechanic's garage and paint shop. The pavement there was quite rough, with some of it actually reduced to gravel. I always wore shorts and a T-shirt to work, so I gingerly sat down behind the car so I could attach the license plate.

The bumper of this car was tight up against the body, tighter than other models that I had put plates on in the past. I eventually had to sit with my legs under the car and my hand wedged between the bumper and the body to get the nut started on the bolt that held the plate onto the bumper. I had just gotten the nut started when I heard the car door slam and the engine start. I didn't think too much of it since Robert's dad had told me he was going to check everything out. I heard the air conditioner come on. I was still trying to get the first nut tight on the bolt, when I heard the car go into gear. I looked up and saw that the backup lights were on.

"He's just checking things out," I thought, certain that he knew I was behind the car putting on the license plate.

The car began to move backward. At first, I was too incredulous to react, but I quickly began to assess my situation and figure out how to get out of my precarious predicament. As the car picked up speed, my right hand became impossibly stuck between the bumper and the body of the car. I was soon completely under the car being dragged through the rough pavement and gravel. I grabbed hold of the dangling license plate with my left hand in an effort to gain more control over my ability to avoid getting run over by the back wheels.

I started yelling, then screaming. I went into a panic. It all happened so fast. Suddenly, the car stopped and I realized that Robert's father was out of the car and several men from the maintenance garage were yelling and running toward the car. Soon, there were people down on the ground asking me if I was alright. I was in shock and don't recall giving them any response.

The next thing that I can recall was being in an ambulance with sirens blaring away and medics looking concerned as they administered first aid. At the hospital, after getting patched up, several people from the Ford agency came into my room to see how I was doing. I looked down at myself, covered in bandages, and said something about looking like the mummy. I could see there was a great deal of genuine concern on their faces, and it scared me. How badly was I hurt?

I was declared ambulatory and released from the hospital within a couple of hours. Robert and his dad told me they would take me home. I was afraid that if my grandma saw me she might have a heart attack. As children we were always warned that grandma had a weak heart and could leave us at any time. I didn't want to be the one who caused her departure. As it turned out she lived into her nineties but I asked Robert's father to go in and tell my grandparents that there had been an accident and despite all of my bandages, I was alright.

The next several weeks dragged by, but I was enjoying all the attention. I didn't have to go to work, but got paid anyway. I was given a car, a 1957 Plymouth, as a gesture of further compensation for my injuries. I had to sign some papers releasing the dealership from further liability, which I was naively happy to do. My grandmother doted on me, which of course I soaked up.

A much less desirable consequence of the accident was the healing process. Some of my wounds were quite serious, involving the removal of patches of skin and muscle. I later learned that all my clothes had been scoured off and my bare body was dragged several yards across rough pavement before the men in the garage caught the attention of Robert's father. He of course had no idea that I was trapped under the car and had only stopped because he thought they were yelling that he was stirring up dust near the paint shop.

The doctors told me that the healing process was creating "proud flesh". As I understood it, the skin was healing faster than the tissue underneath and therefore the flesh in the wounds had to be removed with, in my case, silver nitrate. I can tell you it was a painful process. It was essentially legal torture as far as I was concerned, and I was anxious for it to be over.

After several weeks I asked the doctor if I could be considered released. I told him that I had been asked by my employer to stay in the local area until I was officially released, but I needed to get back to Ohio to enlist in the Air Force. I decided I had been in Florida long enough. It was time to move on. The doctor told me I was indeed "officially released".

# Chapter 18

I told my grandparents and the Ford dealership that I planned to go back to Ohio in a few weeks. It was early March and still cold up north, so I decided to spend a few more weeks in Florida. I was in no particular hurry, and since I was not allowed to work, but was still getting paid, I had plenty of spare time. I started another sketch book of things that caught my interest.

One day I drove my new, old Plymouth down to Clearwater Beach. As I was parking I noticed a couple of chopped Harley Davidson bikes parked close to the beach. I thought they looked very cool and decided I would try to sketch one of them. I walked over and sat on a curb stone close to the bike I wanted to sketch and began drawing. I spent the better part of an hour drawing the big bike, which I realized was more difficult than I originally thought. I decided to capture the essential characteristics of the bike, those that made it unique, and finish it later at home where I could focus on the detail.

Out of the corner of my eye I saw two figures approaching me. I looked up to see what I would describe as stereotypical outlaw bikers, the kind that you saw in the biker movies like *The Wild Angels* or *Hells Angels on Wheels*. My immediate reaction was alarm. I had never met a real, live outlaw biker, but I knew they were the kind of guys normal people tried to avoid.

"Hey asshole!" the largest and most dangerous looking one snarled. "What the fuck are you doing next to my bike?"

"Umm, I'm just sketching it," I said warily, trying to get up off the curb stone.

He pushed me back down before I could get more than a few inches off my perch and grabbed the sketch pad out of my hand. I landed in a most ungraceful manner. I was now in a state of panic, like a rabbit must feel when confronted by a pack of wolves, but I remember worrying about my sketch pad and all the work that it contained. Both of them were looking at me as if trying to decide how best to dismember my body.

The big guy looked at the sketch of the bike. To my surprise, he seemed to be appraising the work and started to slowly nod his head as in approval.

"This is not bad," he said, his voice slightly less intimidating. He showed it to his partner, who scowled in what I presumed was a tacit agreement.

They proceeded to mount their bikes and started them up. The big guy still had my sketch pad.

"Get on," he ordered. I got off the ground and stood there dumbly looking at him. He handed me the sketch pad. "Get on!" he repeated in a tone that clearly brooked no argument. So, I got on the back of his bike. His partner looked over at me with a sneer that made me very uncomfortable.

"You're his bitch," he called with a sardonic laugh. I later discovered that this was a term for guys who rode on the back of a motorcycle, a position apparently reserved for women in normal circumstances.

I looked forlornly at my Plymouth as we roared out of the parking lot. This was probably my last day on earth, I thought, so I started to pray.

The bikers drove outside the city limits and into the expansive back country that dominated the Florida landscape back in those days. They eventually rode up to a desolate looking building that seemed to be miles from anywhere. There were a few large motorcycles parked in front of the place, the only indication that the place was not abandoned. We pulled up alongside of the other bikes. I was ordered to get off. They turned off their bikes and dismounted.

"What's your name?" my biker asked.

"Wolf," I replied meekly.

"I'm Butch," he said. "This here is Pete, but everybody calls him Grinder." This elicited another scowl from Grinder, which I was beginning to think might be his version of a smile.

They both stood there for a few moments, looking me up and down. I had on cutoff jeans, a T-shirt, and tennis shoes with no socks. Judging from the looks on their faces, I apparently didn't measure up to the biker dress code. They were wearing well-worn jeans, well-worn boots, well-worn T-shirts, and the mandatory well-worn leather vests despite the warm tropical weather. The vests sported the "club colors" on the back, which, in their case, was the skull and crossed pistons of the Outlaws. I stood there uneasily, blissfully ignorant of outlaw biker gangs in general, and totally ignorant of the long and violent history of "the Outlaws".

"Go inside," Butch said finally, shaking his head in obvious dissatisfaction. Grinder just kept scowling.

Obediently, I headed for the door. As far as I was concerned I was a captive and the probable victim of some horrible fate yet to be determined. I looked around to see them following me. When I reached the door, I looked back for some additional instruction. They both lifted their chins in a tacit gesture to open the door. The look on their faces had changed slightly to something that resembled mischief.

I opened the door and walked a couple of steps inside a dark space. Temporarily blinded by the stark contrast between the bright sunlight outside and the dimly lit room, I stood there allowing my eyes time to adjust, and at the same moment, the sounds in the room went from raucous to silence. When my eyes adjusted, I could see a dozen or so unsavory men looking at me. Perhaps glowering would be more accurate.

"Who the fuck are you?" one of them bellowed. Several guys started walking toward me with menace in their eyes. Two of the men grabbed me by each arm and began to drag me into the room. They threw me unceremoniously onto a pool table that was in the middle of the room. As I sat there on the edge of the table, terrified beyond capacity for rational thought, Butch and Grinder stepped into the doorway. With the bright sunlight at their backs, only their silhouettes were visible from inside the room. Silence once again permeated the room as all eyes were now on these two men.

"This is Wolf," Butch said. "He's okay. He's an artist."

One more, quick look at me and everybody dispersed, going back to whatever they were doing when I entered. I sat there in shock, still clutching my sketch pad. Perhaps I wasn't going to be murdered after all, at least not yet.

"Hey Wolfman," someone said in a sarcastic tone, "Get the fuck off the pool table."

"Did you piss on it?" someone else said, to much laughter.

Butch approached me as I jumped down from the pool table. He grabbed my sketchpad and started to show it to a few guys standing nearby. At first I panicked, but as each guy examined the sketch of Butch's bike, he looked over at me with something that resembled acknowledgement. Before long, several of the bikers made their way over to me and indicated they would like for me to draw their bikes, variously referred to as hogs, choppers, knuckleheads, panheads, and bobbers.

# Chapter 19

I eventually found myself standing alone and essentially ignored. I made my way to a table against a wall and sat down. I was unharmed and didn't seem to be in any imminent danger. As difficult as it was to fathom, I apparently had several orders for sketches, although it seemed unlikely that this effort would result in any compensation other than perhaps an extended life expectancy. I was in this state of reflection when Grinder shuffled over to my table.

"You want a beer?" he asked.

"No thank you. I don't drink," I replied.

He looked annoyed. "You some kind of faggot goody-two-shoes?" he snarled, and took a menacing step closer to my table. I was still off balance. I had to think quickly.

"Well, I'm not 21 yet," I offered.

"What the hell difference does that make?" he said. We were beginning to draw attention.

"I'm studying to be a priest," I blurted out. "We're not allowed to drink." I don't know where that came from, but it just popped into my head. Having said it out loud, I instantly thought it was a stupid thing to say in front of these guys.

"A priest?" Grinder exclaimed. He looked at me, apparently perplexed. "What do you mean, a priest?" Now just about everybody was looking at me.

"Um, I'm studying to be a priest in New Mexico. I'm here in Florida on a vacation, recovering from an operation. I was working at the Ford agency in Clearwater and the owner ran over me. Now I'm stuck here while I recover from those injuries," I explained, holding up my bandaged hand and pointing to my bandaged knee. "I live with my grandparents." It all gushed out of me in a stream of consciousness, fueled by a growing sense of hysteria.

The room was quiet again, everybody just standing there staring at me. I was afraid I was going to start crying. Butch walked over to me and roughly put a hand on my shoulder.

"Well, Father Wolf," he said. "We could use a little spiritual guidance in this club, couldn't we boys?" There was much laughter.

"Wolf," I said barely above a whisper. "People just call me Wolf."

"Don't worry Father Wolf," he replied. "We'll take good care of you while you finish all them pictures the boys ordered. We're heading up to Daytona tomorrow for Bike Week. You can go up there with us to work on the pictures." There was a general mumble of agreement from the others.

I knew that this proposal was not negotiable, but said, "I should tell my grandparents that I'm going to be away. My grandma has a bad heart. I don't want her to worry."

Butch looked at me for a long time, then he said, "OK, we'll take care of that. There's a payphone in the back, just outside the bathroom," he gestured with his thumb in the general direction of the apparent location of a phone.

I got up and headed toward the back. Butch was right behind me. I found the phone and put a dime in it. I began to dial. Butch was standing next to me, leaning against the wall. It was obvious that he was going to make sure I wasn't going to call anybody or say anything that was going to result in problem for these guys. I realized I was going to have to play this developing situation carefully. I finished dialing by grandparents' number.

"Hello Grandma, it's Wolf," I said. I explained that I was in Clearwater and had met some people. "They invited me to go to Daytona with them tomorrow for a couple of days. I decided to stay with them here, tonight, so that we can get an early start in the morning."

Grandma didn't seem to suspect anything was wrong. I told her I loved her and that I'd see her in a few days.

"Yes, I'll be fine," I said. "My injuries are doing just fine. I'll be okay. Bye."

I hung up the phone. Butch managed to look mildly threatening and magnanimous at the same time. He turned and walked back toward the bar. I came to the conclusion that I was stuck here in this unusual situation and I would just have to go with the flow. I told Butch I was going to go outside and start sketching bikes, and that's what I did.

# Chapter 20

As the day wore on, more bikers arrived, some with women. They looked at me curiously as they entered the building, but nobody bothered me. A few guys came out to point to their bikes, making sure I knew which one to draw. Butch came out a few times to look at my progress and seemed to be pleased with my work. By nightfall there were about fifty bikes parked around the building.

The place was packed and getting increasingly loud and rowdy. It also reeked of stale beer and cigarette smoke, so I stayed outside even after it was too dark to work on sketches. I was getting hungry and wondered where I was going to sleep, if in fact sleep was on the agenda.

A woman came outside and sat down beside me. I glanced at her. She was smoking a cigarette. She wasn't unattractive, but had a rough look. I was pretty sure she could kick my ass if push came to shove.

"You want something to eat Honey?" she asked, looking over at me. I didn't recall seeing any sign of a kitchen.

"Sure," I replied. "What is there to eat?"

"Nothing," she laughed, "but somebody's bringing barbeque chicken and stuff soon. I'll make sure you get something to eat."

"Where does everybody sleep?" I asked.

She took a big drag off her cigarette and exhaled loudly. "Some just pass out and sleep wherever they land. Some pitch tents out back. Some have their old ladies drive in later and they sleep in their cars or trucks."

"Where should I sleep?" I asked.

"You could sleep with me, I guess," she said. I sat upright and spun my head around to look at her with an experesion that she apparently thought was very funny. She laughed, "I own this place. You can sleep upstairs on the sofa. Don't worry Father Wolf, I won't tempt you into sin. Food will be here soon. By the way, my name is Donna. I'm Butch's woman."

She got up and went back inside. I leaned back in a rickety, old chair that I had been sitting in most of the day. I was feeling less frightened, but still anxious about what the next few days would bring. I was generally being left alone. It seemed apparent, however, that I was a prisoner, or maybe I was just some kind of a joke. Maybe tomorrow they would decide that I was no longer worth the trouble of keeping track of and leave me behind. I could find my way back if abandoned, I thought with an ember of optimism.

While my night passed with little personal incident, the same could not be said about the others sharing this remote den of iniquity. Food did arrive as promised, and the ensuing feeding frenzy was a spectacle I would not soon forget. I'm sure I would have not eaten that night if not for Donna. I fell asleep outside in the chair despite the chaos in and all around the building. Donna eventually woke me and led me up an outside stairway to her small apartment on top of the bar. The din below continued into the early morning hours, making it difficult to get back to sleep.

## Chapter 21

I woke up around nine to the sound of bikes. Butch came up to the couch I was lying on and kicked my feet.

"Time to role Father Wolf," he said. "You ride with me."

"What about Donna," I asked.

"She'll be following in her truck," he said. "She and some of the other girls bring the gear we need for this kind of ride. Get something in your belly before you leave. There's some stuff over there on the counter you can have."

I shuffled over to the counter he pointed to, looking for something edible. All I could find was an open bag of stale potato chips and some Cokes in the fridge. "Nourishing," I thought, but decided to consume it in the interest of fending off the potential malnutrition that seemed highly possible over the next few days.

"Catch," Butch yelled as he tossed a pair of well-worn jeans my way. They hit me in the head and fell to the floor. "You need to wear long pants for a trip like this."

I picked up the jeans to see what I was expected to get into. They looked clean enough so I exchanged them for my cut-offs. They were too big, but with the aid of my belt, I was able to keep them up over my narrow hips. I grabbed by sketch pad, pencils, and cut-offs and headed downstairs.

The place was a beehive of activity with preparations. Butch grabbed my cut-offs and sketchpad and handed them to Donna, who transferred them to her truck. She brought back a leather cap that looked like an old aviator's helmet. She told me to put it on and I obeyed. She then handed me a pair of goggles.

"Be sure to wear these so your glasses don't fly off and so you don't get bugs in your eyes," she said above the roar of bikes. She was grinning in a peculiar way, looking at me and then Butch, and shaking her head. I got the impression that she also wondered what the hell Butch was doing, taking me along on this big ride.

"You should see yourself Honey," she said to me, her smile widening.

I felt a hot flush of embarrassment across my face. "I'm sure I look like a dork," I said dejectedly.

"Not at all," she said. "You look like a biker." She turned and headed toward the truck.

Butch gave me a long look and made a snuffing sound in what I interpreted as condescending mirth.

"Mount up Father Wolf," he commanded.

Once underway, I must admit that I began to get into the feeling of the freedom of the open road. All the bikes in formation, roaring down the highway, the wind in my hair, the way everybody looked at us. When the group pulled into a gas station, everybody backed away and cars on the road just passed on by, not willing to take any chances of finding trouble with outlaw bikers. The gang, however, didn't try to start any trouble on these stops. They all gassed up in an orderly and efficient manner. Some of them bought Cokes. Some of them even had conversations with the mechanics who were on duty. Then, at Butch's signal, everybody mounted up and took off in perfect order. It became apparent that Butch was in charge.

We pulled into the Daytona area several hours later. We made our way to the broad, hard packed beach. I was unprepared for the magnitude of this event. There had to be hundreds, maybe thousands of bikes cruising up and down the beach. There were camps of different bike groups everywhere. There were concession stands of every conceivable nature lining the beach.

Butch led the Outlaws to a spot where he decided we would set up our camp. The bikes were lined up and the trucks parked behind them. Several guys set up tents, portable tables, and beach chairs. Coolers filled with beer appeared. The party was on.

I managed to find a relatively secluded spot where I could stay out of the way but still see everything. I used a tarp from Donna's truck to create a makeshift shade cover near the area where the Outlaws parked their bikes. That was where I continued sketching.

There was a continuous parade of bikes and people up and down the beach. People were there to see and be seen. During the day, lots of non-bikers came to the beach to see the spectacle. They cleverly disappeared before nighttime.

The first night was surreal. The activity ranged from run of the mill bacchanal to deranged hell-raising. There was plenty of alcohol consumption, drugs, music, dancing, fighting, occasional gunfire, screaming, and police raids. I somehow managed to avoid getting caught up in the chaos. I eventually crawled into the back of Donna's truck to see if I could get some sleep. I considered taking refuge under the truck but thought better of it when I recalled my little accident at the Ford dealership. I finally fell asleep late into the night.

The next morning I awoke to the combined smells of ocean decay, vomit, urine, and trace elements of things I didn't want to think about. I could hear the ocean waves crashing on the beach, sea birds squabbling over remnants of last night's party, and somebody farting nearby. Ah, nothing like morning on the beach.

I sat up in the back of the truck and took a long look around to assess the aftermath. I discovered Grinder was asleep next to where I had been. I had no recollection of him climbing into the truck, which was a scary thought. I saw that somebody had a camp stove going close by with what looked like a coffee pot sitting on it. A couple of people were sitting in beach chairs nearby.

I got out of the truck and decided the first thing I needed to do was find a bathroom. When I had asked about this the day before, I was told to go into the ocean to "take care of business". I wasn't real comfortable with that option, so I had located something slightly more conventional a couple hundred yards off the beach. The public restroom was not a pleasant place when I first discovered it, but overnight it had plummeted into a state of vile corruption. I stood at the entrance reconsidering the ocean, but decided that I needed to relieve myself quickly. I plotted a path of least disgust, took a deep breath, and plunged forward.

Back at the camp stove I asked if I could have some of the coffee and was told I was welcome if I could find a cup. Finding nothing back at the truck, I opted for an empty Coke bottle that I had kept in a fruitless effort to do my part at keeping the beach clean. I gingerly poured coffee into the bottle, burning my fingers only slightly. I found an empty beach chair and sat back, planning my strategy for locating a more acceptable bathroom.

Things on the beach started to come back to life in the late morning. With little else to do, I resumed my station under the shade pavilion and continued to sketch bikes. Just before noon, a huge member of our biker gang shuffled up to me and sat down on the sand. He went by the name of Muscle Mike and that name suited him. He was well over six feet tall and very muscular. He had long hair, which he typically wore in a braid, and he always sported a headband made from a kerchief. He was covered in tattoos, which he showed off by wearing only a vest. He was a very intimidating guy.

"Father Wolf," he said, "I need to go to Confession." He was sitting cross-legged, elbows on his knees and staring at the ground.

It took me a few moments to process what he said. "Ah, I'm studying to be a priest, Muscle Mike, not an actual priest," I replied in a tentative voice.

"I need to confess a sin right now," he pleaded. He looked up at me with an insistence that seemed to brook no argument.

"Well," I was desperately trying to figure out what to do.

"Bless me Father, for I have sinned," he interrupted, and looked back down at the sand. He was apparently brought up Catholic because that is how the process of Confession starts.

I set my Coke bottle of coffee down and turned my full attention to Muscle Mike, trying to look priestly.

"I boned Hoghead's old lady last night," he blurted out. I looked around to see if anybody was within earshot.

"Boned?" I inquired.

"Yeah, boned. You know, I fucked his old lady. I was pretty drunk and so was she. She passed out and she just looked so good laying there, so I boned her," he confessed, nearly in tears.

I was shocked to the core. I had to make myself close my mouth. I had no experience with sex personally, but I knew enough to realize that Muscle Mike had not only committed adultery, but rape. Hoghead was one of the more volatile members of the gang, so I quickly conjured up visions of a murder as well. I calmed myself.

"Well, Mike," I said, "God forgives those who are truly contrite. If you acknowledge the wrong you have done and determine that you will mend your ways, God will forgive you. Does Hoghead know about this?"

"Naw," he said.

"Umm, do you have any other sins you want to confess," I adlibbed. "like taking God's name in vain, or stealing." I decided to leave out murdering and the other commandments. I didn't really want to know.

"Hell yeah," he said. "I've done all that shit too."

I nodded my head gravely. "OK, say your Act of Contrition, and God will forgive you."

"What's that?" he asked.

"Uh, just say, I'm sorry and will try to do better," I coached.

"I'm sorry and will try to do better," he repeated.

"OK, you are absolved of your sins Mike," I said. "For your penance, think of a good deed and go do it."

He looked up at me with a sincere look and said, "Thank you Father Wolf." He rose and walked away.

As Muscle Mike walked away, I wondered if I was going to Hell for impersonating a priest. The whole adventure just kept getting weirder.

The day wore on and I kept myself occupied with sketching. Activity on the beach increased through the day until the tempo and craziness matched that of the day before. Around five o'clock, Grinder came up to me and handed me a wad of cash.

"Here's some money. See if you can find some pizzas or something and bring 'em back here. Everybody's getting hungry," he said, and walked off.

"OK," I said to myself.

I headed up toward Highway A1A, where there were lots of places to get food. I found a pizza parlor and determined that I could get 27 pizzas with the cash I had. I skimmed enough off the top of my bank roll to purchase a Coke for myself. I recruited a couple of younger kids hanging around outside to help carry the pizzas back to the beach. I offered them $2 a piece, which was enough to buy a small pizza in those days. They were impressed to find that the pizza delivery was for a biker gang and seemed doubly impressed that it was the Outlaws. I was a momentary celebrity for bringing such a gourmet dinner to the camp.

That night was much like the night before, which is to say it was chaos. One of our gang, a guy they called Billy, staggered into our camp all bloody from a fight with a guy from another biker gang, called the Bandidos. I helped to patch him up. He confided in me that he was talking to one of the Bandidos' women, which resulted in the fight.

"I messed him up though Father Wolf," he proudly concluded. "There'll be hell to pay later. Those Bandidos are bad ass. They don't like it when you mess up one of their members."

Oh great, I thought. Just when I thought I might get out of here alive, I will probably end up in the middle of a gang fight. I'd seen West Side Story. I knew how these gang fights went. I retreated to the relative safety of the truck and hunkered down. The sun came up the next morning, however, without anything worse than the sporadic fighting that seemed to be part of the ritual fun inherent in this type of gathering.

Butch was already up and getting his people organized by the time I woke up. He seemed anxious and was hurrying everybody along. I relieved myself in front of the truck. What the hell? When in Rome. I helped get everything packed up and loaded into the trucks.

"Let's roll," Butch commanded. Bikes roared to life in the relative quiet of the early morning. I jumped on the back of his bike.

"What's the hurry?" I asked.

"Word is out that the Bandidos are planning to jump us this morning. There's too many of them here at Daytona so we're leaving before they have a chance to start something," he said.

Butch didn't strike me as a guy who was afraid of much. I decided to assume that he was using good judgement and choosing his battles wisely so he could live to fight another day. Good Grief! I was beginning to think of this barbaric thug as a natural leader. For myself, I was quite happy to avoid any trouble.

# Chapter 22

We left the beach with all the subtlety of a column of Sherman tanks. We exited the city and headed south. I was tired, dirty, and smelly, but I was looking forward to getting back home. I was still under the assumption that I was some kind of prisoner. I had to figure out a way to get Butch to drop me off somewhere so I could escape.

As we rolled into the Tampa, Saint Petersburg area a brilliant idea came to me. I tapped Butch on the shoulder.

"Hey Butch," I yelled over the noise, "Today is Sunday and I really need to go to church. Saint James Cathedral is up ahead on Orange Avenue. Could you drop me off there?" He lifted his chin in what I decided was agreement.

Butch made some signals with his hand to the bikes nearest him and we ultimately turned onto Orange Avenue. He was going to do it, I thought excitedly. As the cathedral came into sight, I pointed and told him that was it. He pulled over, along with all the other bikers. I took off my borrowed goggles and leather helmet and put them in his saddle bags. I stood there a bit awkwardly.

"Thanks," was all I could come up with. I turned to all the others and gave them an exaggerated Catholic priest type of blessing, guessing they probably wouldn't get the joke. They all waved. I looked back to Butch, who gave a quick nod. I turned, walked toward the cathedral and up the steps to the large double doors. I went in without looking back and entered the first pew in the rear. I knelt down and gave fervent thanks for letting me survive the last few days.

The service was the eleven thirty High Mass, which meant that the front of the cathedral was full of nicely dressed parishioners, the church choir in the loft behind and above me, accompanied by a large pipe organ , and the bishop himself who was celebrating the Mass. In those days the Mass was still in Latin and very traditional. The service was about halfway through when I came in. I was grateful that this was the case so I could enter quietly and keep to the back where nobody would see me in my wretched condition. Not only were my clothes filthy dirty and ill-fitting, but my face was smudged with grime and my hair was matted, sticking in every direction from wearing the leather helmet. I could only imagine what I must have looked like.

I remained kneeling during the rest of the Mass, so relieved that my nightmare was over. As the Mass neared the end, I thought it best to leave a little early so I could avoid being seen. In this type of Mass, the bishop leaves the Cathedral by way of the central aisle, holding a large crucifix on a golden staff, followed by several altar boys. The pipe organ booms a stirring recessional, while the choir sings the hymn. It's all quite impressive. This ceremonious recession was just starting, so I stood up to leave, when suddenly the doors at the back of the Cathedral swung open with a loud bang.

"Hey Father Wolf," I heard Muscle Mike's distinctive voice holler. "When you gonna be done? We gotta roll!"

I stood there frozen, still facing the front of the Cathedral. The bishop stopped where he was, looking puzzled and slightly alarmed. The choir, and then the organ faded into silence. Everyone in the pews turned around to see what was happening. I was mortified. A storm of competing emotions overtook my rational being. I spun around to see at least a dozen of the Outlaws standing in the doorway, wide-eyed, opened-mouthed, and seemingly frozen in various positions of surprise. I can only guess that none of them had seen the inside of a Cathedral, in all its opulence.

"What the hell are you doing," I shrieked, voice breaking. "I'm not done yet!"

You could hear a pin drop. Time remained suspended for what seemed like minutes. Slowly, the bikers backed out of the entrance and quietly closed the doors. I turned back toward the front of the Cathedral and let out an exaggerated sigh of utter frustration. I looked straight into the eyes of the bishop with an expression I can only imagine must have looked like, "go ahead, send me to Hell. I've already been there!"

The bishop collected himself, gave a nod to the choir director, and the recession proceeded as though nothing had happened. As was the custom, the parishioners followed behind the bishop's recession in an orderly manner. The bishop, and each person who followed, gave me only a very subtle side-glance as they filed by. I stood there as if on display, accepting the humiliation as though it must be part of my punishment for impersonating a priest and absolving Muscle Mike for his sins. I kept my eyes focused downward accepting the penance.

In a few moments, it became apparent that things were backing up. People couldn't seem to get out of the Cathedral. A low murmur edged through the crowd. Now what? I thought. I risked a look toward the back. People were starting to look at me as though waiting for me to do something. It couldn't be, I thought. I left the pew and started making my way through the crowd, which parted like the Red Sea as I approached.

As I reached the back doors and moved outside to the top of the steps, I could see that the whole Outlaw gang was waiting at the street, looking back at all the people looking at them. The pipe organ and choir were still cranking out the recessional as though nothing was amiss. The scene was surreal. I walked slowly down the steps, retaining as much dignity as I could.

When I was a couple of feet in front of Butch, I said, "Well?"

"Sorry we interrupted your thing in there," he said simply. "Come on, let's get you back to your grandparents." These were the sweetest words I could have heard at that moment. Tears started rolling down my cheeks. I was a wreck. Butch patted me on the shoulder in what I think was a brotherly gesture.

"Come on, mount up," he said quietly, and everybody did so. The bikes roared to life. The boys and girls couldn't help themselves. As we rolled away from in front of the Cathedral, they hooped and hollered with Indian war cries. I heard a few yell, "Go Father Wolf!" as the motley parade passed by. I'm sure the bishop was thinking, "who the hell is Father Wolf?"

We headed across Tampa Bay. When we got to Highway 19, Butch peeled off from the column and headed north to New Port Richey. He signaled the others to keep going on toward Clearwater, where their clubhouse was located. We pulled into my grandparent's driveway about twenty minutes later. I got off the bike and thanked Butch for the interesting experience. He gave me a wry smile and a two-finger salute. I had secured my sketchpad to the sissy bar at the back of the bike.

"Could you make sure that everybody gets the sketches I did for them?" I asked. "I put their name at the top of each drawing, but they'll probably recognize their own bike. Hope they like them."

"You're a good guy Father Wolf," he said. "Good luck." He got his bike turned around and took of down the street.

I turned toward the house to see Grandpa and Grandma standing there, just outside the door, with a bewildered look on both their faces. I walked up to them and said, "Hi."

"Are you okay?" Grandma asked.

"I'm fine. I really need to take a shower and change my clothes, then we can sit down and I'll tell you all about the last few days. I think you'll agree that it's a pretty interesting story," I said.

# Chapter 23

The next week was blissfully uneventful. I visited the Ford agency to notify them that the doctor said I was no longer under his care and that I planned to head up to New Jersey in a few days. I had met a girl in Ohio a couple of months before heading to Florida, who had since moved to the Elizabeth area in New Jersey. We had exchanged a few letters while I was in Florida. I decided on impulse to go visit her before heading back to Ohio.

Robert was at the Ford agency the day I visited and I told him my plans. He told me that he had been planning a trip up North, and suggested we might travel up to New Jersey together. It sounded like a good idea to me. It would be nice to have company on such a long drive.

"I'm planning to leave in the next couple of days," I said. "Can you be ready by then?"

"Sure," he said. "Just tell me when." I had never been to Robert's house, so I didn't know where he lived.

"Where do you want me to pick you up?" I asked.

"On the corner of Highway 19 and Gulf to Bay Boulevard," he replied. "Let's set a day and time right now."

"OK," I said. "Let's make it Thursday at eight a.m. We should get an early start."

"OK, sounds good," he said.

I always thought of Robert as being the same age as I was, but as it turned out he was 17 years old, while I was 18. I did not know this at the time, however, nor did I know that he was essentially running away from home after an argument with his father. Both of these details would ultimately result in big trouble for me.

We departed on Thursday as planned, taking our time in order to enjoy the road trip. We rolled into New Jersey on Saturday afternoon. At a roadside payphone, I called Lynn to announce my surprise visit. I don't think she was as pleased with my surprise as I had fantasized she would be in my daydreams.

"You can't come here to my house," she hissed over the phone. "My mother doesn't like you. She thinks you're a bum."

That kind of hurt, momentarily flashing back to the time when I thought bums were similar to bridge trolls. Why would she think I was a bum?

"Oh, well, could we maybe meet for a couple of hours, see a movie or something?" I begged. "We came all the way from Florida."

"We?" she said.

"Oh yeah," I said. "I brought a friend with me. His name is Robert."

"You're crazy," she whispered into the phone. "OK, I'll tell my mom that I'm going to go over to one of my girlfriends' house. Pick me up at the corner of Westfield and Locust in half an hour. It's not far from the turnpike. Do you have a map?"

"Yes," I said. "I'll find it."

That was not exactly the way I had envisioned our meeting, but I was in good spirits at the thought of seeing Lynn again, despite the subterfuge of our arrangements. I noticed that Robert seemed to be in a glum mood. "What's the matter," I asked.

"Aw, nothing really," he said. Clearly, something was bothering him though.

"We've got some time before we pick Lynn up," I said. "Let's go get some snacks."

We stopped at a little store and got some nuts, chips and sodas. As we were about to get back into the car, Robert suddenly yelled out "Dammit!" and slammed his fist hard onto the roof of my car. He hollered out in pain.

"What the heck are you doing?" I asked, alarmed at the sudden outburst.

He was doubled over in pain, holding his hand with his uninjured hand. I ran around to the passenger side of the car.

"What happened?" I asked.

"I think I broke my wrist," he groaned, still bent over. He started yelling like a possessed person. I presumed it was in response to the pain. I looked around to see that we were attracting the attention of other patrons of the little store who happened to be out in the parking lot. I wasn't sure what to do.

"OK. Um. Get in the car," I urged. I opened the door for him and he slowly sat down on the seat but didn't get his legs in the car. He was clearly in a great deal of pain. I was focused on trying to get Robert calmed down, barely noticing another car pulling up next to ours. When I finally looked up to assess our situation, I discovered that the other car was, in fact, the police.

Ah, I thought, this might be useful, since it was becoming evident that Robert might need medical attention.

"What's going on here?" one of the two officers demanded.

"My friend hurt his hand," I replied. "I think we might need to get him to a doctor. We're visiting from Florida so I don't know where I could take him."

The cop who had asked me this question was giving Robert and me a close inspection. We were both clean-cut boys, wearing nice jeans and plain T-shirts, so I didn't think we warranted such suspicious scrutiny. The other cop was making a note of my license number.

"Let me see your driver's license," the first cop said. "Stay right here." He walked back his cruiser to consult with his partner. The one who took down my license number got into the cruiser and got on the radio.

I told Robert that everything would be alright, that the police would ensure he got some help. He was moaning, rocking back and forth, and holding his bad hand with the good one. After several minutes, both cops approached us and asked for Robert's driver's license. I had to help him get his wallet out of his back pocket. After a quick look at his license, the first cop told me that we would have to go to the police station. I was to follow him.

I got into my car and followed the cruiser several blocks to a police station. I was thinking they would arrange for help for Robert and that I would be asked to wait there at the station until he was patched up.

Once inside I was advised that I was under arrest for transporting a minor across a state line. Robert was hurried away into another room. I stood there in stunned bafflement. I didn't have the vaguest idea what they were talking about. I quickly surmised they must have made some kind of mistake, and tried to explain that I didn't have any minors with me.

"You are eighteen years old. Robert is seventeen, and he ran away from home according to his father," the officer explained. "In Florida, at eighteen, you are an adult. At seventeen, Robert is a minor. When you transported him across the Florida State border, you broke the law. Robert's parents have been worried sick and thought he might have left with you. They knew that you were headed to New Jersey, so a law enforcement bulletin was issued to stop and question you if found."

"I didn't know he was running away," I pleaded. "We worked together at his father's car dealer. I always thought he was the same age as me. I didn't even know there was such a law." I was having a hard time comprehending my alleged wrong doing.

They never actually put me in a jail cell. Instead, I sat in a small room for what seemed like forever, waiting to see what my fate would be. Eventually, the same officer who had originally discovered me in the store parking lot came into the room.

"We've talked to Robert's father," he began. "He says that he believes that you didn't know that Robert was running away, but that you were under a doctor's care for an accident that happened on his car lot, and you should not have left until you were released." I didn't say anything. "He says that he will drop this whole thing on two conditions: that you never see Robert again, and that you come back to Florida until your doctor officially releases you."

"OK", I quickly agreed. "It will take me a couple days or so to drive back."

"He's arranged for you to fly back," the officer said. "There's a ticket for you at the Newark Liberty Airport. Your plane leaves this evening at 7:00 pm. He'll pick you up at the Tampa/Saint Pete airport."

"What do I do with my car," I asked.

"We're going to lock it up here in our impound lot," he replied. "It sounds like you just need to take care of some formalities and then you can come back up here to retrieve your car."

I was numb, still trying to make sense of the situation. I didn't try to defend myself or protest or wonder what going back to Florida would achieve. I essentially just did what I was told. I was given my little suitcase of personal belongings from the car, and driven to the airport by the police. I felt very self-conscious when we arrived at the terminal. I was sure everybody was assuming I was some kind of desperate criminal. The officer escorted me to the ticket counter and made sure that I got on the plane as scheduled.

# Chapter 24

When I arrived at my destination, there was Robert's father waiting for me as promised. I tried to act very humble and contrite, although I didn't feel like I had actually done anything wrong. As we left the terminal, he told me that I had made grievous errors in judgement and he had gone out of his way to help me out after the accident. He expressed his disappointment in my ingratitude. He reminded me that I was not to try to contact Robert. He wanted a signed letter from the doctor indicating that I was released from treatment.

He strode off to the parking lot, leaving me there at the entrance to the terminal.

"How do I get home?" I called after him.

"Call your grandparents," he shouted back over his shoulder.

If this had happened to me today, I would have shouted back that he was a fucking asshole, but in those days I was a very reserved and polite teenager. So, I just stood there trying to absorb all that was happening, not having a clue what to do next.

It was quite late and I didn't want to call my grandparents at this time of day. Not only was I concerned about my grandma's health and the potential reaction she might have to my situation, but I was also embarrassed, humiliated, and bewildered. I also knew that once my grandparents knew what had happened, it was just a matter of time before my parents heard the story. That was a situation I found entirely unbearable. I decided to just stay at the terminal until morning. I saw other people sleeping in chairs, waiting for flights. I figured I would not stand out.

The next morning, I left the terminal and headed toward Highway 19. I decided I would hitchhike back to Clearwater and try to see the doctor. In those days, it was pretty easy to get a ride. Somewhere along the way I recalled it was Sunday and the doctor wouldn't be in until tomorrow. I had to come up with a plan. I decided I would only call my grandparents as a last resort.

When I arrived in Clearwater, on the main drag, it was still early. I purchased a sandwich and a soda from a little café and made my way to a bus stop bench, where I sat down to devise a plan. Perhaps I could stay at the YMCA for a day or two. I was deep in thought when the sound of motorcycles roared into my consciousness. I looked up to see two bikers coming toward the corner where I was sitting. As they drew closer I could see that it was Butch and Muscle Mike. They spotted me and pulled over.

"On no," I said out loud.

"Hey, Father Wolf," exclaimed Muscle Mike, clearly pleased to see me. "What are you doing here? You waitin' for a bus?" My head dropped into my hands in an exaggerated expression of frustration.

"What's up man?" Butch asked in a tone of voice that required an answer.

I gave them a quick version of what had happened and why I didn't want to tell my grandparents. I added that this was about the worst thing that could ever happen to me. When I finished my story, they looked at me with a combination of sympathy and anger. They looked at each other for a moment, then back at me.

"Get on." said Butch. Oh great, I thought. Here we go again. I got on the back of Butch's bike. Sometimes a plan just defines itself.

We drove directly to the Outlaw clubhouse. Butch told everybody who was there what had happened and declared the situation "bullshit". I was taken up to the apartment over the bar, where I made myself at home. Butch told me he was taking care of things. I could tell that he was worked up over my plight. I wasn't sure what he was talking about, but, right then I started to get an uneasy feeling.

Bikers came into the clubhouse that day from wherever it is that bikers come from. More bikers assembled there that Sunday than had come in for the Bikers' Event in Daytona. The abandoned partying that I had witnessed in preparation for the Daytona run was absent this time. Everybody was drinking to be sure, but things seemed restrained.

The next morning Butch got me up and told me to get ready to roll. He announced that he was taking me to see the doctor. Oh, I thought, this is a positive turn of events. My spirits elevated as we headed back into Clearwater. I directed Butch to the doctor's office. He told me that he would be back to pick me up in about an hour.

Inside the doctor's office I explained my reason for the visit and pleaded with the receptionist to try to get a letter of release from the doctor, assuring her that he had already told me I was done with treatments. After some time, the doctor came out to the waiting room, with my release letter. He told me that it was entirely unnecessary for me to have come back, but understood the owner of the car dealership was probably trying to limit his potential liability. He wished me luck.

I went outside to wait for Butch. Now I had to figure out how to get back to New Jersey to get my car. I figured I'd go to the dealership, show the release letter to Robert's father and ask him to send me back. When Butch showed up with several of the gang, I shared my plan with him. He seemed skeptical, but agreed to take me to the Ford agency.

As we rode toward the dealership, several more bikes joined the growing formation. When we arrived, I headed toward the offices. I noticed that Butch and Muscle Mike were following right behind me. I thought to myself that this might cause some consternation within the offices, but what the heck. Having them with me bolstered my confidence. Once inside the office area, Robert's father came out of his big corner office to meet me.

"What do you want, Wolf?" he asked. He was looking warily at Butch and Muscle Mike.

"I have the letter of release from my doctor. I got it this morning. I'd like to go back to New Jersey to get my car," I said.

"OK," he said. Well, good luck," and started to turn around and head back to his office.

"I need a ticket," I exclaimed.

He turned slowly back around to face me. "I'm not going to pay for a ticket back to New Jersey," he said.

"But, you made me come back by plane, and my car is still up there, and I can't afford a ticket," I protested, beginning to feel myself getting angry.

"You owe this man a ticket, pal," Muscle Mike said in tone of voice that sounded distinctively ominous.

"Who the hell are you?" Robert's father said with a condescending attitude.

Butch moved closer to Robert's father, looking like he might be considering breaking him in half. "I've got fifty Outlaws just outside who'd be very upset if they thought that Wolf here got screwed." Muscle Mike made his own menacing move. It was clear the other people in the office were getting uneasy.

Robert's father cleared his throat. "How about giving you the money for a bus ticket to New Jersey?" he asked me. "You go get the ticket and I'll reimburse you."

Butch looked at the nearest young woman sitting at her desk. "How about you call the bus station and get the exact amount of that ticket and we'll collect the money before we leave?" She looked at Robert's father, clearly looking like she was ready to fall apart. He nodded. She called the Greyhound bus station and got the price, $54.72.

"Make that a money order," Butch ordered, and it was done.

As we left the offices and headed for the bikes, I told Butch I was grateful but that I probably wouldn't be allowed on the bus, much less get all the way to New Jersey. "Don't you think that they will call the police and that I'll be arrested at the station?"

"Arrested for what?" Butch sneered. "You didn't do nothing."

"Maybe you'll get in trouble," I said more quietly. Butch assured me that he was more than capable of dealing with any trouble. I was not confident. How in the world did I get myself into this mess? We mounted up and headed for the bus station.

Arriving at the station, we saw three police cars. This is it, I thought. My life is ruined. To my surprise, however, nothing happened. Perhaps the police felt outnumbered, but I was sure reinforcements must be on the way.

I purchased my ticket for a bus that was departing imminently. Everybody at the station was clearly nervous about having so many outlaw bikers in and around the bus station. The cops were outside their cruisers, but seemed to be content with just keeping an eye on things. The bikers were keeping to themselves, not bothering anybody other than an occasional whistle of approval directed toward any attractive young woman unfortunate enough to stroll by.

When the time came, I said goodbye to Butch, Muscle Mike and a few others I knew. Butch told me not to worry, that I would make it all the way without any problems. I sat down nervously at the front of the bus. Everyone was staring at me. I tried to act nonchalant. I was fairly certain that my journey on the bus would be short lived. There was no way I was going to be allowed to get to New Jersey, and even if I did, they were sure to nail me when I tried to get my car from the police station impound there.

The driver closed the door and backed the bus up into the exit lane. He drove the bus out onto the street and we headed up Highway 19. I was on pins and needles. Just a matter of time now, I thought. I heard a growing commotion in the back of the bus. I turned around to see nearly everyone looking out the windows and toward the roadway behind the bus. As we progressed up the highway, where the city turned to rural countryside, the unmistakable sound of big bikes could be heard and growing louder. In a few moments bikes were passing the bus on both sides to form a double column in front of the bus. It was evident that there was a second double column behind the bus.

As we progressed up the route toward northern Florida, more bikers joined the escort. By the time we reached Orlando, there were hundreds of bikers in the formation. Initially, everybody on the bus was showing signs of panic. One middle aged black woman asked me what these bikers were going to do to them. She obviously associated me with them. I told her that they were just escorting me up north and that they weren't going to bother anybody, unless the cops try to stop us, I thought to myself. Within an hour, the other passengers were getting used to the idea of a massive biker gang escort and starting to think that it was kind of cool. Personally, I was holding my breath.

In those days, the population of Florida was only around 6 million, a million less than the city of New York. Outside the major metropolitan areas, there were vast areas of marsh, citrus groves and sugar cane fields. Biker clubs from places as far away as California, Texas, New York, and Canada were expanding their membership. In many parts of Florida law enforcement was spotty and spread out, making this state a prime target for gangs like the Hells Angels, the Outlaws, the Pagans, the Warlocks, and the Mongols. In those days the Outlaws were the predominant biker club, and are still the dominant club in many parts of Florida.

Today, I seriously doubt that my biker escorted bus ride through Florida would have gotten farther than the Clearwater bus station, but on that day in 1967, our Greyhound Bus drove all the way to the Florida/Georgia border with full biker club escort.

As we neared the State line, the bikers began to fall back behind the bus, a few waving at us as we passed them. When we crossed into Georgia, the passengers cheered, and there were no more bikes. Everybody but me showed obvious signs of relief.

I recall the trip from the Georgia line to Newark as one of the longest passages of time in my life. Yet, nothing happened. We pulled into the Newark bus station and there were no police there to apprehend me. I hitched a ride to the local police station where my car was impounded. I asked about retrieving my rusty old Plymouth and was given some paperwork to fill out. I was then handed the keys and a release form. Nobody slapped the cuffs on me and dragged me to a cell. I retrieved my car and drove out of Newark, heading west to Ohio. I never looked back.

When I arrived at the family home, I was greeted with enthusiastic joy and warmth. There was no hint of suspicion that I was a former outlaw biker on the run. It was good to be back in the bosom of my family. After a few days of recovering my senses, I began the process of getting myself enlisted in the U.S. Air Force.

# Part II

## The Warrior

*Then I was a soldier*
*I had a gun*
*But we saved someone*
*I guess we all were heroes*

# Chapter 25

The old man leaned back in his chair, rubbing his face. Writing this book was more work than he had thought it would be, but he had to admit, he was enjoying it. There were some aspects of conjuring up all these memories, however, that could be quite cathartic.

The initial stories of his youth were fun to recall and write about. He had a very fond memories of his childhood, and recalling those days made him feel pleasantly nostalgic. By pure coincidence, he and his wife had attended their high school class reunions a couple months ago. Going back to the old home town, meeting old classmates, seeing the old school, had helped to jog his memory about many of the experiences from those days.

"Old" seemed to be the operative word. So long ago, he thought. So many things had happened since then. The world was a very different place now. How much had he changed, he wondered? Quite a bit, no doubt. Oh well, there were lots of good memories to be sure.

He was now preparing to write the part of the book that involved his military experience and the war. That was a different kettle of fish altogether. It required bringing up some painful memories. He could deal with that though. He always had. He knew that many people who had been in the Vietnam War had a difficult time adjusting to normal life when they returned. For some veterans, their lives had been affected in negative ways.

He had some friends who did not do well after they returned. He wondered how many of their problems were due to war experiences rather than an individual propensity toward some type of compulsive behavior or inherent disorder. Did a person's war experience cause alcoholism or drug addiction? He doubted it, but he didn't want to judge. Nobody had ever heard of Posttraumatic Stress Disorder back then, at least he had never heard about it, but he supposed that was likely part of the problem. A lot of people probably didn't think there was any connection between mental health issues or addiction and the war when a vet went off the deep end after they returned home.

As for himself, he didn't have any problems directly related to his war experience, at least not that he was conscious of. He didn't really think about it much, his personal Vietnam experience that is. Perhaps that was what allowed him to avoid the problems that others had. In fact, he had done such a good job of not thinking about it over the years that he was now discovering he couldn't seem to remember much at all about his time in the war. The stories he had told over the years had focused on the crazy things that happened to him in between the distressing war action he experienced.

In an effort to jog his memory, he dug some old scrap books out of storage and found a suitcase that contained letters from that period of his life. He did some research on the Internet too, but discovered the information about that period required quite a bit of digging. Many things had changed since he was in the Air Force. Individual units, even whole commands were no longer in existence. Bases had closed or had changed their mission focus. Some of the incidents that felt so important back in the 70s seemed to be missing from the history that was available on the Internet.

As he completed his research and prepared to write this section of the book, he also began to recall some of the turmoil that occurred in his personal life during this time. Yes, this was going to be much more challenging to write about than the first part of the book.

He sat up in his chair prepared to begin, but what the hell was that sound? He cocked his head a little. He became aware of a very deep hum. Oh yes, it was definitely there. He had been hearing this off and on for some time, but mostly ignored it. He wasn't sure it was actually a sound. Perhaps it was a vibration rather than a sound, but then he supposed that sound was a vibration after all. Whatever it was, it was incredibly low, almost undetectable. Once you noticed it, however, it was hard to ignore. He couldn't say that it was annoying, but curiously distracting. He wondered if his wife could hear it. He'd have to ask her. He would also have to try to determine the source, but now it was time to get back to work.

# Chapter 26

During the months preceding my entry into the Air Force, I focused on having a good time with my cousins and friends. My friend, Brian, was also entering the Air Force about the same time my enlistment was scheduled, in early December, and we spent a lot of time together. My old Plymouth had given up the ghost since returning to Ohio. While I could borrow my mother's Dodge Dart occasionally, I was pretty dependent on Brian and his 1961 Pontiac GTO for transportation.

Fun in those days was pretty tame by today's standards. The whole hippie, free-love, drug culture thing was just beginning but hadn't quite reached the rural Midwest yet. Neither Brian nor I drank at this transitional stage of our lives. Actually, we tried drinking beer a couple of times, but it didn't set well with Brian. Our second attempt at having a couple of beers with some pizza resulted in Brian suddenly hurtling a stream of projectile vomit in my direction that rivaled the vomit scene from *The Exorcist*. Very unpleasant. We avoided drinking after that incident.

Brian had managed to get himself a girlfriend while I was in Florida, which limited his availability to hang out with me. As a matter of pragmatism, I suggested that perhaps his girlfriend might have a female friend who could be persuaded to go on a double date. Brian came through a few days later when he announced that he and his girlfriend planned to go to a local concert and that she arranged for two of her friends to go as well. Another one of Brian's friends, a guy named Denver, and I were invited to join the group.

The triple date proved to be a momentous occasion, as it turned out. It was on that date I met the woman who was to become my first wife. There was one unusual aspect about the occasion however. The girl I eventually married was supposed to be Denver's designated date. As the evening wore on, it became evident that Tanya, Denver's date, was not interested in him, nor was I having much luck impressing my assigned date. I was being my usual jovial, humorous self, and Tanya apparently found my silly antics entertaining. Perhaps she just found me less boring than Denver. In any case, midway through the evening, in an odd but not necessarily awkward moment, we each tacitly implemented a switch in the pairings for the evening.

Over the next few months, Tanya and I saw each other frequently. She had been a cheerleader in high school and was a pretty, petite blond. I was extremely flattered a pretty girl like her would consider me worthy of her attention. Our brief courtship was quite traditional in a 1950s sort of way. We were both very young and naïve about many things, including sex, so there was no torrid love affair before I had to leave for military service. It seemed like bad timing, meeting this girl just before leaving for Air Force basic training, but she promised to write to me while I was away.

It's hard to overstate what a geek I was at this stage of my life. I was tall and skinny, not particularly good looking, wore black, horned rim glasses, and was always trying to compensate for my physical appearance with an over-the-top goofiness meant to entertain and endear me to others. I was particularly awkward around women, and, in fact, found very pretty women to be almost terrifying to be around. Looking back on it, I suppose I was rather pathetic. Nevertheless, I seemed to have a knack for charming people, and I never shied away from trying to get the attention of others.

Going into the Air Force was not something I spent a lot of time thinking about. My dad had been in the Army Air Corps during World War II. Although he never encouraged me to follow in his footsteps, I inherently felt that anything he did was a good thing for me to consider doing as well. I did think about entering the military in the context of the Vietnam War. There was a draft program in effect at this time, and since I was not going to be able to attend college I knew that there was a good chance I could be conscripted into the Army. I didn't really see myself going in that direction, so I set my sights on the Air Force.

From the day I arrived at boot camp my life began to transform. While the environment there at Lackland Air Force Base, Texas, was stressful, very regimented, and sometimes frightening, I actually flourished. For me, it seemed vaguely familiar. I believe the seminary had prepared me for this kind of strict discipline and regimen, and my propensity to perform in an effort to please others actually worked in my favor. My height of six-foot-two was a lucky attribute ultimately resulting in me being placed at the front of our squadron. This happened to be an initial de facto lead position. I was soon singled out for leadership positions and assignments, and I discovered that I had an aptitude for many things the Air Force apparently valued. I took it all very seriously.

My biggest struggle was with physical conditioning. Not having been athletic in high school, I discovered I was woefully unprepared for the physical rigors of military life. Fortunately, my youth and will to excel allowed me to ultimately morph into something much less wimpy than I was when I started. I discovered something else about myself during this time. I was not competitive by nature. That is to say, I was not predisposed or inclined to beat others at all costs. In fact, I found myself holding back and even assisting others in order to allow my comrades to think they had bested me in physical efforts. This was probably another manifestation of my inherent need to have others like me.

At basic training, new recruits are subjected to an unrelenting barrage of vociferous demands and commands that are given by training instructors who seem to thrive on creating discomfort in other human beings. On frequent occasions our flight would be required to stand surprise inspections, usually at very early hours of the day. Everybody would have to stand at attention at the foot of their bunks in the open bay that served as our living quarters. Because of the early hour, everybody was often clothed only in their underwear.

The drill sergeant would go through each recruit's foot locker with a fine tooth comb, looking for the slightest infraction. Clothes had to be folded exactly and arranged in a specified manner. Razors had to be spotless and toothpaste tubes had to be clean in the neck of the tube, which was no easy feat to accomplish. If the drill sergeant found anything out of place or unclean, he would get within a couple of inches of the offending recruit's face and scream his displeasure. This was a very disconcerting encounter, and some guys didn't handle it very well at all. They usually disappeared from our ranks within a short time.

There was one guy in our flight who I felt particularly sorry for. His name was Willy, and he was a young black man from Mississippi. I knew him to be a good person and serious about getting through basic training successfully. He had more than one encounter with the drill sergeant, and I thought that Willy was being undeservedly singled out. I wondered if maybe there was some kind of racial thing going on, but you don't dare say anything like that in basic training. At one of these inspections, the white drill sergeant found that Willy's underpants were not folded to his satisfaction and he screamed his displeasure at him in a sarcastic, demeaning manner. He made Willy put his underpants on his head and march around the barracks, proclaiming "Ain't I pretty." With Willy's Mississippi accent, it came out "Ain't I purdy."

I could tell that Willy was mortified, but he did exactly what he was told and didn't utter a word of protest. Most of the other guys started laughing. Under most circumstances the drill sergeant would have yelled at everybody to shut up, but he just let them laugh at poor Willy. I felt really bad for him, and later approached him to see if he wanted to talk about it. He told me that it didn't bother him that much. He was determined to get through basic training and would do anything not to get cut.

"I ain't gonna let that ol' white boy goad me into doin' somm'um stupid," Willy said. "I'm gonna get through this and stay outta trouble."

This was the first time I had witnessed what I was pretty sure was racial prejudice and I never forgot that incident. I'm glad to say the Willy made it through basic training. We stayed in contact for several months afterward, and was pleased when he wrote that he'd graduated from the Tactical Aircraft Maintenance technical school at Sheppard AFB. He wrote that he was going on to get more training in aircraft electrical and environment systems. He was a man on a mission and I knew that he would do well.

I was not surprised, but pleased to find myself as a top marksman among my peers, not just in basic training but throughout my military career. My father had taught all of his sons and daughters to shoot a gun when we were kids. I had many hours of target practice with several different types of firearms by the time I entered the Air Force. I also had been hunting with my dad, and had acquired some knowledge about the intricacies of stalking prey and shooting at distant targets. Finally, I had discovered something that I could do really well, better than most, in a career where marksmanship really mattered.

While most of my fellow airmen complained incessantly about military life, I took to it like a duck takes to water. Some of my comrades looked upon my comfort with military discipline as a deliberate attempt to "brown nose the brass", but most eventually accepted the fact that I just genuinely flourished in the military environment. I managed to get along with just about everybody.

As men and women go through the early stages of their basic training, they are subjected to a number of tests designed to determine what they are interested in doing and what they have the aptitude to do successfully. Depending upon what specific type of resources the Air Force needs at any given time, an individual recruit has some modicum of choice in the specific job they will be trained for. In my case, I had high scores in all areas except mechanical.

At the end of my basic training I was steered toward administrative specialties, but I had decided I wanted something more exciting and tried to get into the military police. Unfortunately, more military police were not what they needed at that time. So, I ended up at Amarillo Air Force Base, assigned to the 3320th Technical Training School and placed into the Personnel Specialist training program. After my initial disappointment, I threw myself into my technical training regime and was appointed Dorm Chief, responsible for approximately fifty airmen and the building where we all lived.

Amarillo was a strange place. The Air Force brass decided to close the base down and move its training mission to other bases, such as Chanute AFB, Illinois, Keesler AFB, Mississippi, Lowery AFB, Colorado, Sheppard AFB, Texas and Lackland AFB, Texas. The last technical training classes at Amarillo were scheduled to conclude in late 1968. Much of the base real estate had already been taken over by Bell Helicopter. The net effect of this closure was that the base resembled a ghost town, and that tended to result in a general relaxing of the "spit and polish" discipline normally associated with the Air Training Command. Perhaps as a result of this relaxation and the fact that, as trainees for the job of Personnel Specialist, students could get relatively free access to the Consolidated Base Personnel Office, referred to as the CBPO. The CBPO was equivalent to the Human Resources department of a very large company.

I was always looking for opportunities to satisfy my curiosity and enhance my understanding of anything I was involved in. I spent time hanging out at the CBPO during non-training hours, getting to know some of the people who worked there and occasionally helping out. It was this set of circumstances that allowed me to run across a bulletin indicating that the Aerospace Rescue and Recovery Service, under the Military Airlift Command, was recruiting for Pararescuemen, also called PJs. Since I had access to the Air Force Specialty Code manual, I was able to look up what this interesting sounding job entailed.

My first reaction, after reading the job description and training requirements, was that I would not be able to cut it. I was, after all, not athletic, not tough, and not particularly brave. The more I thought about it, though, the more my imagination took control of my thoughts and I naively felt this would be like a Hollywood role in the Air Force. I also liked the maroon berets with its cool pararescue flash that PJs got to wear. Nothing ventured, nothing gained I thought. I got some friends in the CBPO to pull a few strings and arranged to request a reassignment to pararescue training. Due to my conduct and performance during my personnel training, as well as my extra leadership duties, I even managed to get a recommendation from the tech school commander.

This just happened to be a time when the Air Force's scope of operations in Viet Nam was becoming so large that the demand for pararescue teams was expanding dramatically. They were looking for qualified volunteers, and I was in the right place at the right time.

Little did I know what I was about to get myself into. Amazingly, I was accepted and shipped back to Lackland AFB. I entered into what is known as the "pipeline". The training program was nearly two years long and included courses in parachute jumping, diving and underwater skills, mountaineering, combat tactics, survival in various environments, EMT-Paramedic training, and helicopter insertion/extraction qualifications. The physical demands are extreme, requiring significant capabilities in swimming, running, strength, and endurance. The attrition rate for this training was around 80%.

To my own amazement, and certainly to many others', I made it through the program and became a PJ. I proudly swore the pararescue creed the day I was given my pararescue badge:

*"It is my duty as a Pararescueman to save life and to aid the injured. I will be prepared at all times to perform my assigned duties quickly and efficiently, placing these duties before personal desires and comforts. These things I do, that others may live."*

To say that I emerged a different person would be a gross understatement. I morphed into a young, confident man who I would describe as buff, which is not a description that I ever thought would apply to me. But there was something more. There was a visceral change in how I viewed the world and the military and myself. During the intense training, I experienced the deep camaraderie and connection that develops uniquely among comrades-in-arms within the military. I also felt very proud to be a part of something I considered as noble as the rescue and recovery service. "That Others May Live" is the pararescue creed, and I am sure all of us felt a sincere commitment to that oath. For the first time in my life, I felt I had accomplished something really important.

Toward the end of my training, I managed to get back home and marry Tanya, after properly asking her grandfather for her hand, of course. It was a big, formal Catholic wedding and she made a beautiful bride.

When I came home on leave for the wedding, I stayed at my parent's house. My mother had always been a stickler for good manners, and she made sure that all her children were raised to be good people with good manners. She would frequently remind us what Emily Post had to say about table manners and social graces. We were taught to say "yes sir" and "yes ma'am" to our elders. My mother was especially emphatic about how men should treat women. She often reminded me and my brothers that we should always "put women on a pedestal". By the time I was an adult, that concept was drilled into my head.

My mother was always quite candid with me. I think that conversations between her and me while I was growing up were different than they were with my brothers and sisters. My mother seemed to be comfortable with talking to me about everything. Two days before the wedding she took me aside, telling me she wanted to talk to me about something.

"Wolf, I hope that you are still a virgin," she began.

This did not surprise me, as I was quite used to her talking to me very directly, saying exactly what was on her mind. Still, her abrupt comment made me smile a little sheepishly. "Yes, Mother, I am."

"Do you suppose that Tanya is," she asked?

"Yes, I'm quite certain that she is," I said. My mother had been a nurse during the war, and I knew what was coming.

"Well, you must be very gentle with her on your wedding night," she began her lecture. "As you know, women have a hymen that is intact before they've had sex for the first time. Sometimes a woman's hymen can be torn before sex, but that's not typical. When a woman has sex for the first time, you will cause it to be broken and it can be painful. So you should be very patient and gentle and aware of her experience.

"That's good advice, Mother," I said. "I will be very gentle, but you know, I don't really know what I'm doing since I've never done it before. I promise I will be sensitive to her experience though."

"A married man and woman having sex on their wedding night is a very beautiful thing, Wolf," she concluded. I had heard this statement many times in the past as well.

"Thank you for the advice," I said sincerely. My mother was the sweetest person.

I saw Tanya that evening over at her place. I told her about my mother's pre-nuptial talk, and she thought it was sweet of my mother to think of such a thing, but was surprised that she would talk to me about it so plainly.

We were up in Tanya's bedroom. She was getting her trousseau ready. I would not be allowed to see her after that evening until we met at the altar, approximately 36 hours later. I started fooling around with her and we started getting passionate. I got the bright idea that we ought to practice the wedding night right then and there in order to get the whole hymen thing over with. Amazingly, she gave in.

After we made love, during which I was the epitome of gentlemanly care and gentleness, I was floating on cloud nine. Holy cow! I had no idea that sex was so wonderful. I mean, holy cow! This is something that we should do several times a day for the rest of our lives, I thought. For Tanya's part, I eventually discovered that this initial experience was more like having a hemorrhoid removed without anesthetic. Recovering from my own ecstasy, I asked if it had been painful.

"Not too bad," she said, "but it still stings."

"Oh. Oh, I'm sorry," I said, disappointed that she didn't share my experience. "I tried to be very gentle."

"You were, but it just hurt," she said. "It will be okay."

I took her at her word, but I don't think she was ever able to get over that first experience. Of course, I suppose I have to consider the possibility that I was just not a very sexy guy in those days. I was looking forward to a life of sexual bliss, but it turned out that, in fact, sex was not high on the list of things she was interested in during our marriage. On top of this sexual drought, trying to live on an airman's salary was very challenging, adding stress to the fact that I had taken her away from her home and friends in Ohio. I didn't have the time or the money to take Tanya on a genuine honeymoon. Sadly, the storybook romance started to fizzle early on.

That short marriage, however, did produce one of the most important events of my life, the birth of our daughter, Alexa. Being blessed with this little girl made my life feel more meaningful than ever. She was adorable. Unfortunately, shortly after she was born, I got my orders to go to Vietnam.

# Chapter 27

I volunteered to serve in Vietnam. I didn't think about wanting to go there as a heroic or patriotic thing. While tens of thousands of young men were trying to figure out a way to avoid going to Vietnam, I wanted the chance to get into some action for the sake of the action, and that is where the action was. Of course I knew people were dying there, a lot of people, but I didn't think about the possibility of me dying there, at least not in any concrete way. For me it was more of an abstract notion.

It was my modus operandi to dive into something I wanted to do and deal with the consequences as they presented themselves. Odd as it may seem, the reality of what I was about to get into did not hit home until we were approaching Tan Son Nhut Air Base. We were several miles to the north of the base. I was looking out the window of the airplane and saw what must have been a large battle field. It looked like the surface of the moon. It seemed every square inch of the ground was pocked with a bomb or artillery crater. "My God," I thought, "This is really a war, and that's what it looks like." It was a very sobering moment.

I arrived on Friday, December 17, 1971. I was met at the air base terminal by my unit's first sergeant, a guy named Robbins. He was a large man with a pleasant personality and dressed in a khaki uniform. While this was the same uniform that I was wearing, I was surprised to see him dressed in this way. After all, this was a war zone, and I assumed everybody wore fatigues. I noticed that many others in the terminal were in the same khaki uniform.

"Sergeant Robbins, why is everybody dressed in khakis?" I asked. "I would have thought that everybody would be in fatigues."

"The base commander ordered that all non-combat personnel to wear khakis. Wants to keep up appearances here in the capital. They're definitely more comfortable than the old fatigues. The Air Force has a newer jungle fatigue uniform that's lighter and more modern, but they haven't made their way to us yet," he said with a wry grin. "Most of the time, flight crews will wear fatigues or flight suits, but anytime you are outside the base you are required to wear khakis."

Sergeant Robbins took me to the barracks, apparently called "hooches", where I would be staying. He advised me that he would take care of the necessary paperwork to record my arrival. He added that I would need to report in to the 3$^{rd}$ ARRG headquarters the following Monday. Meanwhile, I could get myself situated and explore the airbase. He told me I would not be allowed to go off base yet. He pointed the way to the 3$^{rd}$ ARRG building, the mess hall, and the NCO Club, then told me where I could usually find him if I needed anything.

There were a couple of guys in the day room of our barracks when I walked in. They introduced themselves and showed me to a room with an empty bunk. There were two bunks to a room and in this room the other bunk was obviously occupied. My absent roommate had spread out to occupy most of the small space in the room. It was necessary to move a few things off of my bunk in order to get myself installed. Within a few minutes I was essentially moved in. I sat down on the edge of the bunk and took in my new home. Pretty dumpy and depressing, I thought, but at least I'm not in some hole in the jungle. I decided to go out and explore my environment.

I had been assigned to the 3$^{rd}$ Air Rescue and Recovery Group, which also operated control over the Joint Search and Rescue Center, known as Joker. Both were located at Tan Son

Nhut Air Base, just outside of South Vietnam's capital, Saigon. I was to spend time there for briefings on Joint Search and Rescue procedures, then I would be reassigned to one of the two rescue and recovery squadrons in Thailand where HH53B Jolly Green Giant rescue helicopters were located. But for the immediate future I was in Vietnam.

The United States had been involved in French Indochina as advisors since 1950. The Vietnam War, as it became known in America, escalated into a real fighting war in the 1960s. By 1968, the conflict had spread into Laos and Cambodia where they bordered Vietnam. This is where we were now bombing the hell out of the North Vietnamese supply route known as the Ho Chi Minh Trail. 1968 was the same year of North Vietnam's Tet Offensive. Though this offensive was ultimately unsuccessful, it marked the beginning of large scale disapproval of the war within the United States. By August 15, 1973, direct U.S. military involvement was over.

So basically, though I didn't know it at the time, I was there for the bitter end. This had two consequences. First, the military action, at least for the Air Force, seemed to be concentrated on the remote and dangerous territory along the Ho Chi Minh Trail in Laos and Cambodia, where the enemy was often well entrenched and fortified. Second, my fellow Americans grew more and more vociferous against the war and they took it out on us poor slobs who were sticking our asses out there and dying. Not an ideal arrangement in my opinion. So, why did I volunteer for this again?

It was a distracting coincidence that I was in the process of getting a divorce during my initial time there in Vietnam. I was wrestling with conflicting thoughts and emotions. Being Catholic, divorce was a very serious and bad thing. I worried what this would mean for my daughter. Nobody in my family, including my extended family, had ever divorced. It was stressful, but once I was in Vietnam it was hard not to focus on my immediate situation and the mission at hand. Losing focus could get a guy killed.

I think that when most people think about war, they conjure up pictures of combat and the terrible cost of fighting the enemy, war movie images. There are also political aspects of war that often overshadow the battles. Both are the essential activities of waging war and they are the things that the media seem to focus on, but these are not the predominate memories that I have of being there in the Vietnam War.

My first and immediate impressions of Vietnam upon my arrival are also my most enduring memories. I had never previously been outside the United States, so being plunked down into this place was nothing an average American kid like me could have ever imagined or prepared for.

The first and predominate sensations were the smells, a combination of charcoal braziers, JP4 jet fuel exhaust, tropical damp mustiness, and the not-so-faint odor of open sewage. Those ubiquitous smells are indelibly stamped into my memory such that if I encounter similar smells today, I have immediate flashbacks of my time in Vietnam and Thailand. Next were the sounds, which were dominated by incessant aircraft engines, the thump of helicopter blades, the pop-pop of two-stroke three-wheeled taxis, and the Vietnamese language, which tended to be spoken in a loud, almost shrill manner. Finally was the tropical weather, which can probably best be described as a blanket of warm dampness that feels like something you are wearing.

There were many hardships that stick in my mind. The tropics are host to a lot of bugs, big bugs, bugs that I don't even want to remember, especially the endless supply of mosquitoes. In all the places I lived or visited in my life, the bugs here in the tropics were beyond counting. I figure it must be where bugs originated.

Everything smelled musty, and it was impossible to be completely dry unless you were fortunate enough to be in an air conditioned building. I recall waking up in the morning and having to flick pools of sweat from my eyes before opening them. The seasonal monsoons resulted in rain that never seemed to stop for weeks. It got to feel like you lived in water. You had to change your socks twice a day in order to avoid foot fungus.

The toilet facilities, especially in Vietnam were quite primitive and distasteful. The community latrines, which included toilets, sinks and showers, had no doors and no stalls. These facilities were frequented by Vietnamese women who served as cleaning staff. There was essentially no privacy. Just about everybody had diarrhea much of the time, so you had to resign yourself to doing your business in front of everybody.

Another vivid memory that I have of Vietnam and Thailand is that there seemed to be very little adult supervision. Wars are fought by young people, I realized. The vast majority of the American military personnel, there in that war, my war, were kids, eighteen to 25 years old. I can recall many occasions where the behavior of these kids, including myself, was less than exemplary and often out of control. There was a lot of alcohol consumption and drugs. I sometimes got the feeling that senior officers turned a blind eye toward much of this behavior. At times I witnessed similar poor behavior from officers, who themselves were mostly in their twenties and thirties.

There was a widespread dislike for the Vietnamese people among the American troops. Behavior toward the host population was often explicitly hostile and despicable. While I suppose one could explain some of this attitude as a reaction to the harsh circumstances of the environment, I can't help but feel that much of it was just an inherent predisposition to the darker side of our human condition. I was often deeply embarrassed by what I saw and heard. I came to understand what was meant, at least in part, by the term "Ugly American". Unfortunately, I was to see a lot of ugliness during my war experience. In fact, there really isn't much glamor in war at all.

Perhaps in some sort of subconscious attempt to make amends for all of this bad behavior, I and a few others managed to find ways to engage the local people in a more constructive and favorable manner. As it turned out, Sergeant Robbins had connections to a Catholic orphanage not far from the Tan Son Nhut Air Base. In fact, the 3rd ARRG provided frequent support to this institution, and I asked if I could help in some way. I vividly recall visiting the orphanage on Christmas day, passing out gifts and candy. As a result of this visit, I got to know some of the Vietnamese people who volunteered there.

This turned out to be an amazing opportunity to get to know much more about the people and the culture of Saigon. During my brief stay at Tan Son Nhut, and during my occasional temporary duty visits from Thailand, I used my local relationships to do things like visit their homes, eat local foods, visit the Saigon Zoo with some of the orphans, and take a boat tour on the Saigon River. I learned that among many Vietnamese there was a lot of reciprocal resentment toward the Americans, but also a desperate hope that we would help make life in Vietnam more normal and end the war. I learned that there were good people and not so good people among the Vietnamese. I came to know of their weariness of the war, and that nearly everyone had some tragic story as a result of the war.

One of the better experiences I had with civilians involved having dinner at a Vietnamese family's home. I was invited by a young woman who worked as a telephone operator on base. I got to know her through her sister who worked as a house maid in our barracks.

On the evening of the dinner, I went to the house and was met by the young woman and her many younger brothers and sisters. The house was occupied by a large extended family that included one of her uncles and his family as well as her grandfather and grandmother. After introductions, I was invited to sit down on the floor at one end of a large mat which was covered with an assortment of food. I knew that this little feast must have cost them dearly, and I felt honored to have been invited. In an effort to show my gratitude I had brought with me a case of beer and a bottle of American whiskey, which I offered to the grandfather.

Grandfather was sitting at the head of the mat, with the father on one side and me on the other. Everybody got quiet and the grandfather began speaking in Vietnamese. I quickly discerned that this was some kind of prayer or devotion directed to the ancestral alter situated next to the mat. The little alter contained statues and pictures of what I presumed were relatives, as well as candles and various other items. After the initial prayer, the grandfather poured three small glasses of some local spirit, giving one to his son and one to me. After a few more words, he gestured that we should drink the contents of the shot glass, which I gladly did. Everybody remained very quiet and solemn. He then made another little speech, gesturing significantly toward the alter. He picked up a small plate and, from a platter of a whole cooked chicken, cut off the head and placed it on this plate. He put it in front of me and made a gesture that I should eat the chicken head.

Now, I knew from briefings and barracks discussions that there were many things that American GIs should and should not do around the Vietnamese people in order to avoid insulting them. I took all of this very seriously and did not want to do anything that would reflect badly on my country or myself, but there was no way in hell that I was going to eat this damn chicken head.

I stared down at the severed head for a moment, then looked around the room to see all these very serious faces looking at me with what seemed like obvious expectations. I looked Grandfather in the eye and said, "I'm very honored sir, but I'm sorry. I cannot eat this." I'm sure that I must have looked stricken. The young woman who had invited me interpreted my apology. The grandfather looked at me in a stern manner for another few moments, then started laughing. Everybody else at the table, especially the young children started laughing as well. There was much pointing and knee slapping. Seems I was the brunt of a good joke by the whole family. I laughed as hard as any of them, and we all enjoyed a most excellent meal.

# Chapter 28

My first experience under fire came while I was at Tan Son Nhut. I was sitting in the 3<sup>rd</sup> ARRG headquarters building when I heard and felt two explosions. Shortly after, alert sirens began to wail. We all headed for a bunker just outside the back door of the building. It got the blood pumping, but the attack was limited to those two explosions. Fifteen Vietnamese soldiers were killed in the attack. There were no American casualties. It was a stark reminder that this was indeed a war zone.

My orders came shortly after the attack. I was assigned to the 40<sup>th</sup> Air Rescue and Recovery Squadron, Detachment 1, at Nakhon Phanom Royal Thai Air Force Base, in northeastern Thailand. I was excited and enthusiastic to be assigned to this unit. These guys were involved in combat search and rescue operations, and this was definitely where the action was.

Although there was not supposed to be a war going on in Laos, that was definitely where the Air Force was conducting intensive offensive operations. The Ho Chi Minh Trail in Laos was the focus of U.S. air power after President Johnson terminated Operation Rolling Thunder over North Vietnam in 1968. Operation Steel Tiger bombed eastern Laos, along the Vietnamese border. Operation Arc Light's B-52 raids included targets in Laos. Operation Barrel Role sent bombers and tactical strike aircraft into northern and southwestern Laos, dropping about 3.4 billion pounds of bombs there between 1968 and 1973. Yeah, that's billion with a "b".

The 40<sup>th</sup> ARRS was responsible for conducting combat search and rescue operations in support of bombing and special operations in this area. Nakhom Phanom was located on the border of Thailand and Laos, and just 75 miles from North Vietnam. This area was considered by the Thai government to be an "Insurgency-Threatened Area" infested with communists, NVA and North Vietnamese Viet Minh refugees loyal to Ho Chi Minh. It was also viewed as a vulnerable crossing point for communist sapper teams. In the vicinity of the Nakhom Phanom Province there had been 2,700 attacks on Royal Thai Guard (RTG) units by communist terrorists in 1970, increasing to 3,400 attacks in 1971. So, this was definitely a hot spot.

The 40th ARRS was originally activated in 1967 and located at Udorn Royal Thai Air Force Base in Thailand. The 40th was moved to Nakhom Phanom, usually referred to as NKP, in July, 1971, just six months before I arrived in Vietnam. It was home to 8 Sikorsky HH53 B and C helicopters, the aircraft that was to be my occasional office. The HH53s were referred to as Super Jolly Green Giants, or sometimes BUFF, which stood for "Big Ugly Fat Fuckers". The HH53 was the largest, fastest, and most powerful heavy lift helicopter in the Air Force inventory at that time. It replaced the HH3, which was also referred to as Jolly Green Giant.

I think a lot of Americans think of search and rescue as similar to what they saw on the TV series *M\*A\*S\*H*, which began in late 1972. MASH helicopters featured a big red cross on the aircraft and operated in conjunction with military ground actions, hoping that the enemy would respect the time honored practice of not shooting at medical evacuation vehicles or aircraft. This is not how we rolled in conducting our combat search and rescue operations in the Southeast Asia Theater.

The HH53 was armor plated on its belly. Its armament included two pintle-mounted General Electric 7.62 mm, six-barreled Gatling-type machine guns, with one at a forward hatch on each side of the fuselage. There was also an M60, 50 caliber Browning machine gun mounted on the tail ramp. When

Joker, the call sign for the Joint Rescue Coordination Center, activated a rescue mission, the CSAR "package" included a Forward Air Controller, usually an O2A Skymaster, two or more A1 Skyraiders armed to the teeth, and HC130 Hercules "King" aircraft used for airborne command and control, as well as HC130s for the refueling of HH53s. If the rescue sight was "active" and required additional help, F4 Phantoms and/or F105 Thunderchiefs were called in. Successfully extracting a downed crew out of the jungles of Laos or North Vietnam was often a full out battle.

Compared to Tan Son Nhut, Vietnam, Nakhom Phanom, Thailand, in terms of its environment, was a like a resort. Further north than Saigon, the weather was sub-tropical and less oppressive. Our hooches here were actually small cabins that housed eight airmen in air conditioned comfort. Each came equipped with a housekeeper. The latrine facilities were much more civilized. We had our own little recreation hooch, which included a bar and a full time barmaid. I figured I was going to be able to endure this assignment just fine.

I entered the squadron lounge, which was known as "The Pit", to see if there was anybody around to introduce myself to. There were a few guys there, playing Pinochle. They looked up as I entered the room. I was standing there, just inside the door to let my eyes adjust to the dim room.

"You must be the new PJ," one of them said. The others stared at me.

"Yes," I said. "Name's Wolf. You can call me sir," I joked, smiling broadly to be sure they knew I was trying to be funny. They didn't crack a smile. Great. Off to a good start, I thought.

I knew the drill. The new guy has to buy drinks and let everybody size him up. "The Pit" was not an official drinking establishment so the members of the squadron who frequented this place had to provide the alcohol from their own resources. Alcohol was rationed in Vietnam and Thailand. Each person got a ration card allowing them to purchase three cases of beer, three bottles of liquor, and three bottles of wine per month. I was carrying a bottle of rum and a bottle of whiskey when I entered the room. I walked over to the bar and handed the bottles to the bar maid.

"A round of drinks on me," I told her. That got everybody's attention and opened the door for the usual questions. "Where are you from?" "What was your last unit of assignment?" "Do you know so-and-so?" Since I was a Staff Sergeant, a couple of the guys wondered out loud how I didn't get deployed to Southeast Asia before now.

"I got a little side-tracked on some military education programs that I was urged to attend," I offered. "The brass at the 41st needed some extra help with getting more PJs trained to fill the increased demand, and I got a TDY assignment to fill in some gaps." I tried to play down the fact that I was singled out to help out with PJ training, an assignment normally given to PJs with more experience and rank. At the time I had been elated to be put on the leadership fast track, but I knew from my earlier experiences most of the enlisted guys you had to work with considered this kind of recognition the result of "brown nosing". Being looked upon as some sort of sycophant here, in a combat environment, where trust and dependence on your comrades could mean the difference between life and death, was definitely something I had to avoid. I steered the conversation in a more productive direction.

"I'll be counting on all the guys who have been here awhile to show me the ropes," I said. They looked a little skeptical.

As the evening wore on, more guys filed into the bar, and I bought more drinks and answered more questions. At some point, a couple of the guys suggested to the room at large that I should prove my worth as a new member of the outfit by meeting Bo Bo. This suggestion was met with suspiciously enthusiastic and boisterous approval by everyone in the room.

"Who or what is Bo Bo?" I asked warily.

"One of the Thai Guard units has a sun bear. It's their mascot. His name is Bo Bo," somebody explained. "The new guys have to go one round with the bear. It's the initiation."

"A bear?" I asked nervously. "What do you mean by going one round?"

"A sun bear," another chipped in helpfully. "It's just a little bear, about the size of a big dog. They put a muzzle on him and gloves, so you won't get mauled or anything." There was much stifled snickering around the room.

"You're a big guy," another said encouragingly. "You shouldn't have any problem taking him down."

I looked around, clueless. "So, what do I have to do?"

"You gotta grab the bear and pin it to the ground," somebody said. "You only get two minutes, then we pull your ass out, lose, win or draw."

I laughed nervously. "Sure, I guess. It's a small bear, right?" Everybody laughed. I began to think that the notion of bear wrestling was probably a joke to see how the new guy reacted, and the best thing to do was to just play along.

# Chapter 29

Over the next half hour or so the place became packed with enlisted men from the 40th. These were not just the guys on flight status, but guys with all kinds of specialty codes required to run the operation. I wondered if the place was always this crowded and lively. My liquor contribution was eventually consumed but the drinks kept flowing. I was given multiple beers and was the object of several toasts, some involving Bo Bo.

I was beginning to think these guys were a pretty great bunch, when somebody burst through the door and shouted, "It's all arranged! They're getting Bo Bo geared up now. We need to get over there pronto!"

The room erupted in loud cheers. Somebody grabbed one of my arms and held it up like a prize fighter. The bar began to empty, and I was hustled along with the momentum of the crowd. A sudden feeling of dread overcame me, the combination of too much beer and the growing reality that I was being shuttled off to fight a fucking bear.

I made some meager protests. "Tonight? Right now?" I whimpered, trying to sound casual. "Don't I get a last meal or something?" That brought great guffaws from what was becoming a mob. We seemed to be picking up more people as we traveled through the base. Somebody had commandeered a bus and met us on the main road. We all jammed in and headed for the Thai section of the base. I was trying desperately not to show signs of the increasing panic I was actually feeling.

When we arrived at our destination, I saw a large contingency of Thai Guards surrounding a cage. As I was ushered up to my fate, I caught my first glimpse of Bo Bo. Well, I thought, he doesn't look so bad. He was actually pretty small, in fact. On all fours, he didn't look like he was much over two feet or so. I sized him up to be 150 pounds at most. He had a muzzle and what looked like mittens on all four paws, as promised. He looked kind of cute. He was all black except for a yellow patch on his upper chest. He rolled over on his back and seemed to be playing with his mittens. The worst thing about this so far was the smell coming from the cage.

There were a number of greetings between the Americans and the Thais, and cases of beer materialized from the bus. It seemed to be quite the jovial event and I was being given a great deal of encouragement and advice by just about everybody, including many of the Thais. The next thing I knew, however, I was pushed into the cage, honey smeared on my face, and the door slammed behind me. The cage was now surrounded by wildly cheering men, in a scene that reminded me of what it must be like at a cock fight or bull fight, or maybe like when Christians were thrown to the lions in Rome.

I turned to face Bo Bo, who had taken on a whole new personality since I had entered his cage. He was now on his hind feet and making sounds and gestures I assumed were meant to warn me that he was about to kick my ass. Even on his hind legs he was still only around four feet tall. I didn't think this was going to be a fair fight, and I felt a moment of pity for this poor caged animal. Just then he dropped to all fours and charged at me. I crouched and prepared to fend him off and grab him around the neck in order to pull him down.

What actually happened is that Bo Bo barreled into me and knocked me down on my back. He immediately started to jump up and down with his front paws on my chest, over and over again. It felt like getting hit with a sledgehammer. I managed to get out from under him and rolled over a couple of times to give me time to regain my balance. Bo Bo didn't miss a beat. He was on me like white on rice. I managed to get him around the neck and was about to fling him down, when he grabbed me around my own neck and kicked me in the gut with both of his hind legs. That hurt, a lot.

The worst was yet to come. Just as I was recovering from the abdominal punch and preparing to give Bo Bo a taste of his own medicine, he stuck out his tongue through a slit in the muzzle and started licking my face. I later learned that sun bears have one of the longest tongues on the planet. This is apparently so that they can get honey out of trees. They are also called Honey Bears I was told. In this situation, I was the tree and my face the bee hive. Now, getting licked by a bear with a ten inch tongue is not like being licked by your dog, Fido. This was a beating in and of itself, and I soon curled up in a fetal ball hoping that somebody would hurry and rescue me. I think I recall yelling out in desperation, "That others may live, dammit!"

After what seemed like an eternity, although I was assured it was only the agreed upon two minutes, I was finally dragged out of bear hell. I was handed a beer and received many expressions of admiration for my feat. It wasn't clear whether the expressions were based on entertainment value or bravado. When I asked if anybody ever beaten the bear, it was revealed that nobody from the 40th had ever agreed to take him on.

"What!" I exclaimed. "I thought this was the standard initiation into the unit."

"Shit no," somebody said. "Never could get anybody to agree to do it."

"I don't recall agreeing," I said, still wiping bear slobber off my face. Everybody laughed and it was apparent I was becoming something of a celebrity now, and so I laughed along to hide my lingering hysteria.

We returned to the squadron hooches, and I spent the rest of the evening showering the big event's residue off of my body. I made a note to tell the hooch maid the next morning to wash the clothes in the laundry bag hanging from the bottom post of my bunk as soon as possible.

# Chapter 30

The next morning it was time to get down to business. I reported in to the squadron commander, Lieutenant Colonel Moore, and was assigned to the flight crew of Jolly 65. A guy entered the HQ office and walked up to me.

"You the new PJ?" he asked.

"Yep," I replied.

"I'm Sergeant Overkill," he offered me his hand. "I'm the other PJ on Jolly 65." He was a sturdy looking fellow, with black hair and movie star looks. He immediately came across as self-assured, cocky, and perhaps a little cynical. I thought it was kind of odd he didn't offer his first name, since his last name was plainly visible on his fatigue shirt.

"Well, my name's Wolf" I said, shaking his hand.

"The guys are calling you Wolfman," he said, with a judgmental look. I gave him a quizzical look. I had just arrived so I didn't think I'd been around long enough to get a call sign attached to me.

"Last night, with the bear," he said flatly. "I wasn't there, but heard about it this morning. Some of the guys are saying a tall PJ took on Bo Bo. They called you Wolfman." I realized that he was overtly sizing me up. He had not let go of my hand, which he was grasping a little too firmly. Good Grief! I thought. Did this guy, my apparent partner, think I was some kind of loose cannon?

I smiled with a small laugh. "Well, last night was pretty weird. I ended up with that damn bear before I knew what hit me. I presume you heard he beat the shit out of me?" I gave another wry laugh.

He eased the grip on my hand and gave me one more appraising look. "Some of those guys are assholes," he said. "I damn sure wouldn't get into the cage with that thing. They took advantage of you having just arrived. In any case, you're like a legend now." He smiled for the first time, which actually looked more like a sarcastic smirk.

"Come on," he said. "I'll show you around."

"Bart," he added. "Name's Bart."

Being in a combat unit, in the middle of a war, does not mean that you are in perpetual battle. On the contrary, most of the time you're trying to find ways to fill the time while you're waiting around for a rescue mission to happen. In our squadron, each person on flying status had to be on stand-by for three consecutive days, then three days off. This stand-by duty was often spent in the Air Rescue Alert Shack, where all of the members of stand-by crews stayed, including pilots, co-pilots, flight engineers, and PJs.

The three days "off" actually meant you worked on non-flying duties. There was typically one actual day that you were free to do what you wanted. This was time I often spent checking out the city of Nakom Phanom and the local area. I also had started working out at the base gym. Bart and I became friends and he introduced me to weight lifting. He also offered to teach me how to box. He felt he was qualified since he claimed he was a former Golden Gloves champion back in his home town of Rock Island, Illinois. But, that's another story.

# Chapter 31

I spent four three-day cycles in the Alert Shack without any incidents. Passing the time when there was no flying could be pretty boring. Guys tried to catch up on sleep, some read, wrote letters, or played cards. On my fifth cycle, in late March, Joker sent us a mission. Major Evans was our AMC, airborne mission commander, and he called the crews together for our pre-mission briefing. Reinforcing my feeling that there weren't many adults in the American forces, Major Evans looked to be around 30 years old, which made him the "old man" of our outfit. He was also my pilot, the pilot of Jolly 65.

In keeping with tradition, the pilots flipped a coin to determine which Jolly would be the low bird, resulting in Jolly 65, my chopper, being designated as the low bird for this mission. In similar manner, Bart flipped the Thai one-Baht coin he was holding, calling "heads" as it spun in the air. It landed heads up, which meant that I would be PJ 1 on the rescue. If someone on the ground needed help, I'd be the one going down to bring him up.

"You ready for this Wolfman?" Bart asked, with that smirking smile of his.

"I admit I'm nervous, but yeah, I'm ready," I replied, trying to appear braver than I felt. He gave me one of his appraising looks that always felt like they were dripping with skepticism.

Since I was assigned to Jolly 65, the designated low bird, it meant that I was even more likely to have to assist in a rescue on the ground since the low bird would be the first to go in and perform the pickup. The second HH53, Jolly 64, would be the high bird and fly above to support the mission and pull our asses out of the fire if the low bird got in trouble and went down.

There was not any time to dwell on the possibilities just yet. Major Evans was getting the briefing underway. The briefing room was a small room adorned with a chalkboard and a map of Laos in the front and a table with a well-seasoned coffee maker in the back. It was apparently a grave error to actually wash the coffee pot because that was believed to ruin the next batch of coffee. Several folding chairs in the room were already full of air crew. We were to be a part of a larger rescue mission in Laos, along the North Vietnam border.

Our team departed NKP around 8:00 a.m. As the "package" assembled in the air from various bases in Vietnam and Thailand, we met up with an HC130 Hercules tanker in an area over the Stoeng Tregng Province in Cambodia for refueling. We were first up, and completed our refueling operation. Sometime later, Major Evans tried to contact Jolly 64 to determine if they were finished with their refueling.

"Anybody in the back get a visual on Jolly 64?" Major Evans asked through the intercom. "I can't get them on the radio."

I was sitting at the M60 located on the tail ramp, strapped with a harness to keep me from accidently falling out of the open ramp. I had a view of all the area behind Jolly 65. I could see a thin column of black smoke quite a distance behind us.

"PJ 1 on the tail ramp. I see a column of smoke at our 180," I replied.

"Roger." Major Evans made a 180-degree turn and confirmed the smoke. When further attempts to contact Jolly 64 failed to get a response, we headed in the direction of the smoke to investigate. Unfortunately, when we got to the site, it was clear that the smoke was coming from the wreckage of Jolly 64. The area immediately surrounding the crash site was an inferno.

We orbited the area until the rescue assets could reorganize for this area. Alternative assets were pulled in for the original mission up north. The A1 Sandys came in and "Sandy low" buzzed the area at treetop level to try to draw any enemy fire that might be there. That was part of their job. Their aircraft were dripping with ordinance. If they got shot at, they blew the hell out of the area. Nothing happened, so Jolly 65 prepared to go in to take a closer look. Nobody had heard any radio contact from the Jolly 64 crew. There was no way to know if there were survivors at this point.

"PJ 1 get ready," Evans said over the intercom.

"PJ 1, roger," I replied. I moved away from my tail gun position and over to the starboard hatch where the hoist was located. I started gearing up. I heard the pilot and the flight engineer over the intercom talking back and forth, guiding the Jolly in near the crash site.

"Four thousand feet, five hundred feet per minute. Three thousand feet."

I realized that I was tensing up. I tried to focus on my training. I checked my medical ruck one more time, thinking about its contents and what kind of situations might require each of the items in that kit. My survival vest felt extra heavy, containing radios, canteens, and grenades. I also had a .45 caliber pistol in a shoulder holster and an M-16 rifle slung over my back. I realized I was unconscientiously squeezing the patch on my tunic. I repeated the pararescue motto, "That Others My Live". I looked over at Bart, who was intently searching the area below his hatch window, hands on the grips of his gun.

"Twenty feet. Ten."

"Roger."

I snapped back into focusing on my job.

"Five. Okay, hover."

"Roger."

I was looking out over the FE's shoulder. FE is what they call the flight engineer. We were just a few feet above the tree tops.

"PJ 1 ready?"

"PJ 1, roger."

"Hold hover."

"Roger."

The FE swung the hoist inside and unfolded one of the penetrator seat paddles down and motioned for me to get on and strap in. Once secure, I disconnected my intercom and pushed outside the HH53, but kept my feet on the chopper's frame. The sound and wind from the prop wash was, as always, overwhelming, adding to my stress. I looked over at Bart, who was now looking back at me. I was already unhooked from the intercom, so he gave me a thumb's up. I got a signal from the FE, tightened my grip on the hoist cable and started my decent to the jungle floor.

By this time I was in auto mode. I didn't know what I would encounter on the way down or what I would find once I hit the ground. The decent seemed to take forever. I let the penetrator hit the ground first to diffuse any static buildup, then got my feet under me and unhooked the harness. I took my M-16 off my back and dropped to a knee to assess the situation in my immediate area. There was no sign of any movement. The sound of the hovering Jolly above and the roar of the passing Sandys made it impossible to hear any potential sounds on the ground.

I made my way toward the burning aircraft, looking all the way for any possible survivors who may have gotten out of the Jolly, but were injured nearby. I saw that the downed Jolly was on its right side. I wanted to get close enough to see if I could identify any bodies inside the aircraft, but the fire was too intense. It was like a blast furnace. We had all just refueled, so there was a lot of fuel to burn. I made a thorough search of the area around the downed HH53, making increasingly larger circles around the burning aircraft, but found no crew members. I tried again to get close enough to the wreckage, but the heat was just too damn intense. If anybody was in there, they were definitely dead, I thought.

I radioed in my status and the unfortunate news that I couldn't find any signs of survivors. I was ordered to stand-by, and that PJ 2 was going to join in the ground search. I continued to look for survivors as well as any possible enemy on my way back to where Bart was being lowered to the jungle floor, but saw no evidence of either.

I gave Bart a quick summary of where I had been and we formulated a plan for a more thorough search. We first attempted another try at getting closer to the burning aircraft, but it was still too hot. We began a methodical search of the area. We eventually found two partially deployed parachutes, but no evidence of the men who used them. This was very disconcerting, since it meant they might have been hauled away, even though it was unlikely they survived. We spent over an hour on the ground looking for any signs of survivors or bodies, but found nothing else. We were ordered to return.

As I was being hoisted up, the devastating reality of situation started to hit me. I knew these people. These were our guys and they were gone. I had to shake off the temptation to dwell on this until later.

The FE pulled me into the chopper and I unhooked the harness. Bart had come up first and helped pull me into the fuselage. He looked me in the eyes and seemed to understand what might be going on inside my head.

"Don't think about it yet," he yelled to get past the noise. "Plenty of time for that later." He smacked me hard on the left shoulder with his right hand in a gesture of support. I nodded my head and gave him a brief smile of thanks. He pulled out a little flask and handed it to me. I opened it up and took a quick pull on the strong liquor. This was usually reserved for rescued crew members, but I guess he thought I could use some reinforcement, and I was grateful.

# Chapter 32

We headed back to NKP. Our part in the mission was finished. After we got back, Bart and I joined others in the Tactical Unit Operations Center to keep tabs on the search effort over Cambodia. A second search and rescue team was sent to the crash site. They reported that the fire was out and that the aircraft was completely destroyed. There were no sign of any human remains.

The area of the crash was heavily contested and very dangerous. The United States had no formal relations with the Cambodian government and in fact did not recognize that government. So it was nearly impossible to get any information on Americans who were killed or captured in that country. We heard the reports that enemy forces were moving into the area where the crash occurred. SAR operations were formally discontinued. There would be no more searches for the Jolly 64 crew. They were declared "Killed in Action/Body Not Recovered".

There was a dark cloud that settled over the entire 40th ARRS that evening. I began to grasp the reality of our loss. One of the guys in that crash had just arrived two days before this mission. He was 20 years old and, like me, it was his first combat mission. Four other guys perished in that crash, all young men, and even though it was evident they had not survived, we had to leave their remains behind. That was an added weight for all of us to bear.

The stress of what I had personally experienced in fulfilling my duties during the search mission also caught up with me. I quietly left the others and wandered to a remote area near a stand of trees. I thought again about how young we all were, and I wondered if all wars were run by old men who sent young men to die in them. I knew I could have been the one in the Jolly that crashed. I looked around to see if anybody was nearby. I wept in uncontrollable sobs. Maybe it was not manly or PJ-like to cry, but I could not hold back the emotion.

The next few weeks were consumed with relatively routine activity. It was difficult to shake off the sadness from the Jolly 64 incident, but we couldn't stop the world from turning. We flew a lot of stand-by missions, where Jollies and Sandys flew orbits over Laos in support of offensive sorties over North Vietnam and Laos. There were some CSAR missions that resulted, including one of the largest rescue operations of the war, but these were ultimately assigned to the 37th ARRS at Da Nang Air Base, located in the northern part of South Vietnam.

# Chapter 33

I wrote frequent letters to a girl in California, named Halley. I actually met her at a traffic light. That's not entirely accurate. I met her briefly a couple of times before the traffic light. She had been the girlfriend of the guy who Tanya, my estranged wife, had taken up with after I left for Vietnam.

I had to return to the U.S. on emergency leave while in Thailand due to some complications with the divorce proceedings. Tanya's lawyer had devised a divorce settlement requiring me to pay more than I earned as a staff sergeant in the Air Force. When I went to the local JAG office in a panic to get some advice, I was told that the Soldier and Sailor Civil Relief Act of 1940 protects active military members from such things. I had to return to the U.S. though in order to get all the appropriate paper work processed.

I was in the process of getting the divorce situation straightened out, when I saw Halley at a traffic light. I honked my horn and gave a little wave when she looked over. She was a very attractive, tall woman with long brunette hair, big brown eyes and one of those little gaps between her front teeth that make a girl look terminally cute. She also had a husky voice that made everything she said sound seductive. I harbored no illusions she would be attracted to me. I was just glad to see somebody I recognized. We got caught at the next light as well and I rolled my window down in an attempt to just say hello. She motioned for me to pull over after we got through the traffic light.

I couldn't remember her name, but surprisingly she knew mine. I guess I was a hot topic of conversation among her crowd due to the situation with her ex-boyfriend and my soon-to-be ex-wife. The fact that this was all happening while I was away at war apparently made for interesting gossip. After exchanging some banal pleasantries, she asked if I'd like to go to a party that evening.

"Heck yeah. I mean, yes, that would be great," I said. She gave me the address and said that she would see me there.

Wow, I thought as she pulled away. I tried not to project too much into the invitation. She was just being nice to a guy she felt sorry for, but still.

I went to the party and had a very nice time. The people there were very different from the kind of people I was used to being around, namely military. These people were what I thought of as hippies. They all had long hair and funky clothes, smoked dope, and were all about peace and love. I found it kind of strange that they treated me just like I was one of them, with no outward indication that my being military and on leave from Vietnam was an issue. In those days, people like these were the kind of people you saw on TV protesting the war.

At the party, I asked Halley out to dinner the next evening, and she accepted. We talked about our lives and former relationships. She seemed so normal and nice. I guess I expected someone who looked so good to be kind of snooty. We exchanged addresses. At the end of the evening she let me kiss her. All in all, those few days seemed like a pretty amazing turn of events. I returned to my duties in Vietnam with a new sense of optimism about the future.

She did write to me, a lot. She actually made a calendar with pictures of her for each month. It was very clever and definitely a morale booster. I was surprised her letters were the kind you get from a girlfriend. I was feeling pretty lucky.

# Chapter 34

I wrote many letters to my parents as well. I was very close to them and loved hearing any news from home. My daughter, Alexa, visited them a few times and they sent pictures of her I probably would not have otherwise seen. It was great seeing those pictures and knowing that she was spending time with her grandparents. She looked a lot like her mother, which is a good thing. If she had looked like me it would have been unfortunate.

One of the letters I wrote to my mother and dad told the story of the day a monkey got into our hootch. This event was quite a distraction to say the least.

I was getting dressed one morning when I noticed something brown by the door, which happened to be ajar. I thought it must be the stray dog that we had adopted several weeks before, so I snuck up to the door to scare him. When I threw the door open I found myself looking at a monkey staring me right in the eyes. Now I want to clarify that this was not a cute, little hurdy-gurdy monkey, and while it was not gorilla size either, it was big enough to scare the shit out of me. I don't know who was more startled, me or the monkey, but we both headed in the opposite direction.

The very next day, a long difficult day, Bart and I returned to our hooch after a badly needed shower. Upon entering I noticed a can of peanuts I kept on a shelf was open and on my bunk. Peanuts were scattered everywhere. I stood there trying to figure out what was going on when Bart yelled, "Look Out!" I turned just in time to see a very large monkey, teeth bared, moving toward me from the top of my clothes locker.

I shrieked like a little girl and quickly backed away. Unfortunately, I had backed myself into a corner and, too late, realized that I had no way to escape. This monkey had me cornered. I was only wearing a towel, having just come from the showers, and felt very vulnerable. I realized this was probably the same monkey I had encountered the day before.

I had previously acquired a couple of those large, carved spoon and fork things that you hang on a wall for decoration. That's where they were, hanging on my wall, within my reach. I grabbed the fork and held it like a gladiator's weapon.

"Come on you bastard," I said in my most commanding and challenging voice, some of my composure having returned. I lunged at the monkey with the fork. That was apparently a mistake. He charged and I barely managed to keep him off me with the fork. He quickly recovered the high ground on top of the cabinet, effectively keeping me cornered.

"Go get someone," I yelled over to Bart.

A few of our guys from the bar came over and tried to help get the monkey out, but I think they thought it was funny and they weren't very effective. In fact, the monkey seemed to be getting more and more agitated.

There was a phone in the corner where I was being held captive. Keeping a wary eye on the beast and holding my fork in a defensive position, I called the security police.

"There's a monkey in my hootch and it has me cornered," I said in what must have been a panicked stricken voice. "It got in here somehow and was getting into some peanuts that I had and now it's pissed off and won't let me out."

"Right," the voice on the other end said. "What do you want me to do?"

"Well, send some APs over here and help us get this damn thing out of here," I pleaded. I think that the guy thought I was pulling some kind of stunt, but I eventually convinced him, along with others in the hootch yelling their validation from afar.

Bart and the others in the hootch made one more valiant attempt to drive the monkey from the place, but that resulted in what I would have to describe as a horrifying shit fest. That is to say, the monkey was apparently beginning to feel a panic similar to mine and grabbed a florescent light on the ceiling to maneuver itself to safety. The light broke with its weight and that scared the shit out of the monkey, literally. It also began to shriek in a most alarming manner and go into a frenzy. All the others fled the building, leaving me still cornered with a large monkey that was now not only pissed but hysterical.

I was beginning to see my life flash before my eyes. I could see the headlines now, "Naked airman killed and half eaten by a monkey in the Vietnam War." I had heard of some GIs getting killed by tigers in the surrounding jungles while on patrol. At least that would be a more glorious, manly way to go. But, a monkey?

The APs finally arrived. I was still cornered. They came in and looked around to assess the situation, nodding sagely and conferring with each other quietly. One guy decided to grab some mosquito netting from a nearby bunk. The other cop took out his baton. They slowly approached the monkey, which got his attention immediately. That was just enough of a break for me to bolt for the door.

I ran around to the other end of our hootch, where I assumed Bart would be waiting. I was somewhat horrified to find that a large number of people had gathered to see what all the excitement was about. There was even an Air Force TV crew there, apparently having caught wind of the incident from the call to the Security Police. Bart was standing behind a nearby tree still wearing just a towel, as was I. I joined him, trying to ignore the stares and laughter.

There was a terrible sound coming from inside our hootch, screaming monkey, screaming cops, glass breaking, large furniture overturning. Then two thing happened at exactly the same moment that caused utter chaos in the entire area. The hootch door burst open. The two APs fell out of the door yelling as if being pursued by Satan himself, followed by the monkey as if shot out by a cannon. At that precise moment a flying squirrel, headed for the tree we were behind, perhaps distracted by the commotion, accidently landed on Bart's back, causing him to drop his towel, running and screeching in surprised terror. I was chasing behind him trying to dislodge the squirrel, losing my own towel. Everybody in the area lost it, and there was a lot of screeching and running as a result.

We eventually recovered ourselves with no physical damage, just mostly wounded egos. When we finally made it back to our hootch we could not believe our eyes. The place looked like a bomb had gone off, and it smelled like monkey shit! We gathered up some cloths and were thankfully able to finally get dressed. We had to arrange for temporary quarters while the disaster that was formerly our hootch could be sorted out.

I saw the monkey a few times after that incident. We eyed each other cautiously. I had no doubt he recognized me, and I'm pretty sure that as he watched me pass by, I could detect a primitive look of vengeance mixed with wariness in his expression. I couldn't help but feel he was contemplating another go at me. We made sure our doors were closed all the time for the rest of my tour.

# Chapter 35

The days rolled on by. Our crew flew many mission that involved flying orbit over Laos when there was a strike mission or a MIG Combat Air Patrol mission going on in the area. This was a standard procedure in case any of our aircraft in these missions were shot down. In reality, any excitement that we experienced on these missions was often related to some mechanical problem with our aircraft or "bingo fuel", meaning that we were running low on fuel and had to either refuel in flight or return to base.

During this period, I was sent back to Tan Son Nhut Air Base in Vietnam on temporary duty. The 3$^{rd}$ ARRG was beginning the initial process of moving from Tan Son Nhut to Nakom Phanom, and that required a lot of details that needed to be attended to. While there, I volunteered to help a couple of administrative airmen destroy classified files and film. Jollies sometimes carried official combat photographers on missions and this apparently produced a lot of film that the Air Force no longer wanted but felt needed to be destroyed.

The incinerator used for destroying classified material was located at the relatively remote, far western end of the base. There was essentially nothing else around this contraption. The perimeter fence was only about 100 yards away, then another 100 yards or so of cleared space, then brush and trees. Upon our arrival, I immediately felt exposed and decided to keep on the alert. I carried an M-16 and had two clips of ammo. Considering the nature of the "mission", this seemed more than adequate.

I helped the other guys get the incinerator ignited, and stood back to watch them throw the material into the receiving hatch. It was a fairly large object, and the receiving hatch was located up high so that a person had to reach above their head to get stuff in it. After a while, I got bored and decided to help so we could get out of this place. As always, it was oppressively hot and humid, and working next to this fire breathing beast made it worse. Within ten minutes we were all sweating profusely and anxious to be done.

There was very little air traffic taking off or landing during this time, so other than the occasional roar of an aircraft engine, the only other sound of significance was the incinerator, which emitted its own infernal roar. We were well away from all of the din that was a normal part of the rest of this densely populated base. So when the first shot was fired, there was no mistaking what it was. The other airmen seemed not to notice, but I immediately shifted into high alert. I moved quickly over to the truck where I had parked my M-16.

I grabbed my weapon and scanned the perimeter. We were very exposed. Another shot, and one of the airmen who was just putting material in the receiving hatch, grunted and slumped over.

"Get down!" I barked. The other airman crouched where he was and the guy who was shot started moaning. A couple more shots were fired. It was difficult to tell exactly where they were coming from. Fortunately, they had to be at least a couple hundred yards away and had to shoot through the brush and trees that provided their cover, as well as through the perimeter fence. Nevertheless, as more shots were fired, bullets were hitting all around us, the incinerator, the truck, and the ground.

I ran over to the incinerator where the airman who was hit was laying. A quick look at the wound in his right forearm revealed that it was not too serious. I pulled him a little ways from the incinerator to keep him from going up in flames. It was intensely hot next to that damn thing. I could see that the other airman was okay but clearly scared shitless. So was I. Guys who claim that their not afraid during combat are full of shit as far as I'm concerned.

I had not brought a radio with me and the old utility truck didn't have one in it either, so we had no way to send the alert. Fortunately, there was an old French bunker installation at this end of the base, staffed by members of the 377th Air Police Squadron. Surely they would notice what was going on and come to our aid.

I didn't have any medical supplies with me, so there was not much I could do for the wounded airman. We had taken off our T-shirts and left them in the truck, so I couldn't even use something like that to bind the wound without exposing myself to the fire. This was supposed to be a routine administrative task. It never dawned on me that I'd encounter a combat situation.

I didn't think that there were many enemy troops involved in this, based on the number of shots coming from the trees. Maybe a small sapper team had decided they just might get away with taking us down and using our uniforms and truck to infiltrate the base? I didn't know, but just hoped there weren't many of them.

I finally saw evidence of where some of the shots were coming from and put a few rounds of my own in that direction. That got their attention and the firing stopped for a moment. I used the moment to dash over to the truck to grab a shirt. As I came back to the incinerator the shots started up again. I returned fire. That was the end of clip number one. I reloaded and turned my attention to the wounded airman, and managed to get his bleeding stopped.

While I'm sure this whole situation only lasted 10 minutes or so, it seemed like an eternity. I saw a couple of M113 armored personnel carriers rapidly approaching from our left. Ah, the cavalry to the rescue, I thought. In an effort to give our guys some idea of where the danger was, I decided to put a few more rounds into the area where I thought the bad guys were. The bad guys returned my fire. That was a mistake. Our guys opened up with their .50 caliber Browning Machine Guns, one on each M113.

I got the other airman to help me get the wounded guy in the back of our truck. I hoped it was not too shot up to start. The two back tires were flat as a result of the little battle, but I thought I could still get the truck farther from the action if I could get it started. It did start and I moved away from the incinerator trying to keep it between us and the enemy shots. Fortunately, there wasn't much firing coming from that direction any longer. Our guys were on top of the situation.

This little incident caused quite a stir at our headquarters. The poor admin guy might have been the only ARRG administrative airman wounded in battle. He was lucky. The wound was not serious, but good enough to assure a Purple Heart and his early return to "the world", as we all called the United States. I was the recipient of a lot of good natured guff for "trying to be a hero during an administrative activity." For me, it was a stark reminder that the war could get personal anywhere, anytime.

The next day there was a commander's call, which is a periodic meeting of all personnel whereby the group commander makes announcements, provides news, and recognizes accomplishments. I was thanked for my part in the previous day's action, which brought on more good-natured teasing by everyone. I was made to wear a metal helmet, given a Chinese machinegun and draped with a bandolier of bullets, both taken from the 3rd ARRG's little museum of captured enemy weapons. I was then "ordered" to guard the big metal container that was used to hold iced-down beer for these occasions. I got the joke and took it with the intended good humor. I was asked to pose for several pictures. Ha ha. Very funny.

The time was getting relatively close when I would be shipping back to the good ole USA. Like many other guys, I was keeping what was called a "short" calendar. These were drawings of something or other, often aircraft, that had little patch-work sections drawn in, like jig-saw pieces. Each little section contained a number, which taken together, provided a visual way to count down the number of days remaining on one's tour. Each day you would color in the highest remaining number. The more the drawing was colored, the shorter you were.

The short calendar that I had was a cartoon drawing of an HH43 Pedro, the helicopter that was used by the 40th ARRS for local base rescue. This drawing was a very stylized version of the Pedro which included a gritted-teeth face on the front and smoke rings coming out of the odd tail pipe that these helicopters used for exhaust. A cartoon bird of some kind was pictured in the upper left had corner of the drawing with feathers flying as the Pedro whizzed by.

The Air Force used these helicopters as first responders, especially when there was a crash that involved a fire or the threat of fire. They were used within a 75 mile range from the base from which they operated. They were a very odd looking aircraft. It looked kind of like a toy. Some called it the "flying shithouse", I suppose because of its boxy shape. It also featured an unusual contra-rotating, twin-rotor arrangement, eliminating the need for a tail rotor, and that curious looking exhaust protruding from the rear of the aircraft. The rotors were made of wood and so they drooped quite a bit at rest, during start-up, and during shutdown. Those who flew in it, however, considered it one heck of a flying machine. The HH43 could take off in just one minute, making it an excellent first responder for nearby accidents. It also held several world records for highest altitude for a helicopter, at 29,846 feet. This helicopter flew more rescue missions during the Vietnam War than all other aircraft combined.

The closer it got to the day I was to depart, the more I thought about the possibility of not surviving. I can't say that I dwelled on it or was distracted by it, but it was frequently in the back of my mind. It certainly wasn't unheard of for a guy to get killed or captured just before it was time to go home. "Sawadee" is the Thai word for "hello" and "goodbye". I attended many sawadee parties during the months I spent in Thailand, and my goal was to make it to my own sawadee party.

A few weeks before my scheduled departure, a CSAR mission was organized that turned out to be one of the more memorable rescues of the Vietnam War. An F4 Phantom jet fighter was shot down during a MIG CAP mission over North Vietnam. The pilot was killed when his plane crashed, but the Weapons System Officer, a guy named Captain Lowe, successfully bailed out. He wasn't able to use his radio that day, and could not get his radio signals through in the days that followed. He was too deep into North Vietnam.

He spent an amazing 22 days on the ground, evading local search parties and local farmers as he alternately hid and worked his way toward the Red River. He was only about 60 miles from Hanoi and five miles from Yen Bai airfield, which was one of the most important and well-defended Vietnamese People's Air Force airbases in North Vietnam. This was not an ideal place to conduct a search and rescue.

On his 22$^{nd}$ day on the ground he was able to contact a flight of American jets overhead, and a CSAR mission was launched that same day. I was on one of the Jollies that made up that first CSAR package, along with several A1Hs, F4s, and F105s to provide air protection. In fact, this turned out to be one of the largest rescue efforts of the war, with over 100 aircraft dedicated to the rescue effort. This was also the deepest penetration into North Vietnam of any CSAR effort. All in all, it seemed to be shaping up as the very situation that I had been dreading, but there was no time for dwelling on the possibilities.

As we drew near Captain Lowe's position, our Jollies and the Sandys came under attack from a MIG. We managed to evade the enemy aircraft by flying down a narrow canyon. The Sandys were also taking heavy anti-aircraft fire and dodging missiles. Jolly 65 took some small arms fire, which sounded like a heavy hammer hitting an anvil as the enemy bullets punched against our armor. Bart and I let loose a few bursts from our GAUs, although I didn't actually see anything specific to shoot at. Since they fire 4000 rounds per minute, they are pretty effective at keeping enemy heads down. A Sandy roared past us, close by, and laid down some its ordinance to help clear our path. Thank God for those guys!

Ultimately, the resistance was just too intense and we eventually became bingo-fuel, so our part in the CSAR mission was called off that day. We returned to NKP in one piece, notwithstanding some damage to the HH53. We were all jacked up from the experience and concerned for the downed flier. A new CSAR effort was already being planned for first light the next day, and we hoped this one would be more successful than ours had been. We knew that it might be very rough and I prayed everyone would get through it. We were advised that we would not be on the next day's mission due to the damage sustained by our Jolly in the first rescue attempt. This had an odd impact on me, personally, as I struggled with conflicting feelings of relief and disappointment.

The rescue mission the next day was successful and nobody got killed or even injured. Captain Lowe was reported to be in pretty decent shape considering that he had been living off the land for over twenty days. Our Jollies flew him to Udorn Air Base because that was Lowe's home base. The Jollies and Sandys made an initial overhead pass in echelon formation. Turned out that just about everybody who was anybody was there to greet him and the rescue team, including General Vogt, the 7th Air Force Commander who had flown in from Saigon for the occasion. I admit I was a little envious, stuck there at NKP, but shared in the pride of a mission well done.

# Chapter 36

The rest of my tour passed without any major incidents. I was ready for my war adventures to be over. I wanted to see my daughter and was anticipating a reunion with Halley. The trip back to civilization seemed to take forever. I flew from NKP back to Tan Son Nhut. From there I flew to Clark Airfield in the Philippines where I had to lay over for three days. From there I flew to Tokyo, Japan, then to Spokane, Washington, and on to Travis Air Force Base in California. From Travis I got a military hop to Norton Air Force Base.

I had asked Halley to pick me up, which she seemed anxious to do. Our initial meeting felt a little awkward. I wasn't really sure how to act. We didn't really know each other that well, yet it felt like we were long lost lovers. Most of our relationship had been through letters, which had grown increasingly intimate over time.

She had arranged a little welcome home party for me with a few mutual friends. I was having a little trouble adjusting to the new normal I now found myself suddenly thrust into. I had dreamed of this day for many months, but the intense life in a war zone over such an extended period had left its mark on me. I felt out of place and I had to focus on controlling my behavior. In Southeast Asia, my environment had been rough and crude. Cussing, chain smoking, heavy drinking, lewd remarks, and rowdy behavior was the normal there. There was also the impact of the constant stress of a wartime job. Then there was the comradery that is unique among men who fight in the difficult circumstances of a war. There was nobody at this party who could even begin to understand any of that.

I am, however, flexible and always anxious to fit in. After a few beers, I felt all of the anxieties about coming home and being with Halley and her friends begin to melt away. I had to move on, and I was determined to make this day the first day of the rest of my life. From what I can remember, it was a very pleasant evening.

I was on an extended leave from my military duties. After a few days in California, I traveled to Ohio to see my family. It was great to see my parents and siblings. We were always a close family and my homecoming from the Vietnam War made the gathering that much more special to me. I think that everybody was glad to see me and have me back home.

My daughter, Alexa, was there as well. I was amazed by how much she had grown. I think she was a little intimidated by me since she probably didn't really remember who I was. She was just a little toddler when I had gone off to war. The last time I saw her, she was in diapers, walking around like a drunken sailor, as toddlers do, with a bottle of milk dangling from between her baby teeth. Now she was eating real food with a spoon and drinking from a sippy cup. Man, she could shovel it in too. She definitely had the Irish family genes.

I made the surprise announcement that I had met Halley and that we were planning to get married in a couple of months. My parents took the news with stoic acceptance. I'm sure my mother was hoping that, by some miracle, I would get back together with Tanya. I avoided any serious discussion of the issue. After all, we were already legally divorced, and she was living with another man. I knew that my mother, especially, was disappointed that my marriage didn't last. I tried as best I could to reassure her that she did a wonderful job raising all of her children, but the marriage just didn't work. I also tried to convince her the new woman in my life was very special and I was sure she was the right one despite the fact I had only known her for a short time.

Halley and I got married a couple months later, as planned, and she moved to Illinois to be with me at my new stateside duty assignment. Scott Air Force Base was the location of one of the three stateside Air Rescue Coordination Centers under the Military Airlift Command. Scott was also the home of the Military Airlift Command. It was a starkly different environment than Vietnam and Thailand. I had to recondition myself to this kind of military life. I thought that the spit and polish nature of the base, as well as its excellent amenities, would please Halley. As it turned out, she was not a good fit for life as a military wife, and she missed Southern California. Heck, Southern California was like paradise compared to the flat, rural country around Scott AFB. It was essentially in the middle of a giant cornfield, which was in turn in the middle of nowhere.

While part of me liked the military life, with all its structure and focus on taking care of its own, another part of me was ready for the next adventure. We decided it was time to leave the Air Force and head back to California. I made this decision without any undue concern for my future or how this choice would potentially change my life. I was only 26 years old. I had my whole life in front of me.

# Chapter 37

The Vietnam War had officially ended for the United States in 1973. We had no direct military involvement after that, and the Air Force was making adjustments to its wartime force. They offered an "early out" program to specific specialties, including mine.

These programs included cross training opportunities to help ensure airmen leaving the military would have a successful transition into civilian life. I took a look at the possibilities and in my typical manner of throwing a dart to see where it lands, I chose the food and beverage industry. Actually, it wasn't quite that cavalier. I had always enjoyed cooking. To my parent's surprise, I once prepared a complete Sunday dinner, including a layer cake from scratch, when I was only 10 years old. I certainly liked drinking. I also understood the inherent social possibilities of being in the bar and restaurant business. In my mind's eye, I saw this change of career as just the right choice for me, and without any more serious reflection or research, I applied.

The people on the base who ran the program had made agreements with various local businesses to participate in this retraining. It was good for the local businesses. They got free help. It was good for the Air Force. They didn't have to do the training. They did, however, have to devise a training agenda that included training goals, specific steps for achieving those goals, and progress reports.

My training was to be conducted at the Karavan Club, a local bar and restaurant that provided cabaret style entertainment, which is a generous term to describe what was essentially striptease. It should be no surprise that this happened to be a popular place for the local military to patronize, which of course the proprietors encouraged, and which no doubt influenced the choice of entertainment.

I started my training helping with the lunchtime shift. I did whatever needed to be done, including washing dishes, bussing tables, stocking the bar, and taking care of deliveries. I didn't mind this kind of work. I realized that you have to start at the beginning and learn all of the tasks that go into running a food and beverage business. I eventually moved to dinner time and the late night entertainment service. I worked and I learned. It didn't dawn on me that the strippers might be a problem with Halley.

"Oh, they're just regular people," I'd tell her when she would make some kind of remark. "They're just trying to make a living," I would say in all innocence. I really didn't have any interest in any of these women. These were women who went by stage names such as "Miss Holly Wood", who I recall actually inviting to Easter dinner because I felt sorry for her having to spend a holiday alone. In truth, this kind of woman made me very uneasy and uncomfortable, but I guess that in retrospect Halley probably didn't buy that.

At the end of my program, I got some kind of certificate and felt ready to begin my official career in the food and beverage industry somewhere in the wild blue yonder. With a few lingering pangs of regret, I left the Air Force and we headed for Redlands, California. Thus began the tumultuous period of my life that I refer to as my "pirate days".

# Part III

## The Pirate

*Then I got a real job*
*Got a pretty wife*
*Had a pretty good life*
*Who could ask for more?*
*But, then I was a pirate*
*I had a boat*
*And I loved to float*
*To islands in my dreams*

# Chapter 38

He had finally finished Part II of his book. Like the first part, this had been an interesting journey back in time. He was still surprised about how much he had forgotten, and prying it out of his memory had been a chore. He wondered if his memory was fogged due to age or some kind of Freudian-psycho thing going on. Maybe he was suppressing memories that were associated with things he didn't want to remember. Bullshit. No, there was nothing wrong with him, dammit.

Now it was time to start thinking about years between the war and the beginning of his "real job", his career. He had taken to referring to that time as his "pirate years". He had done some amazing things during that time. Some people might say they were stupid things that wasted a lot of time, time he could have been getting an earlier start on his career. Maybe some of them were stupid. They were certainly good examples of how impulsive he could be.

He had found a letter from his second wife during his research for Part II. It was an outpouring of her bitterness toward him due to the eventual breakup of their marriage. She said that he was selfish, irresponsible, impulsive, and careless, among other things. This was a bitter pill for him to swallow, but he knew that she was right. That was probably how people close to him must have felt as he swashbuckled his way through that part of his life.

He had regrets. Now that he was older and mature enough to look back on his life with candid reflection, he felt remorse for the pain he had caused people who cared for him. He thought that, at the time, he just felt the need to live life and explore, and why couldn't everybody just keep up. Now, however, he realized that he was not the kind of person he always thought he was or wanted to be.

This would be an interesting part of the book to write, he thought. One thing was becoming clear, now that he was recalling his past, his life got more complicated as the years passed. Another revelation about himself had become evident, his mediocrity. He was reminded of the character Antonio Salieri, the court composer for the Austrian Emperor, Joseph II, in the movie *Amadeus*. In that performance Antonio ultimately realizes that he had enough talent to understand and appreciate what can be attained, but not enough talent to achieve the highest levels of his pursuits. Unlike Antonio Salieri, however, the old man was not pissed off at God for his lack of talents. He had come to grips with his limitations a long time ago. He knew that he was blessed with just enough talent to accomplish a lot of things that made his life interesting.

Perhaps all of his failings and misdirection are what would hopefully make this a good story, but he wished that he was writing about somebody else. It was all a little too revealing, he thought. He reminded himself that the story was, in fact, fictionalized, so anybody reading it would have to wonder if this was really about him.

He decided that before he began writing the next part of the book, he would try to find out more about that damn sound he kept hearing. He asked his wife if she could hear the sound. At first she said no, but later told him that she thought she knew what he was talking about. Yes, she thought she could hear it after all, but it was very subtle, and she didn't always hear it. The old man agreed that the sound wasn't constant.

Coincidentally, a neighbor who lived on the nearby mountaintop dropped by that very afternoon and asked if they could hear this really low sound.

"Yes," they both said, surprised. "We have been noticing it for a several weeks now.

"I called the power company, the Sheriff, the FAA, and the Navy," the neighbor said. "I haven't gotten any satisfactory answers. I think they thought that I was crazy or hearing things. The power company and the Sheriff eventually sent somebody out here. They admitted they thought they could hear it, but told me that it wasn't anything they could explain."

"I hear two distinct tones," the old man said. "I actually duplicated them on my electric keyboard. They're both an F sharp, but one is an octave lower than the other. I don't think that necessarily explains anything, but I think that it means that it's an actual sound, not something that's just in our heads. Of course what we're hearing is much lower than what I can produce on my keyboard. I think that it's a subsonic sound that's just within the range of human hearing, at least for some humans."

The neighbor looked at the old man with a curious expression, as if trying to determine if maybe he was pulling his leg.

"Well, I think it's something the Navy is doing," the neighbor said. "It's probably some kind of surveillance aircraft, maybe a drone. Who knows what kind of technology they're using. It could be harmful. I'm going to keep looking into this. We need to know what's going on."

The old man and his wife shook their heads in polite agreement. After the neighbor left, they both agreed that they thought it was unlikely that it was a military experiment this close to a populated area. True, they did live way out in the back country, but there were still quite a few people who lived out here. The old man thought that it was more likely something to do with the power lines that ran through the canyon where they lived. Maybe it was a geological phenomenon producing a vibration that was audible. It was interesting, but it was time to get back to the book.

The old man went back up to his little desk. He had established his "man cave" up in a guest room of their large house. It wasn't a man cave in the traditional sense, at least not like any he had seen. There was no bar or pool table or even a TV. One side of the room was simply a guest bedroom. The other side contained his electronic keyboards and his desk. The room also had a comfortable chair where he could listen to his audio books. The room essentially served as a place where he could get out of his wife's hair when he was doing some of the things he liked to do, including reading, writing and playing music.

He sat down and brought up his computer. It would be easier to just write about the adventures and leave out the difficult personal relationships, but he guessed that wouldn't be good form. People want to read about the salacious details of personal failures. Gore Vidal once said "It is not enough to succeed, others must fail." The old man thought that people liked to point to the failure of others as a reason for them to never try anything outside their own comfort zone. He was sure that was why the scandal rags, like the *National Enquirer*, were so popular.

Well, he could bare his soul, admit his mistakes. That, after all, was part of the adventure, was it not?

# Chapter 39

The original reason that I decided to start my new life in Southern California was that this was Halley's home, and I wanted to please her. We had briefly considered relocating to Central Ohio, where I was originally from, but of course California was a much more attractive location. I loved California. For me, it epitomized all that I felt had passed me by in life so far, beautiful weather, beautiful people, beautiful mountains. It seemed like the center of the new, evolving counterculture that I found so fascinating. Of course, by the time we arrived into the Redlands area, the counterculture and moved on into popular culture, but it was all still new to me.

We moved into some cheap apartments in a little town called Yucaipa, just outside of Redlands. While at the time I didn't see anything particularly odious about having Bart move in with us, I realized later that this was a big mistake. Bart and I had become very close during our Vietnam War experience together and the bond we shared was like that of brothers. He had also left the Air Force and settled in his home town of Rock Island, Illinois. He got married there, but that relationship didn't last very long and he decided to try his luck in California. He asked if I could help him out with a place to live until he got settled, and I had immediately agreed. You just always come to the aid of a comrade, and that was that.

I was too distracted or too insensitive or just too stupid to recognize the potential strain on my marriage that this arrangement might have. Halley was very sweet and accommodating, but was not happy with the situation. I knew that she was not very fond of Bart. He was inherently cynical about most things and could be crude. We both drank a lot in those days. I think we were still behaving like we did during our warrior days. He was also, no doubt, feeling the raw edges of his recent divorce.

We were both arrested one evening, in the apartment parking lot, after returning from a little bar just a few blocks away. Halley had met us at the bar, but wanted to go home early, so I had driven her back home and then, against her wishes, went back to the bar. As a result, we had two cars to get back to the apartments, mine and Bart's, so we were both busted. Halley had to come bail us out of jail, and she was not happy. Bart moved out shortly thereafter.

I buckled down to getting my new life in order. One of my top priorities was to find a job. I was naively optimistic about my prospects, based primarily on my over confidence in the meager training I had received. After a few initial disappointments, I decided that I would overcome my apparent culinary shortcomings with my leadership capabilities, of which I was supremely confident.

I eventually ended up applying for a position at the Tartan Bar in Highland, a small city just outside of San Bernardino. I told the owner that I had just completed two terms in the Air Force and that I had received advanced leadership training as well as the cross training program in restaurant services. I assured him that I was a quick study and that in very short order he could count on me to help him manage things, assuming he needed that kind of assistance.

He listened to me with what appeared to be an amused look on his face. At the end of my little speech, however, he asked me about my restaurant training and experience, and actually gave me a pretty good grilling, no pun intended. Finally, he told me that he would give me a try and that he wanted me to start the following day. I'd begin by helping him at the bar for lunches.

"Yes, sir," I said enthusiastically. "You won't be sorry, sir."
"You don't have to call me sir," he said.

"Yes, sir," I replied. We both chuckled.

The Tartan was a full service restaurant as well as a bar. It had a fairly large kitchen and a decent menu. The décor was typical of the heavy, men's club style prevalent in those days. There were no windows. The chairs and booths were black faux-leather, and there was a large circular fireplace in the middle of the floor at one end of the place. Kilts of various tartan patterns and sporrans were framed and hanging on the walls to give the place a Scottish look.

You have to start somewhere, I thought as I drove home. I was anxious to tell Halley the good news. Now I just had to learn how to be a bartender. At the Karavan Club my bartending experience had been limited to opening beers and making the occasional rum and coke. On my way home, I stopped at a book store and asked if they had a Mr. Boston Official Bartender's Guide. They did! My dad had this book at home when I was growing up. He kept it in a drawer in the dining room buffet, and I would look through it as a kid, thinking that it was a pretty cool book. It not only had drink recipes, but also provided information about the basics of bartending. Just what I needed.

I reported for work the next day, stressing over the need to remember all of the possible drinks that people might order. When I arrived, the owner gave me an orientation tour of the facilities. In one of the drawers on the bar back, he showed me his copy of a Mr. Boston Official Bartender's Guide. I gave a laugh of relief and pulled the copy I was carrying out of my back pocket. He smiled and looked mildly impressed.

The first couple of weeks went smoothly. I had to stock up the bar at the beginning of my shift and then help out wherever I was needed. Sometimes I'd bring a food order out from the kitchen, refill water glasses, bus tables, and even make a few drinks now and then. The lunch drinkers mostly drank highballs and beer. Nothing complicated about that.

The owner moved me to working the supper shift. This was much more work and a lot more to learn. I wanted to learn more about the food, but by necessity, remained focused on the bar. As I knew I would, I learned quickly. Soon, I was essentially the main bartender, working six nights a week. There was another, older guy who worked on weekends. Within four months, the owner was comfortable having me close the bar at nights, doing inventory, and dealing with the daily receipts.

My gregarious personality made it easy to schmooze with the customers, and I made pretty decent money from tips. Tips, as I discovered, were the main source of income for bartenders and waitresses. I learned some of the tricks that helped to fatten the kitty each night, my kitty that is. One of those tricks was free pouring liquor. It wasn't much of an effort to learn how to pour the exact amount of liquor in a drink without using a shot glass.

Once I convinced the owner that I could come within a gnat's ass of matching the amount in a jigger by free pouring, he was comfortable enough to let me do it. He knew that customers thought they were getting more if the bartender free poured. On some occasions I would in fact give a special customer a little heavier pour, and make it up on another drink, usually one that was ordered by a dinner guest and consisted of a lot of phoofy mixers.

I was grateful for the owner's trust in me and the chance he'd given me to get my new career figured out. I wasn't making enough money though. The Tartan was essentially a neighborhood establishment, with a lot of regulars and not much of a night time bar crowd. Weekends were better, but the place was pretty much empty by 10:30. Halley got a job at a local clothing store, helping them with the bookkeeping and other business needs. We were getting by, but just barely. I was working nights and she was working days, so we didn't get to see much of each other. Sometimes she would come visit me at the Tartan and we would share the free supper that I got as part of the job. We were young and in love, so life was still good.

One day, a young, serious looking man came into the establishment at the end of the lunch rush. He walked up to the bar and sat down next to the waitress station. He ordered a Tom Collins, which in those days was a relatively typical mixed drink. I noticed he was watching me intently as I mixed the cocktail. When a waitress came up to place a table order, he watched me again with what seemed like more scrutiny than normal.

I cleaned some glasses, straightened up the bar a little, and started polishing a wine glass before putting it back on the bar back. I stood in front of the stranger and gave him a big smile.

"How is the Collins?" I asked.

"It's good," he replied. "I noticed that you free pour here."

"Yes sir," I said. "So, are you new in this area or just passing through?"

"I live in San Bernardino," he said. "I'm looking for a bartender."

"Oh." I was taken by surprise. "Having any luck?"

"Not so far," he said, stirring his drink more vigorously than was normal, I thought.

"How long have you been working here?" he asked.

"Not very long," I replied. "I started here a few months ago. I just got out of the Air Force. This area is my wife's home, so we decided to settle here after getting out. I went through a cross training program that the Air Force offered just before I was discharged." I suddenly felt like I was being interviewed and felt compelled to provide more information than would have ever volunteered to most strangers.

He nodded his head and looked as though he was processing this information. "What did you do in the Air Force?" he asked.

"I was in search and rescue, a PJ," I explained. Not seeing any sign of enlightenment on his expression, I ventured a little more detail. "You know, guys who fly around in big helicopters and go down to rescue people who are in trouble. In Vietnam, it was mostly guys who got shot down and were hiding from the enemy in the jungle. It was an interesting job."

He looked at me for a long moment with what seemed like a glimmer of reluctant admiration, or maybe it was something more like, "why in the hell would anybody do something crazy like that." He stayed for a while longer, watching my every movement. Finally, he made a motion for his wallet indicating that he was ready to pay his bill. I put his check down in front of him and he gave me a ten. I gave him change and thanked him for his business and wished him good luck on his search for a bartender. He laid a five dollar bill on the bar, then his business card.

"If you're interested, come by the Smuggler's Inn and ask for me," he said, and headed for the door. Just like that.

I looked at the five. Nobody ever left a five dollar tip for a single drink. In fact, I couldn't remember anybody leaving me a five dollar tip, ever. I looked at his card. It read "Carl Short, Bar Manager, Smuggler's Inn, San Bernardino." Wow! I put the card in my wallet, concerned that the owner might see it. Suddenly, I felt vaguely disloyal.

I tried to concentrate on my duties, but I had a hard time not thinking about what it would mean to have a position at the Smuggler's. That was one of the premier night spots in the whole Inland Empire. How would I get a chance to go to Smuggler's and take Carl up on his invitation? I worked every night except Sunday. I wondered if he would be there on a Sunday. I realized that I could follow up with a call. His number was on the business card.

When I got home that night, I woke Halley up to tell her what happened. She asked me if I thought that would be a good move. I told her that I didn't really know yet, but it sounded like an opportunity to make more money. She asked about the impact of leaving the Tartan. That was a consideration of course. I hadn't been there very long but felt a sense of obligation, but at the end of the day, we had to make sure we were looking out for ourselves. I assured her that I would have to get more information before making any decision.

# Chapter 40

I made arrangements to meet Carl on a Sunday evening, which he was willing to do. I wanted to go there at dinner time to see what kind of business they did on a Sunday. I had never been in the Smuggler's Inn because I couldn't afford to eat or drink in a place like that. It was next to a hotel so there was always that built-in clientele, but it was also a "hot spot" for people of means, at least more means than I had.

It was plush by my standards, with a large, richly appointed dining area, and a lounge off to the side. The waitresses wore little green costumes with very short skirts that were supposed to look like wench outfits I supposed. They were definitely interesting. The hostess at the door was very attractive and attentive. I told her who I was and that I was there to meet with Carl. I caught her giving me a quick appraising second look, and told me that Carl was in the lounge waiting for me. She escorted me to the bar where he was sitting.

The bar was also well appointed and very "cool". The room wasn't large, no more than twenty stools at the bar, but I immediately noticed that there were two waitress stations, one at each end of the bar. There were two bartenders and both were busy. The lounge contained maybe two dozen small cocktail tables, and was about two-thirds full, with most of the bar stools occupied. The far wall was the kind that you can fold back, opening up the lounge to the dining area.

Carl got up and shook my hand, thanked me for coming by. He introduced me to the bar staff. Of course, everybody was sizing me up, but not in any kind of uncomfortable way.

Everybody was good looking. Everybody was so professional and self-assured. I wasn't sure if I would fit in, yet here I was by invitation.

Carl gave me a quick review of their operation. He told me that on Friday and Saturday you couldn't get into the place. It could get three deep at the bar and that it was not uncommon for the waitresses bring up 15 to 20 drinks per order. They had a drink order protocol to make it easier to remember and more efficient to fill. I was impressed. I was terrified. I could not imagine that kind of volume.

Carl then gave me a tour of the whole store, including the kitchen, which was a really impressive operation. It was humming with activity since it was right at the dinner rush, very organized chaos, if you can imagine such a thing. He showed me the storage area and the liquor room. They apparently moved a lot of drinks. The liquor and wine inventory was extensive, and the wine area was amazing. It was the first time I had actually ever seen a wine room, with bottles stacked on top of one another in their own cubby holes, lots of cubby holes. It looked like something I had only seen in pictures of French wine caves. Cases and cases of beer were stacked high in one of the walk-in refrigerators. This was definitely a big operation.

He ushered me through the dining room, where well-dressed patrons enjoyed what looked like extravagant dinners. In the back corner of the dining room was a small service door. We entered a little room that consisted of a small service bar and shelves stocked with glasses, napkins, stir sticks and the like. The bar was organized to be efficient, with just about everything at arm's length.

"If you decide to come on board with us, this is where you will start," Carl said matter-of-factly.

I tried not to look disappointed, just nodding slightly. "Ok," I said.

Perhaps he detected some hint of let down in my voice. "This is where all new bartenders start, so that they can learn the ropes," he continued.

That made sense. I quickly realized that I was not up to the level that these people obviously were, and couldn't just walk behind the main bar on day one and expect to be successful. He explained that the service bartender got paid minimum wage, but that the waitresses were supposed to share their tips. I processed that for a few moments. I made double the minimum wage at the Tartan, and got my own tips. This offer, however, was an opportunity to take things to the next level. I was sure of it. I could never hope to get this kind of experience at the Tartan.

The thing was, I didn't really have a long term plan. I knew that I was just feeling my way through life at this point. Was this something that I should grab onto, or should I stay with the more conservative position at the Tartan? Given my impulsive nature and my desire for finding something, I don't know, more glamorous I suppose, this seemed like an opportunity that I shouldn't pass up.

"When would you expect me to start?" I asked.

"I know you would need to give your two-week notice, so let's say in two weeks," he said. "You would start on a Tuesday at 3:00."

I thought for another moment. "Would it be okay if I let you know in a couple of days?" I asked.

"Yes, that would be fine," he said.

We shook hands and I went outside and got into my car. This was happening fast. Why would I not take this job? It was clearly a step up from the local tavern I was employed in now. The potential at Smuggler's seemed hands-down much greater.

I discussed it with Halley that evening, but I had pretty much made up my mind. She didn't have any compelling reason not to go for it, but she didn't seem that enthusiastic either. I decided not to press her about any subtle misgivings she might be having. It was onward and upward as far as I was concerned.

# Chapter 41

Two weeks later I was working at Smuggler's Inn. The first week was terrifying. A Tuesday evening at the Tartan would have been slow and boring. Here at the Smuggler's it was busy, and the waitresses were in no mood to tolerate a new bartender who was trying to figure out where everything was and how things worked. I had to swallow my pride several times.

"Don't garnish my drinks, Honey," one waitress told me impatiently.

"What?" I said, confused. At the Tartan, I always garnished all the drinks. That was part of what a bartender did. I told her so.

"Not here, Honey," she said in a tone that I would use when speaking to a small child.

On another occasion, a waitress ordered an unusual drink, one that I didn't know how to make. I flashed her a deer-in-the-headlight look and hoped that there was a Bar Guide back here somewhere. She rolled her eyes and listed out the ingredients, while busying herself with other tasks. I quickly recovered and made the drink.

At the end of the first evening, I felt humbled and wondered if I would even be allowed to continue working there. The waitresses all seemed inconvenienced by my learning, and I was sure that they would complain. I was assuming that I wouldn't get tipped either.

As I was cleaning up, one by one the waitresses came back to the service bar and gave me a tip share. They all thanked me and told me I did okay for my first night. One girl told me that she thought I was nice, that most bartenders weren't very pleasant to work with. I could see how some guys might get grumpy under the stress. Being nice and pleasant seemed to be a valued disposition at this place and might account for the nice tips that I received. I made a mental note.

Each successive evening was busier than the previous evening. On Friday, that little service bar was mayhem. The place was packed and the drink orders came in faster than I could have imagined. I had to put myself into a totally focused state of mind, like I used to do on a SAR mission. Think, rely on your training, act fast, and don't hesitate to ask for help if you needed it. It was nerve wracking but also exhilarating. Carl came back once during the height of the rush and asked how I was doing. I told him I was holding down the fort. He smiled and went back out into the thick of the battle.

The next evening, Saturday, was totally nuts. It was so busy and the lounge was so crowded that even the cocktail waitresses were coming to the service bar for some of their orders. They said they couldn't get up to the bar to place their drink orders. They introduced me the drink order protocol they used in the lounge. These girls were generally calmer and seemed more worldly than the food waitresses who normally used the service bar. They looked like movie stars to me. Very attractive.

At the end of my shift, which came with the end of dinner, around 10:00, I was told to come out to the main bar as the bar back. The bar back was the guy who got ice, washed glasses, and resupplied anything that was running low. They generally did whatever the bartenders told them to do. I was a little dismayed, given that I had worked my ass off in the service bar and was looking forward to going home at a decent hour.

As I approach the lounge I began to understand why they needed help. The place was a madhouse. There was a band playing up on the stage, adding to the cacophony in the place. The folding walls had been pushed back, tripling the size of the lounge area. It was a struggle to get to the bar. I was given a verbal list of instructions by Ken, the head bartender. I scrambled to get things done, then attacked the dirty bar glasses. They came in and stacked up almost as fast as I could wash them. People crowding at the bar where trying to get me to take their order, but I knew that I was only the bar back and tried to explain to patrons that I would get a bartender to take their order as soon as I could. It was crazy!

When I finally got things under reasonable control, Ken came over and thanked me for giving them a hand.

"Happy to help," I shouted over the din.

Over the next couple of hours, I watched in amazement as these bartenders put together an amazing number of drinks faster than I would have thought possible. In between making drinks they were trading quips with customers and entertaining them with what's called flairing. Flair bartending involves doing fancy tricks with bottles, glasses, shakers and the like. It's kind of like juggling.

A couple of times a customer would order several drinks called a "hot stinger," which was white crème de menthe mixed with brandy in a shot glass. The customer would order one for themselves and one for each bartender. An elaborate toast would be made, and each bartender would knock back the drink with great flair, and then toss their glass to the opposite bartender, the glasses crossing each other in the air across the length of the bar. The customer would then throw his or her glass up in the air toward one of the bar tenders who would catch it, sometimes behind their back, and slide the glass down the bar gutter to be washed. I would merely stand back, out of the way, hoping not to get hit in the head.

Both bartenders wore look-alike shirts that were very modern and chic. Think 1970s modern. The shirts were unbuttoned to mid-chest to expose gold chains. Their hair was stylishly long and they both wore mustaches. I, on the other hand, wore a white shirt, no gold chains, and had relatively short hair.

These guys were cool, like rock stars. I wanted to be one of these guys.

I got home very late. Halley was worried. There were no cell phones in those days. I told her what happened, which she seemed to accept as the potential new normal. I told her that we should count my tips for the week to see how we did. I purposely stashed all my shared tip money in a box without counting it all that first week. I was anxious to see how much it came to. It felt like more than I was used to. We counted it together. It wasn't as much as I hoped it would be, but it was definitely okay, just a little more than I might have made at the Tartan. I reminded myself that this was just the start. Things would no doubt get better.

# Chapter 42

It wasn't long before I got the chance to work the main bar during the week. The slowest day at the Smuggler's Inn was busier than the busiest day at the Tartan. My bartending skills got better and I started morphing into the bartender look that I wanted to emulate. I practiced flipping bottles, glasses and shakers at home. I wanted to fit in behind the bar and I wanted to be as cool as the other guys.

Within a couple of months I was one of the main bartenders, working the weekends and hauling in the money. The tips were amazing. I might take home $60 in a single night. That seemed pretty extravagant in those days. My Air Force pay at the time I was discharged in 1974 was under $6000 a year. I was on track to make over $7000 in 1975, so I thought that I was Mister Got Rocks.

Styles in the second half of the 1970s were characterized by bell-bottom pants, turtle-necked shirts, flowered shirts, long hair, sideburns, platform shoes, leisure suits, and Farrah Fawsett style hair for women. Rock and roll was getting into its second generation and the disco scene was strong due to the movie *Saturday Night Fever*. Lava lamps, black lights and bean bag chairs were big. Then there were the drugs and sex.

This was a time of expanding horizons for me, but it was also a time that created many roads best untraveled. Despite my potential and opportunities for growth, I was in many ways like a babe in the woods. My personality was very susceptible to the many temptations that went along with the bar and restaurant scene. I wanted to be cool, I wanted to be the center of attention, and I wanted people to like me.

Drugs were ubiquitous and everybody was having sex with everybody else. Being married and being incredibly busy at work until everybody else went home, probably saved me from devolving into a complete state of debauchery, but I occasionally had opportunities that I was too weak to pass up.

Perhaps I was also dealing with a subconscious need to make up for something that I thought had passed me by earlier in my life. Maybe I was dealing with some latent anger over the breakup of my first marriage, or maybe I was compensating for some bitterness related to my war experiences. At the time I wasn't thinking about any of that though. I was just determined to have a good time, and I wasn't thinking that I was doing anything that was really that bad.

I eventually rose through the ranks and was offered an assistant manager's position at another of Associated Host's big restaurants, called The Beef Rigger, in Orange. Associated Host was the parent company for Smuggler's Inn. This was another big break from my perspective. Now I got to deal with all aspects of the food and beverage operation. I got to use my management skills and I got to have more control over operations.

Orange was 50 miles away from Redlands, where we were living. I had purchased a Yamaha 650cc motorcycle with my new found financial success, and decided that I would travel to work in Orange on the bike, leaving Halley with our only car. This was often a challenging mode of transportation. The California nights at 2:30 in the morning can be quite cold, and I would often be chilled to the bone by the time I got home. I would try to snuggle up to Halley to get warm, but she would scream and tell me that I was like an ice cube. So I'd huddle on my own side of the bed, shaking with a body temperature that was probably near hypothermic.

On weekends, I would have to close on Saturday night and open on Sunday morning. I was forced to make arrangements to stay at the hotel, which was part of the Beef Rigger complex. This arrangement, of course, was not helping to strengthen my marriage.

One day, an amazing thing happened. A man walked into the restaurant and asked if I would be interested in working with the Griswold Company. Griswold's was a 12-acre complex in Claremont, California, that included a hotel, restaurants, and shops. They also had a couple of establishments in Redlands. It was privately owned by Sandy and Betty Sanford, and they were looking for new talent. If I was interested, I would have to successfully complete a rigorous training program at their private culinary school.

I still didn't have a professional career plan, but I recognized this as another golden opportunity to put my evolving career into high gear. I had no idea what a culinary program was, but I was sure that it would be very useful. I agreed to come in for an interview.

I was accepted into their management training program, which required the candidate to successfully complete every section of the culinary training program and then some. I learned all about food safety, sanitation, preparation, ordering, inventory, portion control, and on and on.

# Chapter 43

My first kitchen assignment was banquet preparation. The kitchen was industrial, equipped with mixers the size of washing machines. Ovens were numerous and large. Long stainless steel tables provided space for up to a dozen cooks and assistants to prepare and assemble plates for large numbers of guests. I once made twice baked potatoes for 500. The effort and coordination that went into preparing a quality meal in this volume was impressive.

My next assignment was the pantry. That was where I learned to make dressings, salads and desserts. Then there was the bakery, then the grill. After that, saucier training, where I learned to make sauces, as well as stews, hot hors d'oeuvres, and how to sauté food to order. This became my favorite specialty and I excelled in this area of food preparation. The final stop in the kitchen was the line, working with the other cooks and chefs to prepare lunches and dinners to order. It was fast, it was furious, and it was stressful, but it was a great experience and, man, I loved it.

I felt a sense of disappointment when I was required to move on to the beverage portion of the training. I thought that there was little I could learn, since I had been bartending in one of the top lounges in Southern California, but I was wrong. They had me skip the bar training and put me into sommelier training. This was a whole new world to me. My wine experience prior to this had been the occasional partaking of Boones Farm or Spanada Sangria. I had more recently been working my way up the wine scale with Mateus and Lancers.

Sommelier training in the mid-seventies was not what it is today, at least not in the United States. There were much more formal programs and certifications in France, Italy, and Great Britain in the 1970s, but the North American Sommelier Association program was still a few decades away. At Griswold's the sommelier program focused on the development of wine lists, the delivery of wine service and training for the other restaurant staff. Working along with the culinary team, the sommelier paired and suggested wines that best complement each particular food menu item. That entailed the need for a deep knowledge of how food and wine, beer, spirits and other beverages work in harmony. Of course, a professional sommelier also works on the floor of the restaurant and is in direct contact with restaurant patrons. I was taught how to determine and work within the taste preference and budget parameters of the patron.

I also had to learn how to drink wine that wasn't sweet or fortified. My first reaction to the initial tastings was that I didn't like wine very much. Why would anybody drink this stuff, I thought? As I continued my training and drank more wine, however, I quickly began to develop an appreciation for fine wines.

Finally, I was directed to work as the assistant manager at the Griswold's County House, in Redlands, working with the current manager to learn all of the business related aspects of managing a large, upscale dinner house. My experience at The Beef Rigger, made this task relatively easy, and within a couple of months I was promoted as the new manager. There was an article in the local paper which included my picture. I thought that I had reached the pinnacle of my career in the food and beverage industry.

I changed the lunch and dinner menus to include special items that took advantage of my love of sauces and French style cuisine. I also added table side service for Caesar Salad, Scampi, and Steak Diane. One of the things that I really wanted to do was to begin providing special events to take advantage of the large banquet space that the building offered. I ran this by the owners and they approved. I organized bridal fairs and a disco fashion show. I added a Sunday brunch buffet. Things seemed to be going great and I was making a pretty good salary, more money than I had ever made in my life.

I started having entertainment on Fridays and Saturdays, usually local bands playing pop and soft rock. Around the Christmas holidays, I decided to do something special and put together a small musical stage show that required a temporary runway. It wasn't very big, maybe twelve feet long, protruding from the existing stage. I had a crew come in to build the runway a couple of days before the show was to begin.

That crew was in the place, putting this thing together, when one of the waitresses came running into my office to tell me that she thought that Elizabeth Taylor was in the lounge. The Country House was located just off Interstate 10 and was probably the last outpost of civilization before Palm Springs, where many Hollywood celebrities went to get away from Los Angeles in those days. Other famous actors had visited the restaurant in the past, so having Elizabeth Taylor in the lounge was certainly within the realm of possibility.

I wanted to get a look at this famous star if she was indeed there, so I went out to the lounge and decided to use the pretense of inspecting the runway construction as an excuse. The room was empty except for staff and three people sitting at a table close to the new runway. The construction crew was not working on it, so I assumed it was finished. I casually walked around it looking as if I were scrutinizing every detail, casting furtive glances to the table to see if I could verify that it was Miss Taylor. I went up on the stage and decided to walk down the runway which would get me quite close to the visitors. Apparently, the final construction was not complete, because just as I came near the table the damn runway collapsed. Fortunately, it went in the opposite direction of their table, but I ultimately landed on my back, nearly under one of their chairs.

Looking up, I could clearly see that it was, in fact, Elizabeth Taylor, who was just at that moment looking quite alarmed.

"Oh," I said, "I'm very sorry. Apparently, this thing is not finished."

"Are you alright?" she asked with genuine concern.

"Oh, yes. Yes," I replied, still lying on the floor. A table tent had come off the table during the accident and landed on the floor next to me. I picked it up and impulsively handed it to her. "I don't suppose you would consider autographing this?"

She gave a hearty laugh and took the card. She took a pen out of her purse and signed the card, "Thanks for the excitement, Elizabeth Taylor." I got up from the floor, very red-faced, and thanked her.

"I will take care of your bill Miss Taylor," I said. I wasn't sure if I should call her Miss Taylor or Mrs. Burton. Liz and Richard had just gotten remarried recently and it was all the news.

I put the autographed card out in our lobby, in a locked display case. Everybody loved telling the story over and over to our customers.

# Chapter 44

Halley and I had moved to Redlands around this time and rented a really great old house in town. Given our current state of stability and steady income, we decided to buy a house and we both agreed that the one we were renting was ideal. The owner was willing to sell. I was eligible for a VA home loan, but we needed $2000 as a down payment. We couldn't figure out how to raise the money.

For reasons that I cannot explain, I went out and bought another house that we could afford without showing it or discussing it with Halley. I think that my only excuse, in retrospect, is that in the mid-70s chauvinism was alive and well, and I was probably guilty of thinking that the man should take care of things like buying a house. Halley hated the place.

I am ashamed to say that I was oblivious to any of the signs of domestic trouble in my life at this time. I was on a roll and I was focused on business and success. I decided to put on a big rock and roll show at the Country House. I used local talent for entertainment on Fridays and Saturdays in the lounge, and I used an agent to locate and book these acts. I told him about my idea and asked how I might go about putting something bigger together. He told me that some "B List" talent might be affordable and available since many of these people lived in Southern California. I was surprised to discover that the so-called "B List" acts were very recognizable and famous.

"So, what do you consider affordable?" I asked.

"You could probably get some of these old rock and roll acts for a couple thousand dollars," he said.

"Hmm. Well, that's a little rich for our situation here at the Country House," I replied.

"Well, let me look into it, and I'll get back to you," he said.

A couple weeks later, he dropped by the Country House and reviewed the results of his research with me. I was pleasantly surprised with what he had come up with. I went through the list and came up with a show that I thought could be very successful and, after some quick arithmetic, one that I thought I could afford.

The headline act would be The Platters. These guys did *The Great Pretender*, *Smoke Gets In Your Eyes*, and *Only You*. The Platters were the first rock and roll group to have a Top Ten album in America. They were also the only act to have three songs included on the *American Graffiti* soundtrack that fueled an oldies revival still underway in the mid-1970s. Radio stations were still playing their songs.

The opening acts would include an Elvis impersonator, one that I was assured was very good and quite popular. Can't go wrong with Elvis, I thought. The next opener would be Bobby Day. He was famous for his 1958 solo hit, *Rockin' Robin*. In 1972, Michael Jackson released a new album called, *Got To Be There*, which included a cover of *Rockin' Robin*, and that song became a hit single. That version of *Rockin' Robin* was still playing on the radio. He also did *Over and Over*, which had been popularized by the Dave Clark Five in 1965, and that song was also still playing.

The banquet hall would hold 200 people. If I charged a $10 cover charge and could fill the room, I could cover the cost of all three acts. The Country House would make its money in food and drinks. I decided to set up two portable bars in the room, with a limited number of drinks that could be ordered, no fancy drinks. I would have to keep things simple. I could devise a special, low-cost food menu especially for this show, one that would be relatively easy to prepare and serve. I would charge $7.50 for any one of three different meals on that special menu. I would bring in every employee we had for the event, including all of the part-time banquet people. I would have to rent lights and sound equipment. There would be no live band. The acts would sing to recorded music. It was a big undertaking and, despite having no practical experience with a production of this scope, I was sure I could manage it.

I put the whole show proposal in a document which I presented to the company's general manager. It included all of the logistical details, menus, costs, expected revenue and profit. I proposed a date that worked with all of the artists, and included copies of the entertainment contracts. I also described a proposed media and marketing plan. I got the approval. Everybody at the Country House was excited and we got to work on getting it all put together.

Because we were bringing in name acts, it wasn't difficult to get newspaper and radio coverage. We didn't have to spend money on advertising in those media. I made up fliers and had busboys go around and put them on windshields in parking lots. We had table tent cards on all of our tables, and by such methods we were able to keep the marketing budget very small. I hoped that enough people would hear about this show that we could fill the venue. It would be embarrassing if not enough people showed up to cover our costs.

One of my employees told me about some old searchlights that we could rent for $50. Searchlights were used fairly often in those days for big sales or events, and presumably directed people's attention to something they should look into. What the heck, I thought. Leave no stone unturned, and I made arrangements to have two searchlights there in our parking lot on the big night.

The day finally arrived. We were all nervous, especially me. What if hardly anybody showed up? We didn't have any advanced ticket sales. It was all pay at the door, first come, first served. What if the acts didn't show up on time? What if they came drunk? I had heard unsettling stories about some entertainers not taking small venues seriously and arriving late, or intoxicated, or both.

A half hour before the banquet doors were to open for the show, the searchlights were turned on. Several people had come in for dinner off of our regular menu in the dining room and had purchased tickets for the show. This was encouraging. I had two hostesses on the door to handle the hoped for crowd. I tried to be everywhere at the same time to make sure all was ready. The acts showed up when they were supposed to and were the epitome of professionalism. We went through sound checks and lighting checks. My talent agent showed up, and helped organize the stage logistics, for which I was extremely grateful.

People started coming in for the show, lots of people. They came in by the droves. One of my hostesses came up to me and told me that the parking lot was getting very full, and asked where people should park if the lot filled up. Crap! I hadn't given parking any thought at all. I sent a young man that I used for fixing things around the store to help direct traffic. His name was Seth. I told him to send people to the adjacent Smorgasbord lot if ours filled up. The Smorgasbord was also a Griswold store, so that seemed like a legitimate alternative.

The place filled to capacity, and still people were coming in. Good Grief! I thought. I hadn't counted on too many people. I ordered a few more tables to be squeezed in and opened up an adjacent patio just outside the banquet room. We quickly set up space heaters around the patio to take some of the chill out of the night air. We had everything we needed. It just hadn't occurred to me that we would have such a turnout.

Finally, we couldn't fit another soul into the place, and we had to start turning people away. Somebody found me and told me that the police were in the lobby and wanted to talk to the manager. Now what, I thought. It seems that we were causing a traffic back up and they wanted to know what our plan was for dealing with it. I just stared at the cop with a blank look.

"Um. I don't know, officer," I said dumbly. "I had no idea that so many people would come tonight. We can't legally fit another person into this building. The only thing I can think of is to turn off the searchlights and put a barricade up at the entrance. Can I get any help from the police?"

The cop gave me a withering look. He turned around and left without another word. I gave orders to turn out the lights and to put up some parking cones at the parking lot entrance. The show was about to begin and I had to run in and get things started. I was the Master of Ceremonies.

I made my way to the stage and stepped up to a microphone. I greeted everyone and thanked them for coming. Everybody inside looked happy, despite the fact that we had packed them in like sardines. I introduced the Elvis act, and stepped off the stage.

I went into the kitchen, where I found mayhem. The chef was angry. Too many orders, not enough help. I calmed him down and helped to get things a little more organized.

I went out to the main bar, where there was more chaos. The waitresses were up in arms. They had to come to the main bar to fill orders for things like margaritas. I reminded them that the show drink menu was limited and that they should not be taking orders for blended drinks. They were on the verge of rebellion. I told them that I would work on it, and got a couple of busboys to dig up some spare blenders and the mixers for the banquet bars.

I checked back in the banquet room, where I was told that customers were complaining that it was too hot. Apparently the stage lights and the close quarters of so many people were heating things up. I went to turn the AC down, hoping that the people sitting close to the open patio doors wouldn't get frozen.

On it went. I kept an ear out for the acts, so that I could run in to thank the departing artist and introduce the next act. Thank

God, nothing was going wrong on stage. If there was a next time, I would have to find an alternative solution for the MC, although that was one of the best part of this whole show, being the focus of everybody's attention, basking in the lime light for my fifteen minutes of glory.

The show finally finished. I thanked each of the performers and told them what a great show it was. I bought them all a drink and then rushed out to the front door to say goodbye and "thank you" to all of the customers. Everybody seemed like they had a good time and enjoyed the show. I received many suggestions about what I should do next time and what performers to bring in.

"Yes, that's a good idea," I said. "Thanks for the suggestion. Drive safely. Thank you. Good night."

When all the customers had left, I rounded up the employees and thanked everybody for a job well done. I offered everybody a drink on the house. All the tempers had settled down. The waitresses and bartenders were very pleased with their tips. It was very late when we finally got the place cleaned up and back in order. I knew everybody was tired and I myself felt like I did after a SAR mission, completely spent.

The next day was Sunday and my assistant manager was in charge that day, but I came in to go over the receipts for the previous evening. I was anxious to see how we did. It was a stellar outcome. We broke the revenue record for a single day by a mile. We easily covered all of the additional costs and maintained or exceeded our food and pour cost targets. Employees were coming into my office to ask if I had heard any of the radio reports about the show. Seems that we were getting some very good exposure in the media.

The general manager called from Claremont to see how the evening had gone. I gave him all the preliminary numbers and quick review of the show. He was very pleased and assured me that he would pass on the good news to the Sanfords. After I hung up the phone, I leaned back in my chair and reflected on all that I had achieved in such a relatively short time since leaving the Air Force. I was only 28 and seemed to be on track for success. I felt good. Then disaster struck.

# Chapter 45

Two weeks after the big show, I was advised that my assistant manager was going to be moved to another location. That was a disappointment because he was good, but that was the nature of this business. The good people move onward and upward, so I was glad he was going to his next step. I planned a little going away party for him on a Monday afternoon, in between the lunch and dinner rush.

Before that day arrived, Halley told me that she wanted to talk to me. The way she said it made me think it was about something serious. We took a drive in the country and she told me that she was not happy with me or our marriage. She listed a number of things that were making her unhappy and how I had disappointed her on several occasions. I realized that this was much more serious than I had anticipated.

I thought about our relationship and I knew that I wasn't being a very good husband. I was, in fact, having an affair with one of my hostesses. Our marriage had been pretty rushed after I returned from the Vietnam War. I was on the rebound and had not given enough serious thought about getting married again. I didn't want to be alone, and Halley was a very sweet, very beautiful woman, but we didn't really know each other very well when we got married.

I should have begged for forgiveness. I should have come to my senses and refocused my attention on making our relationship work, but I didn't. I was very sad that our time together seemed to be coming to an end, but my selfishness got the better of me. I was young. I was successful. I had things that I wanted and needed to do. I was more confident than I had ever been. The other woman I was seeing was a beauty queen and had already been selected to compete in the upcoming Miss California beauty pageant. Her image of me was untarnished. It was not the end of the world for me. I tried to convince myself that it would be a new beginning. Halley moved out.

On the following Monday, I had the bakery make a cake for our little farewell party for the departing assistant manager. I had all of the employees gather to say goodbye. I asked Seth, my young helper, to go to the wine locker and get two bottles of champagne for a small toast. I told him to give the keys to the assistant manager when he was done, since I was off that day.

This kid had been hanging around the place since I had started several months before. He seemed to be a sort of orphan, and I thought of him as kind of a Peck's bad boy. That is, he didn't seem to have a home with parents. I'm not sure how old he was but guessed he was probably 18 or so. I thought that he probably lived in his old, beat-up van. Once, at a Christmas party, he offered Halley and me a toke on a pipe filled with marijuana, which we accepted. What we did not know is that he had sprayed PCP, also known as Angel Dust, on the marijuana. As a result, both of us had a very unpleasant hallucinogenic experience. Once I recovered and discovered what had happened, I wanted to kill the little bastard, but he eventually ingratiated himself back into my good graces.

Seth was not an employee, but I often paid him to fix things, which he seemed to be good at doing, or to run errands for me. He became a fixture around the place. So, giving this kid the keys to the wine locker and asking him to fetch some champagne was not a particularly unusual thing. It turned out to be a bad and deadly decision though.

After the little reception, I left for the day. The kid did not immediately return the keys as instructed, but rather went back to the wine locker and helped himself to a few more bottles of champagne. He shared his booty with a couple busboys. The assistant manager realized what was going on and ordered Seth off the premises.

Meanwhile, two of our regular customers were in the bar waiting for their 16-year old daughter to join them for dinner. She was walking from a nearby friend's house. As she approached the restaurant's parking lot entrance, she was struck by a vehicle and killed. The driver of the vehicle left the scene. I learned of the accident the following day when I arrived to work. I was heartbroken for the parents.

For the next few days, I saw no sign of Seth. I had some things that I wanted him to do, so I was mildly annoyed that he wasn't around when I needed him. I asked a few employees if they had seen him lately or heard anything from him. One of the busboys said he thought that Seth might be sick or hurt.

"Really?" I asked with some concern. "Do you know where he lives?"

"He doesn't really live in any one place," came the unsurprising answer, "but his van is over at this guy's house that we sometimes go to see." This was an apparent obtuse reference to some nefarious character and activity that I probably didn't want to know about. "He's in his van and won't come out."

That's odd, I thought. Perhaps he had a drug overdose or went on some kind of binge that he was recovering from.

"Well, if you see him, please tell him that I have some work for him," I said. I returned to my paperwork dismissively. The busboy continued to stand there. After a few moments, I looked up.

"Is there something else?" I asked. I noticed that this young man was behaving in a very unsettled manner. "Do you have something that you need to tell me?"

"I think that Seth was in some kind of accident," he said haltingly. He was looking at his shoes and rubbing his hands together. "The front of his van is smashed in and the windshield is all cracked. He's acting really weird, kind of freaking out."

I immediately got a very queasy feeling in the pit of my stomach. "Do you have any idea of what might have happened?" I asked in a hushed voice.

"I wonder if maybe he hit that girl who was killed here on Monday night," he replied reluctantly, almost in a whisper.

"Shit," I thought out loud. We both didn't say anything for a few moments. I was trying to gather my thoughts. "You apparently know where he is." It was more of a statement than a question.

"I can't tell you. I can't, just really can't," he whined. "The guy who lives in the house ...where Seth is parked..." He trailed off, not finishing his sentence. "It's just a very bad situation."

"Look," I said. "You cannot withhold this information. If you think that there is some connection between Seth and the girl who was killed, you have an obligation to speak up. I appreciate the courage it took for you to come talk to me about this, but I will have to contact the police so that they can check this out"

He looked up in alarm. "No. I can't," he said in a desperate voice.

"Think about her parents. They need to know what happened," I reasoned. "I'll help you through this. I'll be with you when the police come to talk to us." I picked up the phone and called the local police. The young man dropped heavily down in a chair next to my desk.

"I knew that girl," he said. He had tears in his eyes. "She was in my class at school."

The next few days were like a bad dream. The police found Seth and his van. Skin, blood, and hair found on the front of his vehicle validated our suspicions. Seth eventually broke down and confessed to hitting the young girl as he was leaving the Country House parking lot. He said he didn't see her because it was dark and she was wearing dark clothing, which was apparently all accurate. He panicked and left the scene. It turned out that Seth was a minor and a runaway. He admitted getting into the wine locker and drinking that afternoon.

I advised the general manager of the situation. I knew that this was not going to be good for me. I should have never let this kid work around the premises without a formal employment arrangement. In fact, if I had known that he was a minor, he would not have been allowed to work here at all.

A week later, Griswold's general manager came to the Country House and told me that my employment was terminated immediately. Perhaps I should have anticipated this, but I was stunned. He explained that although they knew that I had no direct connection to the accident, it had happened on my watch and the company had no choice but to distance themselves from me. He told me that their insurance company had advised them that they needed to take this action. I could see that he was not pleased to have to do this to me, but I knew that he had no choice.

I went home to an empty house. I called Halley and told her what had happened. While she was sympathetic, she didn't offer to come over and make everything alright. How in the world had everything come apart so quickly? Now what was I going to do?

# Chapter 46

My friend, Bart, had moved to Fairbanks, Alaska, several months prior to my onslaught of misfortune, and he had suggested that I come up there to join him. He told me that there was a fortune to be made up there on the Alaska Pipeline. I probably wasn't going to find another restaurant management position in this area given what had just happened. I'd have start over as a bartender in some obscure tavern again. I didn't want to go back to Ohio.

I felt like I had been disgraced and there wasn't any place that I could think of where I could go to come to grips with my failures and lick my wounds. Alaska, however. Now there's a place where a guy could go to lick his wounds and figure out a Plan B. I made up my mind to make the journey. I wrote Bart a letter to let him know I was coming and that I would need his help to get established. He wrote back to tell me that he was glad that I was coming and that he would see me soon.

I told very few people that I was planning to go to Alaska. I put the house up for sale. I asked Halley if she would take care of things in my absence. There were some loose ends that would require somebody I could trust. I told Connie, my mistress beauty queen, that I was going. She was upset and told me that she wanted to go with me. I was flattered, but in a rare act of chivalry for me in those days, I told her that Alaska was no place for a woman like her, and besides she had the whole Miss California thing happening and was about to enter California State. I decided to hedge my bets, though, and told her to give me a few months to see how it was up there, then we could decide whether or not she should join me.

Although I was down in the dumps after all that had happened, heading up to Alaska felt like a new adventure just starting to unfold. Once again, my impulsiveness was the primary driver in my decision to go. Also in my typical fashion, I did not invest much effort into planning this move, but rather just let life unfold before me as I blundered along my way. It was already winter in Fairbanks. I realized sometime later that Fairbanks is within the Arctic Circle, so winter there is not at all like winter in Southern California, or any place else that I ever lived for that matter. In fact, I knew very little at all about Alaska, other than it was very far away and that it was a potentially good place for me to go to do penance.

I arrived in Fairbanks in the late afternoon, expecting to find Bart there to greet me at the airport and take me to wherever he lived, as we had arranged. I did not find him anywhere at the airport. I waited in the baggage area, thinking that he must be delayed, but felt certain that he would eventually come for me. He never showed up though. I spent the night in the tiny terminal, trying to convince people that someone would eventually pick me up.

The next morning I talked a trucker into giving me a lift to the city. Fairbanks is not a large city, so I thought that it would not be too difficult to find Bart. After all, I had his address. The truck driver was kind enough to drop me off close to that address. I was traveling light. I had only my Air Force duffle bag full of clothes and a few essentials. I looked around for the street number on one of the nearby buildings, but couldn't find it. It seemed odd to me that this part of the city was commercial. All of the addresses in this general area were stores and businesses of various types. Maybe there was another street with the same name someplace.

I had been living in Southern California, so I didn't have a lot of Alaska worthy cloths. Fortunately, Halley had given me a really cool fur-lined coat for Christmas the previous year, you know, in case I ever needed to go to a place that was really cold. I was glad to have this coat on me right then but it was still not enough. I had no gloves and just regular street clothes under the big coat. It was damned cold.

I walked into a saloon that was close to where Bart's address should have been. It's warm in here, I thought. I looked around as though I was looking for somebody. Since it was only mid-morning, there weren't a lot of people in the place. Finally, a grumpy looking bartender asked me if I was looking for something. I told him of my plight and that I was confused because the address I had didn't seem to match the kind of neighborhood that I would have expected. I took Bart's last letter out of my pocket and showed it to him.

The bartender gave a humorless laugh. "That's the address of this place alright," he said. "Sometimes guys use this address to get their mail. I remember this guy, dark hair, mustache."

"Yes," I exclaimed. "That would be Bart. Do you know where I can find him?"

"Hell, he could be anywhere," he answered. "He might be out on the pipeline, or someplace else. Who knows?"

"I came up here to meet him, and he was going to try to get me work on the pipeline," I said. I stood there for a moment, trying to figure out my next move. "I don't have a lot of money. Can you recommend a place I can wait for a few days, a cheap place?" I looked around the barroom. "In fact, I'm a very experienced bartender. Perhaps I could find a job tending bar for a while."

He coughed out a hoarse, sardonic laugh and gave me a good looking over. "We have a place you can flop, right here, upstairs. I could use a bouncer at night and you look like a guy who can take care of himself."

This bartender was the kind of guy you would not want to meet in a dark alley. He was not attractive, and he was huge. It seemed to me that he was more than capable of doing any bouncing that might be needed, but I decided not to look a gift horse in the mouth.

"Ok," I said. "That sounds like a good deal. Where do I put my stuff?"

He looked me up and down again, and gave another hoarse laugh. He motioned me to follow him and headed for a door at the back of the room. We entered a cozy, cluttered little apartment. Not bad, I thought. He turned around to look at me.

"This ain't it," he said gruffly. He went to the back of this room an opened another door, which lead to an alley outside. There was a rickety old stairway the led up the backside of the building. "Up there," he pointed. "There's no lock. Just go on in." He turned and went back inside.

I stood there a moment, looking at empty space that he had just left behind. I turned and looked up the stairs. Okay, what the hell, I thought, and climbed to the top. Sure enough, the door was unlocked. I stepped in and looked around. It was essentially an attic. Boards had been carelessly nailed down across the joists. Four twin sized mattresses lay on the floor, each with a couple of worn blankets folded up at the bottom. There was nothing else in the room other than a few bits of trash here and there. The ceiling had not been finished, and I could see roofing nails sticking out here and there, each with its own little icicle dangling from the tip. It was cold up here. There was one bare light bulb hanging from a wire in the middle of the room. It was on. I didn't see any way to turn it off.

I wasn't sure if I could actually survive in this place, but at that precise moment I didn't seem to have much of a choice. I chose a mattress and threw my duffle bag on it. It didn't look particularly clean, but I thought that it was probably too cold for any bugs to be living in these things. I would have to carry anything that I considered valuable on my person. Who knew who came up here? I assumed that anybody sent up here to crash was probably of questionable character. Well, then again I was here. Good Grief! Had it come to this?

I went through my duffle bag and stuffed whatever I considered valuable in my pockets. I went back downstairs. I decided I should go around to the front of the saloon. I didn't feel comfortable walking through the apartment. When I got back inside, I asked the bartender what time I should report for work. He told me I needed to be on duty from 8:00 to 2:00. I nodded.

It hadn't occurred to me before, but I asked him if there was any mail for Bart. He told me that there was not. I asked him where he would suggest that I go to get some warmer clothes and where I should go to get something to eat. He gave me his recommendations, so I headed back out to the street. It was dark outside, but apparently at this time of the year there was not a lot of daylight. It was around 4:00 pm.

It was cold and getting colder. First order of business was to get some extra socks, a sweatshirt and some gloves. I found the place the bartender directed me to. It was several blocks away, and I was freezing by the time I found it. That was probably a good thing, since now it would be easier to determine what I would need to keep me warmer. I looked at some boots as well, but didn't feel that I could afford them. I purchased several items and went looking for a diner. I hadn't eaten in over 24 hours and was starving.

I found a dumpy little diner a couple blocks away. It was crowded so I figured that might be a sign that the food was edible. Every item on the menu was fried food, with the notable exception of a hot turkey sandwich with mashed potatoes. I ordered the hot turkey sandwich. I was so hungry, it tasted like one of the best things I had ever eaten. When I got the bill, I discovered that living in Fairbanks, Alaska, would be expensive.

I had to pay as much for that sandwich as I would have for a scampi dinner, prepared tableside at the Country House.

I got back to the saloon around 6:30. I decided to just hang out since I had no place else to go other than my depressing, deep-freeze room. It was warm down here. The smell of smoke, stale beer, and other assorted unpleasant odors hung heavy in the air. The place had more patrons in it now, and there was a jukebox playing country music. Things seemed calm enough. There were no women in the place. It was going to be a long, boring evening. I had to find Bart. I was not going to be able to tolerate my current situation for very long.

At 8:00 the bartender walked over to where I was sitting and pointed to a little stand next to the main door. There was a stool next to the stand. He handed me a baseball bat.

"That's your station over there," he said, pointing. "You keep this bat in plain view. If things get to a point where I need your help, I'll let you know. Don't hit anybody in the head unless they have a gun. Go for the gut if you can, otherwise the legs. No drinking while you're on the job. None, understand?"

I stared at him, mouth open. I was trying to think of something to say, perhaps get a bit of clarification on the whole gun thing.

"Understand?" he barked.

"Uh, yes, yes. Yes, I understand," I stuttered. Guns?

"If you get hungry, there's some moose jerky behind the bar. Just ask for it," he offered.

I nodded blankly. "Thanks," I said. Moose jerky. I'm sure that must be a great delicacy up here. I had never consumed any jerky of any sort in my entire life, so I was only vaguely aware of what it might be or even look like. I wondered if a person could survive on a diet of moose jerky alone. I was beginning to feel the edges of despair gnawing away at the back of my mind.

That first night passed with relatively little disruption to the drunken disorder that apparently passed for normal in this place. I only had to provide bouncer backup twice, but didn't actually have to bash any heads, guts or legs. Just showing up with the bat seemed to convince the combatants to reduce the argument to simply cursing and an exchange of slurring innuendos.

By the end of the night, however, I was a nervous wreck. Still I was reluctant to leave the warm bar room for my cold attic. Partly as a stalling tactic, I decided that I should have something in my stomach, so I asked about the moose jerky. It was in a large glass jar and looked like nothing I had ever seen before. It reminded me of what you might see on a rotting carcass in the middle of a road. It was dark, almost black and felt like leather.

I pulled the smallest piece I could find out of the jar, not sure if I could get myself to actually take a bite. The bartender was watching me. Did this guy work here around the clock? I decided that I should try it. After all, I lived in Alaska now and if this is what people ate, I'd better get used to it. I took a tentative bite and discovered that it was actually quite good. Hmm. Who would have thought that anything this ugly could taste good, I thought? The bartender offered me a beer, which I happily accepted.

Eventually, I had to go up to my room. I was very tired, but still dreaded the thought of trying to sleep in that place. I stepped outside to make my way around the building. It was snowing. The temperature was certainly well below freezing. Oh great, I thought. I hurried around and went up the stairs and went inside the attic. There was a guy on one of the mattresses snoring away. His boots were sticking out from under the blankets he had wrapped himself in. There was a bottle of something brown next to his head. The room reeked with his smell.

I stood in the room, next to my mattress, thoroughly disgusted and growingly depressed. Well, there was nothing for it tonight. I would just have to deal with my situation. Following my new roommate's example, I left all my clothes on and laid down. I used my duffle bag for a pillow. It didn't look like it had been tampered with. I pulled up the available blankets, curled in a fetal position and surprisingly fell quickly asleep.

# Chapter 47

I awoke in a state of disorientation. I felt like I was in a refrigerator, a smelly refrigerator. The snores from my roommate snapped me into recalling my situation. I looked at my wristwatch. It was 9:30 am. I had to go to the bathroom really bad, so I was going to have to get up. I realized that I had no idea where the bathroom was, other than the latrine in the saloon. I sat up and looked around the attic hoping that maybe there was a toilet up here. No such luck. I got up, keeping the blankets wrapped around me and headed for the door. It was still dark outside, or maybe it was a dark grey. I looked at my watch again. Good Grief! When did daylight actually happen in Alaska? I could tell the sky was overcast, but it was no longer snowing. I went down the stairs, not sure where to go. There was a couple of inches of fresh snow on the ground, making everything look clean and fresh. I went around to the front of the building, but the door was locked. I went back to the alley. I couldn't wait any longer, so I went behind the stairs and relieved myself. I guessed that this was probably not unusual around here.

I decided to go to the diner, where I could not only get something to eat, but get warm. I went back up to the attic to put on some extra socks, as well as my new sweatshirt and gloves. I made it to the diner in about fifteen minutes by walking at a very fast clip. That helped me get warmed up a little and by the time I entered the place I was wide awake and ready for some warm food.

I had to conserve my cash, so I looked for something on the menu that would not be too expensive but would fill me up.

Pancakes seemed like it would be just the ticket in my circumstances. I was encouraged by the portion that came to my table. Large cakes in both diameter and thickness. A large syrup dispenser was also delivered, which I intended to make liberal use of. The feast was topped off with a large cup of strong coffee, not as bad as we used to make in the Air Rescue Alert Shack, but close. The brief recollection of the Alert Shack made me recall that Bart was missing in action. Where the hell was he?

I saw a newspaper on the window ledge that looked like it had been read and left by another customer. I got up and retrieved the paper, looking around to see if anybody might object. I sat back down and dug into my breakfast. I scanned the local paper to see if I could get a sense of what was going on around this place. "Jimmy Carter's win over Gerald Ford represents first candidate from the Deep South since the Civil War". "First megamouth shark discovered off Oahu, Hawaii". That's all big news, I thought sarcastically. The second page headline read, "Alaska Pipeline Nearing Completion". Oh great. My timing is just great. Why did I listen to Bart?

I put the paper down. This news was ruining my gourmet breakfast. I needed to develop a plan. Maybe I should just cut my losses and go back to California or Ohio. If I waited very long, I wouldn't have enough money to purchase a plane ticket. I couldn't take much more of my current accommodations. I decided that I would stay for three more days in hopes that Bart would eventually show up. I figured that there had to be some logical explanation for his tardiness. After that, I would head back to California. I still had a house there and my motorcycle. And, it was warm there for God's sake!

The next two days and nights were perhaps the longest of my life. There was no place to go during the day. If I did try to venture out, it was too cold to get very far, and there just wasn't anything to do or see within my range on foot or within my slim budget. Sleeping in the attic was like a nightmare. The time I spent in the saloon working was, by contrast, at least perversely entertaining and warm.

No women ever came into the saloon while I was there. It was a place for hard men whose primary purpose for coming to this place was to get drunk. There was a pool table which was perpetually in use and often the source of vociferous disagreements.

On what I was determined to be my last night in this place, a burly guy came up to my little bouncer stand and proceeded to tell me in slurred speech what a pussy-little-piss-ant I was and where he thought my baseball bat should be shoved. He was clearly intoxicated, and seemed intent on causing me trouble. I started watching for a gun.

I have never been a fighter. I hate fighting and do whatever I can to avoid getting into a fight. Up to that moment, I had only been in one fight in my life and that was in seventh grade in Albuquerque. Three Hispanic boys caught me out behind the school gym as I was leaving school to walk home. We had just moved to New Mexico, and I was trying to get used to my new environment. I didn't really know anybody yet, but apparently during lunch that day one of these boys thought that I had said something about his girlfriend. I didn't see how that was possible since I didn't recall talking to anybody at lunch, but he was insistent in his accusation.

As he continued to harangue me over this imagined infraction, his two friends positioned themselves on either side of me. Other kids were forming a small crowd that encircled us. I suddenly became aware that I was about to get beat up, and I guess I went into fight or flight mode. Before I had any time to process this properly, the kid in front of me slapped me hard across my face.

I was always tall for my age and was already six feet tall by the time I was in seventh grade. So, I towered over all three of these boys. Maybe that's why they thought it would take three of them to handle me. Of course, I was like Mr. Pipe Cleaner man, being very skinny, with long legs and arms. I was born with hands the size of a baseball glove. So, I probably looked like a goofy, geeky guy that could easily be pushed around. Turned out they were wrong.

The slap triggered a reaction in me that I could only call berserk. I was carrying a couple of schoolbooks on top of a clipboard when all this happened. I absent mindedly hurled them, quite accidently, into the face of the kid on my left, chipping a couple of teeth and ripping his lip wide open. At the same moment, the kid on my right grabbed my right arm, which caused me to reflexively kick out with my right foot, unintentionally catching him in the groin. The instigator in front of me lunged. I grabbed him at arm's length, which kept him from connecting his flailing fists with my face, and threw him on the ground. I immediately jumped on his chest and began to strangle him with my very large hands. I was strangling him so hard that one of my thumbs dislocated. The stabbing pain caused me to stop chocking him, probably saving his life and sparing me from spending the rest of my childhood in the reformatory.

My eyes filled with tears. The pain was excruciating. I was still sitting on the kid's chest. I was vaguely aware of his pleading for me to let him up, but I couldn't move. He couldn't breathe. Some of the other kids were trying to convince me to get up, that the little bully had had enough. I realized that several kids were asking if I was okay. I heard one kid say that he heard these other guys fought dirty. I didn't know what that meant exactly, but I think they thought it had something to do with my apparent pain. I heard somebody else tell me that they had my books. A couple guys pulled me up and said that they would help me make sure I got home okay.

On the way home, I made up a story about how my thumb got dislocated. I wasn't sure how my parents would react to me fighting in school, but assumed it would not be good. After that, I was treated like some kind of big-man-on-campus around the school. I never got bothered by anybody there again.

So, here was this big, ugly, drunken asshole, standing too close to me and apparently looking for a fight. I realized that I was shifting into fight or flight mode. I did not want to have to deal physically with this guy, but I wasn't about to let myself get beat up either. I had been working out steadily for the past four years. I had received hand-to-hand combat training in the Air Force. I was six feet, two inches tall, weighed around 210 pounds, and I was sober. I figured that I could probably handle this man if I didn't let him hit me.

I calmly told the man that I didn't want to fight him and that he should calm down. He gave me a very disgusted look and made as if he was going to turn around and leave. I knew what was coming. He suddenly spun around with a wild, haymaker right hook aimed at my head. I simply grabbed his swinging arm, pulled him close to me, letting his momentum turn his body enough for me to get behind him and wrap my left arm around his neck. Still holding on to his right arm I squeezed hard on his neck with my left arm and used my leverage and weight to bring his head down hard on my little stand. He was disabled, but now I was pissed. I was in the process of deciding if I would just choke him to death or bash his brains out on the nearby wall. I calmed myself down a little and pushed him over to the wall next to my stand. I slowly rubbed his face against the brick wall.

"You ready to calm down, asshole," I hissed.

"Aagh!" he roared back, flailing wildly and impotently with his left. He couldn't reach me from the front due to the way I was holding him, so he tried hitting me around his back. That maneuver managed to hit me ineffectively in the upper leg and butt, but I considered it to be the wrong answer, so I pushed his face harder on the rough brick. I knew that it must be taking off skin. He screamed. He'd had enough.

The Neanderthal bartender hustled over along with a couple other patrons who were still in fairly sober condition.

"Let him go," the bartender said in what I thought sounded like a pleading tone.

I let loose of him and pushed him away to ensure that he didn't get a swing in during the break. He bent over, holding his neck and face, roaring with rage and pain. I thought that he was going to take me on again, but he just stayed bent over huffing and puffing and groaning. The bartender gave him a few minutes to recover, then told the guy he could leave peaceful like or he could go out with the cops. He chose option A.

After the guy left the saloon, the bartender stood there a moment looking at me.

"Fuck," he said. "I knew you could take care of yourself. I knew it."

At the end of the night, I drank a couple of beers and savored some moose jerky. I told the bartender that I was concerned that the guy I messed up might be laying for me, and asked if I could go upstairs through his apartment. He readily agreed. I also told him that I was going to go back to California the next day if I could get a ride to the airport. I had given up on Bart showing up. He told me that I ought to give it one more day. Sunday, tomorrow, was the day that guys would usually come in to check on their mail, especially if they were working out on the pipeline.

"Sunday is their only day off," he said. "They come in on Saturday night and go back on Monday morning."

"You mean he might be here in town right now?" I asked.

"Might be, but those guys don't come into a place like this on Saturday night," he said. "They go to the big places that have entertainment and a few women."

"I take it there aren't many women up here," I said.

"No," he replied. "Most of the females who are here are married or still kids. There's a few available though." He snuffed a coarse laugh. "It's about two hundred to one though. Maybe more. Anyplace there's women, there's trouble. It's like a hundred bucks fightin' over one little doe. They aren't necessarily pretty either. The women, I mean." He chuckled, like he was recalling something funny from the past.

"Ok," I said. "Sounds like I'd better wait until Monday. Thanks."

He led me through his apartment. He picked up a nice, thick blanked from a chest at the foot of the bed and handed it to me. "Gonna be colder tonight," he said.

"Thanks," I said again. I was starting to warm up to this guy. There was nobody in the attic tonight, thank God. I laid down with all my blankets and felt reasonably comfortable. I was drained after the adrenaline rush from the earlier altercation. I've been in Alaska for five days and have already been in a fight. There's practically no women. There's only a few hours of daylight in a day, and it's colder than a well digger's ass. What was I thinking?

# Chapter 48

The next day, just as predicted, Bart shows up at the saloon. I was sitting at a corner table reading the newspaper, when a group of burly guys came tumbling in from the snowy weather. I looked up. They were all wearing coats with hoods lined with wolf fur. They all went up to the bar asking about mail, and ordering beers. The bartender told one of them that there was somebody here looking for him, and gestured with a nod and a look toward my table. The guy turned around to see who I was. It was Bart.

"Well, fuck me naked," he exclaimed smiling. Bart always did have a way with words. He came over to greet me. "What are you doing here?" He was holding out his hand.

I stood up. "What am I doing here?" I said a bit too loudly. "You knew I was coming. You were supposed to meet me five days ago. Don't you remember? You sent me a letter assuring me that you would pick me up at the airport." I did not extend my hand in greeting. I hadn't thought about what I would do or say when and if Bart ever showed up, but I was feeling angry at this moment.

Bart's smile transformed into that smirky smile of his, like this was all a big joke. "I thought you were coming this week, this coming Wednesday," he said. There was no apology in his voice.

I shook my head. "Damn it, Bart," I said looking down and shaking my head. "You don't know what I've been through. How could you have forgotten when you were supposed to meet me?" I looked up at him. He still had that damn smile on his face.

"Well, let me buy you a beer, old buddy," he said, and grabbed me in a bear hug. It was hard to stay mad at him. Here he was. I was saved.

He put his arm around my shoulder and ushered me over to the bar where the others were watching our exchange with interest.

"I want you guys to meet my friend, Wolfman," he said by way of introduction. "We were in Vietnam and Thailand together. We flew together on search and rescue missions. He's one bad-ass motha' fucka'. He actually wrestled a bear up in Nakom Phanom."

I was now laughing with embarrassment, which I knew made me look like anything but a bad-ass motha' fucka'. The bartender contributed his version of my altercation with the drunk the night before.

"Kicked the guy's ass!" he exclaimed. "Never took a swing at the guy. Just put the guy in a headlock and wiped the wall with the guy's face. Thought he was going to kill the guy, but he let him go."

The beer started flowing. I was in the mood to let my hair down, but was anxious to get out of this place. After a while, I asked Bart where he lived. He told me that he lived with his girlfriend when he was in town.

"I will be able to stay there with you guys, won't I," I pleaded.

"Of course," he said. "I'm sure it'll be okay."

"Do you mean that she doesn't know I'm coming?" I asked.

"I told her that you would probably be coming up someday," he said, without apparent concern.

"What about getting on with the pipeline?" I asked. "What's the situation there?"

"Well," he said, "things are getting tighter. The project is nearing the end, and it's harder to get a position, depending on what you do."

"I read about it in the local paper," I said. "What kind of people are they still looking for?"

"Welders, truckers, heavy equipment mechanics mostly," he replied off-handedly.

"What about, maybe, like cooks," I asked hopefully, "or some other less trade-specific job?"

"Maybe," he said, "but you gotta belong to the union to get on with the project. That's the hard part. You basically got to buy your way into the union. Costs around $500."

Five hundred dollars was a shit-load of money in those days. There was no way I could afford to pay that, especially with no guarantee that I could even get a job. Besides, I apparently hadn't thought about the now obvious need to have some kind of relevant trade experience. Still there must be something I could do.

"Well, what are you doing out there?" I asked.

"I'm with a contractor who is responsible for putting down the insulation when the pipe goes underground," he said.

"Maybe I could do that too?" I asked.

"Yeah, maybe," he said casually. "They sometimes put temporary help on if they need to fill a vacant position or we need to make up some time."

"So, Bart," I said, "you know that I came up here because you told me that there were pipeline jobs and that everybody was making money hand over fist. I can't afford to be up here if there's no work." I was starting to get that sinking feeling again.

"We'll go out there tomorrow and see what's what," he said, showing no signs of concern. "Don't worry. We'll get you squared away."

We arrived at Bart's place late. I met his girlfriend, who didn't seem too pleased to see me. I was shown to a little room with a mattress on the floor, amid lots of other stuff. The room was apparently used as a storage place. Well, at least it would be warm and I could turn the light off.

Very early the next morning, Bart got me up and quickly out the door. A car with two other guys pulled up in front of the apartment building where Bart lived. We drove to an airport close to Fairbanks, one of fourteen airports built specifically for the pipeline, and boarded a private plane which took us down to an area closer to Valdez than Fairbanks. This area was really out in the wilderness, but the construction area was impressively large, with lots of temporary buildings, tents, equipment and supplies.

We headed toward a construction type trailer that served as the personnel office for this sight. Bart got me signed in as a temporary, unskilled laborer. I didn't feel very accomplished in this environment, a big ego deflation from the lofty position I had been fired from just a few weeks before. I was also woefully unprepared as far as clothing went. I was told that if I was sent out that I'd be issued artic clothing, such as boots, gloves, pants and coat, all designed to keep a person from getting frostbite.

I ended up working two shifts that week, essentially just carrying material to the crews who knew what they were doing. It was cold, just below zero degrees Fahrenheit. The special clothing helped, but I still felt cold after being out in the weather for more than an hour. One of the guys told me that in January and February, when the temperatures could reach 40 below or lower, they would only let the workers out in the cold for about 30 minutes, then they would be replaced by a second crew. That exchange went on throughout the entire shift. I couldn't imagine what 40 below would feel like, yet, but I would find out later.

I wasn't able to get out on a temporary assignment after that first week, so after a month, I told Bart that I couldn't afford to keep doing this. I appreciated his help, but I needed to do something that generated a steady income. His girlfriend worked at a local Safeway grocery store, and she said she would see if they needed any help. I got an offer to work as a night stocker. It paid pretty good money, so I took it.

Night stockers work from 10:30 at night until 6:30 in the morning. Given how the whole day-and-night thing works in Alaska, the midnight shift hours weren't really that bad. It was a mind numbing job, but it was physical and allowed me to eventually get my own place. Well, it was not exactly my own. It was a basement apartment with three bedrooms. Due to the housing shortage caused by the pipeline, there was a requirement that rental units had to be shared. I'm not sure that was a law or anything, but that was the deal I was offered.

My roommates were good enough. They were quiet and went about their own business. We occasionally got together during the summer months and grilled something outside. Since it's pretty much daylight all the time in the summer, we could have a BBQ anytime, day or "night".

When I wasn't working or sleeping, I focused on working out at the gym located at the nearby University of Alaska. I met a guy there who was training for the Mister Alaska contest. I started training with him, which gave me more incentive to hit the weights harder than I ever had in the past. This was the beginning of an eventual decision to train as a bodybuilder and compete.

The house in Redlands was eventually sold, as was my motorcycle. Halley helped take care of the transaction details. We talked about the possibility of getting back together and about her coming up to Alaska, but that never happened.

# Chapter 49

While in Alaska, I discovered that there wasn't a lot to do. There were very few women, so finding someone to date was nearly impossible. The main pastime in Fairbanks was drinking. Saturday nights were the main event in this game. A few guys would get together just about every Saturday and go to one of a dozen or so saloons to listen to music and drink. Most of these places brought in bands from the lower 48, as the rest of the United States was called. Most of these bands were County Western. The bands brought out what few women there were on Saturday nights. Just as my original benefactor, the bartender at the saloon in town, had warned, "anyplace there's women, there's trouble."

Just about every Saturday night, wherever we went there was a big bar room fight, the kind you see in the old cowboy movies. It would almost be funny, except that the consequences of not protecting yourself during one of these mass brawls were substantial. I had to fight my way out of many bars during my time in Alaska. My objective was always to just escape, but that often meant fighting to get to the exit door. I really did hate fighting, but I was honing my fighting skills out of necessity and getting plenty of practice.

There is a tourist attraction in Fairbanks, called Pioneer Park. There are lots of Alaska oriented attractions there, including a place called the Palace Saloon. This place was all decked out to look like an old west saloon and it featured a dancehall style show that included a small troupe of dancehall girls. These ladies were dressed in costumes that include corsets and lots of petticoats and such, and at the end of their performance they would line up and do a cancan number.

Weary of the usual Saturday night fight, Bart and I decided to check out the Palace. Since it was a tourist attraction, we assumed that we could enjoy a peaceful evening. I even bought a special white, embroidered shirt for the occasion, and impulsively bought a small bouquet of flowers, which I planned to give to my waitress, assuming there were waitresses.

We arrived and were ushered to a small table next to the stage. In fact, we did have an attractive waitress wait on us and I offered her the flowers. She seemed quite pleased with the gesture. I then ordered their best bottle of wine. Bart ordered a beer. Within a short time the place became packed, mostly with middle-aged tourists, who were there to see the dancehall show. Right up front, center stage, was a table where four loud, obnoxious Irishmen sat. They had apparently been there for some time. They were obviously drunk. I tried to ignore them, but the way our table was positioned my line of sight included these guys.

The show began with a comedian, then an old time piano player, and a short skit about some historical figure. The Irishmen were rudely heckling these performers, shouting "bring on the dancing ladies." I was getting irritated despite my efforts to ignore them. I think that many of the tourists thought it was part of the show, since they seemed to be laughing at these assholes. The performers on stage were valiantly tolerating the disturbances.

The dancers finally came on stage and went through their chorus line routine. One of the Irishmen kept getting out of his chair and moving up to the bottom of the stage as if to grab the dancers' legs when they were in the midst of their high kicks or the rond de jambe. The other three guys would grab him and sit him back down at the table. I was surprised that the bouncers, who were evident at the front door, did nothing to restrain this guy. I was embarrassed by the Irishmen's behavior.

The conclusion of the chorus line act was also the end of the show. I was having my second glass of wine, and expressing my disgust at the behavior of the Irish assholes to Bart, when I suddenly realized that the most inebriated of the group, the guy who was grabbing at the dancers' legs, was standing right in front of me. He was babbling incoherently, directing his comments to me. He was standing very close, too close for my comfort.

I looked at him, attempting to understand what the hell he was trying to say, when he suddenly bent over, put both his hands on my knees, which positioned his face a couple of inches from my own. I abruptly stood up in alarm, pushing him back with my hands on his shoulders. This had the effect of sending him backward to the floor as if he were a plank of wood. His feet never moved from their original position. He hit the floor with a thud, banging his head. He was out.

In an instant, his buddies were on me. Fortunately, I was a pro at barroom fighting by this time. One of the guys got behind me and was trying to get me in a choke hold, while the other two were wildly flailing punches that I was blocking with my arms. I managed to grab one of the guys in front of me and got him in my time tested headlock. I dragged that guy, along with the bastard behind me over to the corner of the stage, which was very close to our table. I used the combined weight of myself and the guy in the headlock to smash the guy behind me into the corner of the wall. I could hear a cry of pain come from the guy in back. The third Irishman was landing all his punches accidently to the head and body of the one I had in a headlock.

All of this took place in a matter of seconds, and before you could say "North to Alaska", the bouncers were there breaking things up. The two that had been physically attached to me dropped to the floor. The third guy rushed over to what turned out to be his brother, the one that I had pushed away from me. He was still knocked out cold.

Two of the bouncers grabbed me and started shuffling me toward the door. I shook them off with a great show of indignation just as my waitress came running up to assure them that I was just defending myself and that the Irishmen had started the whole thing. The bouncers stood there a moment looking at me with suspicion, ready to rip my head off at the slightest provocation. I reached down and picked up my chair, straightened myself out in an exaggerated manner, poured a little more wine in my glass, and said, "I intend to finish this fine bottle of wine, if you don't mind." The waitress moved close to me as if to protect me from the bouncers.

Incredibly, people in the audience started applauding. The waitress, the bouncers and I all looked at them, then each other incredulously. The bouncers turned their attention to the obnoxious Irishmen, while I took a sip of my wine. The waitress laid her hand on my shoulder.

"Are you okay, Honey?" she cooed.

I guess the flowers worked. "Yes," I said. "I'm fine. Thank you."

I suddenly realized that Bart was not there. I looked around the room to see what had happened to him. I saw him standing outside the swinging doors of the saloon entrance, looking in. He saw me looking at him, my hands spread open in a gesture of "what the fuck?" He reluctantly made his way back inside and to the table.

"Thanks for the help," I said, as sarcastically as I could manage. In his defense, our strategy in these situations had always been to beat a fast exit to the door, out of harm's way. I continued to stew another few moments when I became aware that the Irishman that I had pushed away from me was still on the floor, unmoving. His brother was yelling at me, over and over in his strong Irish brogue. "I'm a vengeful man. If you killed my brother, I will have my vengeance." At first I thought it was kind of funny, but then I heard sirens in the distance. "Shit," I thought.

The waitress came over to ask if Bart wanted another beer. I asked her if there was a back way out. She pointed in the direction of a rear exit. I told Bart that we had better get out of there, that if the guy on the floor was seriously injured, we'd have to deal with the police. I gulped down the remaining contents of my glass and we made our escape.

The fighting thing was getting old, very old, and I was about to give up the Saturday night ritual when we discovered the Malemute Saloon in Ester. Ester is a little gold mining town about ten miles northeast of Fairbanks. There wasn't really much there of interest other than the saloon. A few of us from the grocery store went there one Saturday night. It was very rustic.

The Malemute had a little tiny stage and a small dance floor that was basically a bunch of rough two-by-twelve planks nailed to the floor joists. Not all of the nails were doing their job, so it was kind of rickety. As you walked into the place it was immediately obvious that the left side of the room was taller than the right side of the room. If you went to the end of the bar on the right side of the room, somebody my height had to stoop down a little in order to avoid hitting his head on the ceiling. We were told that this was a result of the Great 9.2 Alaska Earthquake of 1964. Since the Malemute was reported to have burned down in 1968 and rebuilt, that story was suspect. No matter, though, it had a good feel to it.

The weekend entertainment at the Malemute included readings of Robert Service poetry and Blue Grass music. Folks referred to in Alaska as "bush people", came in from their remote cabins in the surrounding wilderness to dance on Saturday nights. The bush people themselves were pretty interesting, quite rough, but peaceful enough if you didn't bother them. Probably the main attraction of the Malemute, however, was the barmaid, Kyle. That is certainly why we kept coming back.

Kyle looked like Farrah Fawcett. She was very attractive and sweet, with a big, Farrah Fawcett smile. She made conversation with everybody like they were all good friends, including our motley crew. Everybody loved Kyle, and we would all vie for her attention when we patronized the saloon. We knew from our conversations with her that she was the daughter of a North Dakota pig farmer. She had come to Fairbanks with a guy who worked on the pipeline, but had broken up with him. She stayed up here because she liked Ester and the independence. We also knew that she didn't have a current boyfriend.

She didn't put up with any shenanigans though. She carried a .38 caliber pistol on her hip at all times and kept her pet dog, who looked very much like a wolf, behind the bar with her. Flashing her brilliant smile, she would occasionally remind people that anybody who tried to get behind the bar without permission would have to be carried out. We all believed she meant it.

The local Retail Clerks Union, which all of us at Safeway belonged to, was planning their annual summer picnic around the time we discovered Kyle and the Malemute. A bunch of us decided that we should invite Kyle. After some discussion, it was also agreed that only one of us would get to take her to the picnic as our date. This subject often reached obsession levels when it was discussed among our little band, which was often. Somebody decided that we ought to have a pool where each person would put in $10. Whoever got Kyle to go with them to the picnic would win the pool. Of course, having Kyle to agree to go with you would be like winning the lottery.

By the time that the picnic was only one week away, nobody had won the pool. Saturdays were always busy and it was the only time we ever saw Kyle. Any conversation with her was in between her efforts to make and deliver drinks to all the customers. It occurred to me that nobody had actually ever asked her to the picnic. I realized that they were all trying to figure out how to approach her on this invitation as if they were asking her for a date. That had been the original concept in our little contest after all.

I hadn't personally asked her because I didn't want to suffer the almost certain rejection that I presumed would result. Any woman who looked like a movie star was unlikely to want to go out with me. As I sat there at the bar that evening though, I suddenly realized that I didn't have to ask her out on a date. I could merely invite her to the union picnic. I had strategically positioned myself close to the place behind the bar where Kyle made the drinks. It was the only place where she stood still for more than a moment or two. The next time she came to that spot to fill a drink order I went for it.

"Hey Kyle," I said with as much confidence as I could muster. "Our union is putting on their big annual picnic at Graehl Park next Sunday. Going to be lots of good food and beer. Want to go?" I put on my best smile and held my breath.

"Sure," she said immediately. "That sounds like a lot of fun. What time?"

"It starts at 11:00, but we don't have to be there exactly at that time," I said. "I think it goes until 3:00 or 4:00. I don't have a car, but I could meet you at the Safeway store whenever you want to go. I can get you in."

"Ok," she said. "That would be great. How about 11:30?"

"11:30 it is then," I said triumphantly. I looked at my gang, who were all looking at me with shocked, wide-eyed expressions. They were speechless.

There was a sustained moment of stunned silence from my friends. I have to say, it was one of my most triumphant moments. Just the look on everybody's face was beyond value. I was $100 richer, but the real prize was showing up at the union picnic with one of the best looking women in Fairbanks. Word spread quickly. It was like the Queen of England was going to attend.

My glory was short lived. Kyle met me at the store as planned. She was driving a 1972 Ford F250 Custom Sport, which was like having a limousine up there. When we arrived at the park, I escorted her up to the check-in table to get our badges. That was pretty much the last I saw of her until it was time to leave. She was practically legend within the local union and everybody wanted to meet her and talk to her. My "buddies" made sure that they got plenty of opportunity to introduce her and bring her beers and food. At first I was a little put out, but ultimately I had to laugh at the whole scene. After all, I wasn't really her date, and the way everybody was making such a fuss over her struck me as crazy.

At the end of the afternoon, she managed to get away from the throng that seemed to perpetually surround her and found me drinking a beer at one of the picnic tables. She looked very happy and animated from all the attention. She had a big smile on her face, showing all those nice white teeth. There was a breeze blowing the long, curly hair back off of her lovely face. She was a looker alright.

"Hello," I called out as she approached. "Having fun?"

"Yes," she said breathlessly, "but I need to get back to open up the saloon."

"Ok," I said. "Would you mind dropping me off at my apartment? It's on the way."

We hustled toward her truck, saying goodbye to people as we made our way. It was quite the send-off, like we were celebrities, well, like she was a celebrity.

"I didn't get to see much of you today," she said gaily as we drove off.

"No," I said. "You were very popular. I hope everybody didn't pester you to death."

"Oh, I had a great time," she said. "Thank you so much for inviting me. It was good to get out and do normal things, like normal people do." She was still smiling that movie star smile of hers. I thought she must have genuinely enjoyed the afternoon. The comment about doing "normal things" stuck in my mind though. It never dawned on me that she might be living a relatively cloistered life there in Ester at the Malemute Saloon, and that she might feel a little cut off and maybe even lonely.

She dropped me off at my apartment. I told her that I lived in the basement apartment, kind of like a Morlock. I didn't think she would make the connection with the creatures who lived underground in the H. G. Wells novel *The Time Machine*.

"Oh I loved that movie," she said, "but you don't look anything like a Morlock." We both laughed.

We said goodbye and I went to my room and laid down on my bed. It had been a good day. I couldn't wait to hear what people had to say at the store tomorrow. As I lay there, however, a subtle feeling of loneliness came over me. I missed the company of female companionship. I wanted to call Halley, but she wasn't very happy with me, so that would no doubt end up having the opposite effect on the mood that I was looking for. Maybe I had done enough penance up here. Maybe it was time to think about going back to civilization and get on with my life. I couldn't imagine any kind of bright future for me in Alaska.

A week later, Kyle showed up at my door, early on Sunday morning.

"You want to go camping?" she asked.

"Uh, well sure," I said hesitantly. "I don't have any camping gear, and I am scheduled to work on Tuesday night." What the hell was this all about? "Uh, where?"

She was all smiles, and I was pretty certain that those smiles would make any man willing to do anything she wanted. "I'm heading down toward Denali, no place in particular. I have to be back on Tuesday too."

"Ok," I said. "Let me throw some clothes and stuff together." Wow! This was an amazing surprise.

So, off we went, camping. It was a great couple of days. She was affectionate while we were together on that trip, and good company. She took me to places in Alaska that I'm certain I would not have otherwise ever seen. Of course, such a short time is inadequate to see all the wonders of the largest state in the Union, but what we did see was impressive. Alaska is so vast that it's really hard to comprehend, even when you there trying really hard to take it all in.

On Tuesday night, at work, I casually mentioned that Kyle came by on Sunday and took me camping. The guys looked at me for a moment, then laughed. They thought I was bullshitting them. I just smiled and gave my head a little tilt, as if to say, "whatever".

I wish I could say that Kyle and I started having a romantic thing after that, but we didn't. I would see her at the saloon on Saturday nights when I visited with all the other guys. I was not really in a position to date anybody since I didn't have a car and not very much money, but I didn't think I was up to the task anyway. Kyle never asked me to do anything again, but was always very friendly when I saw her at the saloon. For her, I think that I was a brief encounter with what she considered normalcy. For me, she was a big boost to my ego.

# Chapter 50

By October, it was already starting to be winter again in Fairbanks. I wasn't sure I could take another winter up here in the Arctic Circle. I was just barely making enough money to survive and pay a portion of my child support. I didn't have a car or much of anything else to show for my year in Alaska. If I was going to put my life back together, it had to be someplace else. I just wasn't sure where. I had burned my share of bridges in California, so that probably was not ideal. I really didn't have any prospects in Ohio other than the opportunity to be close to my family.

I had been writing letters to my parents, my sister Violet, and my brother Bear while I was in Alaska. Bear was having his own issues, having recently divorced from his first wife and now considering relocating from Nebraska with his second wife to Washington. My sister, though, was living in a penthouse apartment on Pompano Beach, Florida. Florida sounded pretty good compared to Fairbanks, Alaska in October. We discussed my coming down for a visit in our letters, but I was beginning to think about something more permanent. I floated the idea of moving to Florida. I thought I could get back into the food and beverage industry there. She agreed to help me out, so I made up my mind to go seek out whatever adventures awaited me in Florida.

I arrived in Fort Lauderdale on October 31, Halloween. I met Violet at the arrival curb with my duffle bag, containing all that I owned. I was wearing blue jeans, heavy boots, a denim shirt, and my fur lined buckskinned coat. I had a flask, which contained whiskey for any potential medicinal needs, attached to my belt by a leather strap. My hair was long, past my shoulders, and I sported a very full beard. My sister did not recognize me. My appearance was the antithesis of what one typically sees as the typical Florida tourist.

I walked right up to my sister and said "Hi." She looked at me for a long moment before it finally registered with her who I was. She let out a long screech and grabbed me for a big hug.

"My God, she exclaimed! "Is that really you? You look so different." She kept saying "Oh my God" a lot, as we made our way to her car. Had I changed that much?

So, it was not a car, actually. She was driving a 1970 Ford E-200 camper van with a pop-top. It was not the kind of vehicle I would have thought my sister would drive, but there it was. I thought it was pretty cool actually, but it didn't seem to fit her style. I made a comment to that effect and she told me that she usually drove her Triumph TR6, but thought that I and my luggage would not fit. I didn't know what a TR6 looked like, but it sounded cool.

As we drove from the airport, we caught up on each other's lives. As we passed certain places, I asked what they were. Fort Lauderdale was dramatically different than Fairbanks. It was so big and modern looking and tropical. I asked my sister what she did for entertainment. She listed a few clubs that were popular. She told me that there was a big Halloween party happening at one of the places and that a couple of her friends were planning to go. I asked her if she wanted to go.

"Aren't you anxious to get home?" she asked.

"I could use a drink, actually," I said. "It's been awhile since I did anything fun."

"Well, that place is just ahead on the left," she said. "I guess we could drop by. It's supposed to be a costume party, and we're not dressed up, although I think that most people would think that you are in some kind of costume." She looked over at me and laughed, "Aren't you hot in that getup."

"A little," I laughed back, "but not that bad."

We pulled into the club's parking lot. It was crowded inside and full of attractive women, maybe more women than the whole population of females in Fairbanks, Alaska. Many of them took no pains to conceal the long, appraising looks they gave me, or more probably my "costume". I definitely stood out in my Nanook of the North get-up. All I needed was a harpoon.

We found Violet's friends in the crowd. They were very impressed with her big brother, if all their chirping about my appearance was any indication. They were unreserved in their flirtations, very unlike the guarded behavior of any young woman in Alaska. I was flattered with the attention and compliments. I had been in Florida less than an hour and my prospects were already looking pretty darn good it seemed.

I didn't have much money, and neither did Violet, so we didn't stay long at the party. We drove on up to Pompano Beach and to her apartment. I was not prepared for the kind of place that she called home. It was called the Pompano Beach Club, and it was like a resort. She lived in the South Tower, on the penthouse level, which was on the 27$^{th}$ floor. There were two floors in her apartment. She pointed to a mattress on the floor, next to a sliding glass door that led to a tiny balcony. From this vantage point you could look out onto the ocean. If there was anything on the planet that was so diametrically different than my dreary basement apartment in Alaska, I couldn't imagine what it would be. Seems I was destined to live the rest of my life sleeping on a mattress on the floor though, but in this place I could live with that.

I asked her how she could afford a place like this, since I was pretty sure that she was working as a waitress. She told me that she had roommates, but the one who normally slept on the mattress assigned to me was gone back up North for a while. I was really impressed with the place and told her so. She found a bottle of wine in the galley sized kitchen, and we settled on the couch to catch up.

It was really great to be here with my sister. I missed my family and missed civilization. As we talked and the wine settled my mind, I felt reassured that moving down here was a good idea. I had a lot to get figured out, but this was going to be a much better place to get myself back on some kind of track than Alaska.

# Chapter 51

I spent the next week or so getting my bearings. I started looking for a job. I thought that I should be able to get work in the food and beverage industry here. My disaster in California would not be known here and, like Southern California, this area had lots of restaurants and clubs. I didn't have to look far for my first job.

The Pompano Beach Club provided many amenities for its residents, including a Recreation Center that supported a bottle club lounge. A bottle club is a private club where the members provide their own alcoholic beverages. The bottle club in the Recreation Center was a very nice room, richly appointed with a 180-degree panoramic view of the ocean less than a hundred yards away. They needed a bartender. That was the good news. The bartender had to work for tips, not so good, but at least it was a place to earn a little money while I looked for more gainful employment.

The lounge was a good place to meet people. I discovered that many of the residents were "snow birds", people typically from New York or Canada who used the condos in the North Tower and South Tower as a winter residence. There were also some notable people who lived there year around, including Lawrence Sanders, who wrote many best-selling mystery books, such as the *Anderson Tapes* and the *Deadly Sin* series. The very distinguished Professor Claude Stern, who told me that he used to hang out with Sigmund Freud and do cocaine back in the days just prior to World War I.

Managing the lounge at the Beach Club was one of the best jobs I ever had. The patrons loved me, the work was easy, the ocean view was inspiring, the commute was a trip down the elevator and I could lounge around by the pool next to the bar when I wasn't working. There was also a gym that I could use in the Recreation Center. The one drawback was the money. There was just not enough of it. The tips I was getting were just not cutting it. I needed to make enough to pay my share of the rent, put gas in the gas guzzling Ford Econoline, and pay child support.

My sister worked as a waitress at the nearby Backgammon Club, which also included a nice restaurant. I asked her to try to see if she could get me a position at this establishment. I told her that I could do anything that they needed, but nothing was becoming available. One day she told me that the boat yard behind the restaurant was looking for help, and that maybe if I could get on there I would be in a good position to jump on any restaurant job that might become available. I knew absolutely nothing about boats, but she told me that it paid five dollars an hour, which would add up to more than I was making at the bottle club.

I went down to the boat yard to check things out. I met the dock master, a guy named Gil. He introduced me to his assistant, Bob. They were both pretty rough, and I could tell that they thought I was under qualified. I found this humorous since the job required no skills at all other than a willingness to do all the crappy, menial jobs in the yard that nobody else wanted to do. By their body language and manner of talking, I could tell that they both thought they were Billy Badasses. My sister had informed them that I had just come down from Alaska and that I was a weightlifter, so I think they were forced to admit that I had some backbone. They ultimately signed me on and immediately assigned me a hull cleaning job.

Cleaning the hull of a large boat is a significant undertaking. At this yard, the boats were hauled out of the water using a traveling boat lift. This is a large machine on wheels that is motorized and capable of lifting boats out of the water using big canvas straps. Once the boat is out of the water the lift is driven by an operator to deliver the boat to a convenient place in the yard where it is placed on boat stands. That's the easy part.

Once the boat is on stands and has dried for a few days, the hull is pressure cleaned and then all of the barnacles have to be scraped off of every surface, including shafts, propellers and rudders. This is not pleasant or easy work. In some cases, where the barnacles have been attached to the hull for a long time, sanding or brushing with a steel brush might also be required to ensure that all of the calcified material is removed. You have to be careful not to damage the hull surface. Once all the barnacles are removed you have to coat the hull with special paint that helps to discourage them from attaching again.

I think that the only other job I ever had that was worse was in Nebraska, while I was in the Air Force. I took on a part time job changing semi-truck tires at a truck stop, in the winter. That job was like working in frozen Hell, where I had to use a blow torch to melt ice and snow off of lug nuts to remove the giant, heavy, dirty, wet truck tires. Yes, that was a worse job.

Nevertheless, I excelled at boat hulls. Gil and Bob grudgingly admitted that I was worth my wages, and they began to give me other, less awful jobs to do. After I had been there a couple of months, they would ask me if I'd like to go with them to one of the local bars on the Intracoastal Waterway for beer on Friday nights. This was cool because they would get to these bars by boat, not just any boat, but one of the really fast, sexy speed boats they worked on. I made just enough each week to invest five dollars, the cost of a single pitcher of beer, to the cause. That was pretty much the extent of my weekly entertainment at that time.

I came to know a lot about boats and boating. Sometimes I would help Bob with mechanical work that he did at the yard. At the epitome of my boat yard career there, I participated in the delivery of boats. My job was to pilot a second boat to the delivery site while Gil or Bob would pilot the boat to be delivered. We would then take the second boat back to the yard. This was a big deal to me. I had never driven a boat prior to this, and it was fun. All these boats were motor yachts, no sail boats, or "blow boats", as Gil and Bob called them disdainfully. Frankly, I thought that the sailboats were more alluring, but I definitely liked the big motor yachts.

Occasionally, we would work on a Cigarette or Scarab. These were very sleek, very fast speedboats. On a few occasions Gil and Bob would take them out to test them and the mechanical work that they had performed. I got to go on a few of these tests, and they were about as thrilling a ride as I think you can get.

I found myself getting hooked on boating and I wanted to get one. However, that day would have to wait, because like anything fun, owning a boat involves a lot of money. Meanwhile, the boatyard job provided lots of opportunity to play boat without paying.

I wondered what my job was called. I asked Gil about it and he only laughed, implying that the job didn't warrant a job title. One day, while I was sitting on the ground, under the hull of a large motor yacht, scraping barnacles, I witnessed an altercation on the nearby docks. One of the combatants pulled out a knife and stabbed the other man and took off. Later, when the police were there, they asked me a bunch of questions. I was apparently the only witness. They were writing down the things I said, and one of the cops asked me what my position at the boat yard was. I told him what my duties were and he said, "Oh, you're a roustabout," and wrote that down on his pad. Hmm. So that's what I was.

# Chapter 52

I knew that a career as a roustabout was not a long term solution to getting my life back on track, but I was a little reluctant to run out and find another job. One of the unexpected but happy benefits of working at the boat yard, other than the joy of learning about boating, was that it was just outside of the restaurant where my sister worked. It was a busy place and there were lots of waitresses who also worked there.

My typical uniform when working on boats consisted of a pair of cutoff jeans and slip on canvas boat shoes. I became quite tan from all the outdoor work and I was buff from several years of weightlifting. I had trimmed my beard to something less mountain mannish, but my hair was still quite long. I was apparently quite an attraction to many of the young women inside the restaurant, who would come take a surreptitious look at me from time to time.

My sister kept me advised of who was expressing interest. I would use this intelligence to ask some of these girls out on a date. Since I was poor, I had to be pretty inventive in organizing a date that I could afford. This typically involved a walk on the beach and a bottle of inexpensive wine. That would usually result in an invitation to my date's apartment. This arrangement seemed ideal to me, but then I met Sharon.

Sharon was one of the waitresses at the restaurant, but she was different. She seemed to have her head on straighter then the other young women. She had a life plan. She was working her way through college. She was also a little older than the other girls, and was a single mom, raising two daughters on her own.

She was smart, but she was vulnerable. I was surprised to find myself feeling the strong urge to help her and protect her.

I stopped dating any other girls and started spending more time with Sharon. I often ended up at her place cooking dinner for her and her daughters. Employing my somewhat rusty culinary skills, I managed to impress them with some amazing meals. I should probably clarify that it was usually Sharon who was impressed. The little girls, I discovered early on, were much happier with hotdogs or mac-and-cheese from a box. Good Grief!

Sharon's daughters, Susan and Natalie, were very cute and well behaved, and we got along quite well. I didn't really know how to act around kids, but these girls were about the same age as my daughter, Alexa, and they reminded me how much I missed her. I also started to realize how much of my daughter's growing up I was missing. I began to start thinking more deliberately about what to do with myself.

My last days at the boat yard began with a weekend trip to the Florida Keys with Gil and Rob. They asked me to go with them to hunt lobster. This sounded pretty exciting, and I had never been to the Keys. Although I knew nothing about hunting lobster, I readily agreed to go. We headed down to the Keys on a Friday, after work, pulling a small boat behind Gil's truck. It was summer, so the days were long, allowing me to see what things looked like down there. We traveled down to Key Biscayne and got on the Overseas Highway. This road connects Miami with Key West and takes travelers through the tropical savanna environment that defines the Florida Keys. I was very impressed. It was so tropical and exotic.

We stopped at Sugarloaf Key, several miles outside Key West. There was a campground there and we proceeded to set up our camp upon arrival. Gil and Bob acted strange, but I didn't think that this was actually that unusual. They weren't drinking beer, though, and that was pretty uncommon. They were anxious to get their boat in the water, so that became one of the first orders of business. The boat had been loaded with diving gear and several coolers filled with ice prior to leaving Pompano.

We sat around our campsite until quite late into the night. Nobody spoke of lobster. I felt like something was going to happen, but didn't ask any questions lest I expose my novitiate status as a lobster hunter. Neither Gil nor Bob had asked me if had ever had any experience, so I wasn't sure what their expectations were. Finally, at some apparently secret signal, they both got up, looked at me and quietly announced it was time to go.

We made our way to the boat. It was made clear that we had to be quiet, and when we got into the boat I was perplexed by the continued stealth of moving it out and away from the dock using a paddle. We were well away from the shore when Gil finally fired up the engine. It was as dark as the inside of a cow's belly. I couldn't imagine how they knew where they were going, but once again, at some mysterious signal, the boat was stopped and the anchor dropped. It wasn't until this moment that I was filled in on the plan and what my role was to be.

Gil and Bob started getting their diving gear on. As they geared up Gil described the mission.

"We're going down to harvest lobster," he said in a very conspiratorial tone of voice. "When we come up, you take the bag and dump the bugs into the ice chests. Don't make any noise up here. If you see or hear anything suspicious, you give three tugs on this line." He was holding a slim nylon rope.

"You got it?" he asked quietly.

"Yes," I whispered.

Within a few moments they were in the water with what was apparently the paraphernalia needed to hunt lobster. They had underwater lights, a funny looking contraption they called a bully net, a fiberglass pole, and a large net-like bag. They swam on the surface for some distance, then dove. I could see evidence of where they were because they turned their lights on once they were at the bottom. The water in this area was not very deep, maybe less than thirty feet, and quite clear.

It was dark and quiet there alone in the boat, and I was feeling nervous. I wasn't positive, but I felt like we might be doing something we weren't allowed to do. After some amount of time that seemed like an eternity, the guys surfaced and swam up to the boat. They handed me the bag. I pulled it up into the boat with some difficulty. It was full of lobster and they didn't seem to be happy to be in there. I opened one of the ice chests and tried to dump the contents of the bag. This was a bit of a chore since the bag was essentially a net with fairly large spaces between the netting. These were Spiny Lobster and they have lots of protrusions that catch on these holes, not to mention my fingers.

I finally got all the beasts in the chest and gave the bag back to Rob. Since they made no effort to get back into the boat, I presumed that they were going down again. And so they did, time after time. Each dive took a little longer, as they went further away from the boat with each successive run. At one point, they did both get back into the boat, but it was only to exchange their empty air tanks for full ones. The hunt went on for what seemed like hours, but I lost track of time. When they finally ended their hunt, they removed all of their diving gear and stowed it away, along with all of the hunting gear.

There were six large ice chest full of lobster. Bob asked me to help him stow these chests in a small cabin at the bow of the boat. He then covered the chests with various items, which included blankets, life jackets, and cushions. It was clear that they were hiding this catch. When we got back to the dock, Gil immediately went to get the truck and ordered me to follow him. When we got to our campsite, he told me to pack up the tent. We were apparently leaving immediately. It must have been around 3:00 a.m. so I was now pretty sure that we were doing something illegal.

Gil took the truck and trailer to the ramp and got the boat loaded up. When he and Bob returned, we quickly stashed all the camping gear into the back of the truck and headed back up the Overseas Highway. It was nearly 9:00 a.m. when we got back to Pompano. I headed back to my sister's apartment to try to get some sleep. I got a call from Bob later that afternoon, asking me to join them for a lobster and beer fest. I took down the address he gave me and headed over.

The party turned out to be a bacchanal of sorts. There were people there that I didn't know, but everybody seemed like nice people, not the sort of company that I would have associated with Gil and Bob. There was no shortage of beer, and a bottle of tequila was making the rounds. There were a lot of lobsters being served with buckets of drawn butter. I ate lobster until I thought I might be sick. Yet, most of what Gil and Bob had caught had been sold to several local restaurants. I never did see the entire catch all at once, but I imagined that there might have been a couple hundred.

It was at this party that I discovered what we had done was completely illegal. Night diving for lobster is forbidden, as are bully nets. The lobsters were not measured, which is not legal, and many were not of the minimum size for harvesting. We also did this a week before the two-day sport season for lobster actually started. No wonder there were so many lobster available. All of this was revealed with a great degree of boasting and bragging, and received without any evidence of moral culpability by those partaking of the illegal feast. Of course, I was included in the latter group, but was starting to get a growing feeling that I had compromised my own standards of conduct. I tried to convince myself that I was innocent because I didn't really know what I was doing.

The final straw for me came later in the evening. I came across Bob, who was standing in a small coat closet in the hallway. I realized that he was relieving himself.

"What the hell are you doing Bob?" I asked incredulously.

He finished urinating and turned around to look at me. He was clearly very drunk. "Somebody was in the bathroom," he said defiantly, and staggered away.

I stood there in disbelief. I decided that it was time to leave. I went to my van, my sister's van, and headed for home. As I drove, I thought about where I was at this point in my life. These were not my kind of people and I was not making any progress. I didn't own a car or a place of my own. I didn't have a decent job. All I really had to my name was a duffle bag full of clothes. I had two failed marriages and was behind on my child support. The one thing that I did have was my family, including my daughter. It was time to move on. I knew that I was capable of much more.

# Chapter 53

The following week I found a job as a maître d' at a jazz club, called Bubba's. It was a classy place that featured a three piece jazz group. The fare was haute cuisine and the table setting was impeccable. My background in the industry was received by the owners with great enthusiasm. I liked the place and enjoyed working there, but once again the money was not adequate to cover all of my financial responsibilities.

Shortly after taking the job at Bubba's, I moved in with Sharon. My sister was disappointed to lose me as a roommate, but glad that I had found somebody to help me anchor myself. Sharon seemed glad to have me live with her, but reluctant to give in to all of the emotional commitments that went along with that arrangement. As for me, well once again, I was just letting life sweep me along in its currents.

As it turned out, one of the most significant turning points in my life happened as a result of knowing Sharon at this time. She was attending classes at the local community college, and was determined to earn a degree. I accompanied her to the college registrar's office one day, where she went to line up her classes for the next semester. The place was crowded so I found a seat in a waiting area until Sharon got through the tedious process. I had nothing to occupy my attention so I was just sitting there checking everything out, when I spied a rack of one page descriptions of academic programs that the college offered.

I walked over to the rack and scanned the titles for a moment. The one that caught my eye was something about computers. I picked up the paper for a closer look. I took it back to my seat and looked through the description. It was describing the curriculum for Computer Information Technology. I looked over the individual courses and thought to myself that I could do that. I had taken some basic courses from the University of Maryland while on active duty, including English and some math courses. I wondered if those would count toward a program here at this college. I knew that I could get educational benefits through the G.I. Bill, which under the 1977 Readjustment Assistance Act had been raised to $311 a month.

I looked up to see where Sharon was in her process, and spied a counter close by that read "Veterans Assistance" on the sign that hung over it. Acting on yet another totally impulsive decision, I got up from my seat and walked over to the counter and told them I would like to sign up for this program, and handed the person behind the counter the sheet I had just read. Although I hadn't given any previous thought about this, I was going to college. Over the next couple of weeks, as I went through the process of enrolling, I knew that this was an important decision and I set my mind on getting it done.

When Sharon finished what she was doing she saw that I was at the counter and was quite surprised.

"I had no idea you were considering going to college," she said.

"Neither did I," I admitted. "I just now made the decision."

She looked at me with a combination of amazement and disbelief in her expression. I just shrugged and told her that sometimes these things just come to me and I feel that I have to take action right away.

"You know, one of those things that seem worth doing. I don't usually plan them so much as they just present themselves to me every once in a while."

She told me that, of course, she thought it was a great idea and kept laughing all the way back to the car.

"What?" I asked.

"You are amazing," she said still laughing lightly.

"I know. It's hard to be humble when you're great," I joked. She laughed again. She apparently found me quite humorous.

I realized immediately that the job at Bubba's was not going to be compatible with college efforts. I thought that I ought to try to find some kind of entry position in the computer industry. I realized later that the Associates Degree that I was about to work toward, was the sort of thing that most people needed to get that first entry position in the industry. Since I didn't know any better, I applied for a computer operator position at the Winn-Dixie regional offices which were located in the Fort Lauderdale area. I got asked in for an interview and met Rusty, the computer center manager.

I had never been in a computer operations center, and was really impressed by what I saw. These were the days of big iron, truck-sized IBM mainframes and all its peripheral IO systems, such as printers, disc drives and tape drives. All of these machines were big. The computer and its sub-systems took up an entire large room, one wall of which was almost entirely glass. It was referred to as the "fish bowl". Out in the adjacent room were dozens of key punch operators, sitting at big, noisy key punch machines, which generated punch cards that would ultimately be ingested by the big card reader in the fish bowl. Off to one corner of this outer room was a smaller room with glass windows on all four walls. This is where Rusty sat.

Rusty was a robust man with red hair and a red beard. He had an unlit cigar sticking out of his mouth, which was set in what looked like a permanent scowl. He moved like he was in a hurry. I sat down in his office and he reviewed my application with a transparent look of skepticism.

"You don't have any computer experience," he said bluntly, throwing my application down on his desk and looking at me like I was some kind of fraud trying to put something over on him.

"No, sir, I don't," I began, "but."

"What makes you think that you could handle the work here?" he barked.

I kept looking him in the eye. I smiled. "Well, I'm taking courses at Broward Community College toward my Associates Degree in Information Systems, and I'm a fast learner. Give me a chance and I'll be able to do anything here that needs to be done."

I caught the hint of a smirk on his face. "I see that you have some military experience. What'd you do?"

"I was in search and rescue," I replied. "Flew a lot of missions in Vietnam and Laos. I figure that if I could make it through PJ training and survive the war I could do damn near anything." I decided that this was the kind of guy you had to be very direct with and I tailored my reply to what I thought was a nod to his type of personality.

"Huh," he said, looking back down to my application. "I was in 'Nam, H Company, 75th Infantry."

"Oh, a Ranger," I said in a tone of admiration and nodding my head in acknowledgement.

"Damn right," he said, clearly proud of his service and impressed that I recognized his unit. "Ok, I'll try you out on the polling systems. We poll all of the stores in our division each night to get their orders. It don't take a rocket scientist to run 'em, but it's a good place to learn how everything else works."

"Thanks," I said.

We discussed schedule. I told him that I had to be able to attend classes during the day, but I could work in the evenings if that worked for him. He told me that the job he was offering was during the night shift, between 5:00 pm and midnight. He said that I should be able to get some study time in during my shift since a lot of the job was just babysitting the machines. It sounded ideal.

The next four years were probably the hardest of my entire life in terms of work, effort, and the intense focus required to accomplish all that was needed to be successful at everything that

I was trying to do. I was a full time student by day and working full time at night. In between, I was training at the gym two hours a day, six days a week, studying, and trying to be a good family man.

After my first two semesters at the community college, I was invited to join Phi Kappa Theta, the national honor fraternity. Since I was older than most of the students attending the college, and perhaps due to my military experience, I was encouraged to take a leadership position in the local fraternity. I was elected chapter president by the end of my first year, and with the help of our faculty sponsors was awarded a full scholarship for my second year. The catch was I had to keep my grade average above a 3.5. That was not a big challenge for me. I never considered myself a particularly smart person, but I found that most of my courses were interesting and I invested the time necessary to get the grades. I graduated from the community college with a 4.0 grade average and the top student in my class. That got me another full scholarship for the next two years of college at Florida Atlantic University, and an invitation to join the national honor fraternity, Phi Kappa Phi.

I certainly wasn't the smartest guy in the university, but I was older and more focused on scholastics than many of my classmates. I had to keep a very high grade point average in order to keep my full scholarship. I basked in the favorable attention that I got from faculty due to my academic performance.

The one class I definitely did struggle with was Quantitative Methods. My professor for that class was the kind of guy who looked like a mad scientist. He was quite thin, wore big round eye glasses, and had white hair that stuck out in every direction. His style of teaching was eccentric, moving back and forth at the front of the class in a manner that reminded me of Groucho Marx. He would write long, complex formulas and notes on the blackboard, then suddenly erase it all before anybody could get it all copied to their notes. He only gave two grades, A or F, pass or fail. He gave eight single question quizzes during the semester and a final exam. If you failed one test your grade average suffered greatly.

I got the math, but I often selected the wrong formulas because I seemed to have a knack for applying logic that did not match the problem. The logic seemed perfectly legitimate to me, but nevertheless, if you didn't come up with the answer that the professor was expecting, you got an F. Every time this happened I pushed the legitimacy of my choice of formula and debated passionately with the professor. While everybody else in the class hated this, the professor seemed to enjoy sparring with me. It was to no avail, however, I would still get an F.

This course was going to ruin me. I tried to drop the class, but I waited too long and the administration denied my request. I approached the professor and explained why failing this course would be a disaster for me. I begged him to maybe let me take it over so that I didn't have the black mark on my scholastic record, but he would not do it. He simply told me that I was over thinking the problems, and that I should keep trying. Great, I thought, that helps a lot.

If this had been any other course, I would have probably received a C, and I could live with that but this was not any other course. I felt that I was doomed. I continued to attend his classes and redoubled my efforts to pick the correct damn formulas by not over thinking. At the end of the semester, I was surprised to find that the professor had given me a C for the course. I was so grateful and surprised that I went to see him. He told me that he recognized that I was intelligent and that he enjoyed our debates so much that he decided to pass me.

I stayed on the Dean's List every semester for my junior and senior years. I graduated summa cum laude. College was, without a doubt, the hardest thing that I had ever done in my life, but I had done it and I felt good about it. Sharon graduated the same time I did with a degree in Accounting. She continued to study for the CPA exam. I think that we helped each other to stay focused during those challenging years. I know that she helped me stay motivated.

During these college years, I got very serious about my weight training. I decided to join a local gym owned by a former Cuban national weightlifting coach, Rafael Guerrero. This was a real, blood-and-guts training gym, frequented by serious athletes. The place gave me a greater sense of motivation, and the training that I received from Rafael was unavailable anywhere else. Despite the fact that I was not genetically designed to be a competitive body builder, that is what I decided to do. The main reason I chose this path is that it gave purpose to all the work I was putting into the training. My main competition was with myself, to achieve improvement and develop myself to whatever my potential might be.

I entered my first novice bodybuilding contest in 1980, at the age of 32. I won second place, but the best part of that effort was seeing how I looked. I was no Arnold Schwarzenegger for sure, but I looked good. I continued to compete a couple times a year for the next nine years. The discipline and focus required to prepare for a contest helped me to apply those same mental skills to other pursuits.

My duties at the Winn-Dixie computer center grew over those same college years. It was not long before I was managing the night shift operations inside the fish bowl. The rapid development of increasingly more powerful, more sophisticated computing technology forced Winn-Dixie management to consider upgrading their systems. My scholastic work in computer science provided me with the opportunity to offer advice and opinions in some of these corporate discussions. I helped with the replacement of the old, noisy chain printers with newer technology, as well as updates to the reel-to-reel tape system to make storage and retrieval of individual tapes easier.

During my tenure at Winn-Dixie, I was able to get my sister a job in the fish bowl, doing the same job I did when I started. The technology had changed considerably, but the polling process was still the same. I left the fish bowl after I graduated in order to begin the next phase of my computer science career at a computer systems development company.

During my four years at college, I worked on trying to be a good partner to Sharon, a good stepfather to Susan and Natalie, and a better father to my daughter, Alexa. I brought her out to visit me in Florida once a year during this time. I realized that we didn't really know one another and that made me feel sad, but I thoroughly enjoyed what little time we had together. I can only imagine what she must have thought about me during this time of my life. I was definitely not the normal, everyday sort of dad.

One year, I arranged for her to fly out from Arizona, where she and her mother were now living. I went to the Fort Lauderdale airport at the appointed time and went to the Delta gate where the flight from Phoenix was due to arrive. In those days, you could go to the terminal gates to greet incoming passengers. When the plane arrived I waited anxiously to see her, but she didn't get off. I worried that something might be wrong with her. Maybe she got sick during the flight. I asked the person at the gate about her status, who advised me that my daughter was not on that flight.

"What do you mean?" I asked in panic. "I know that she left Phoenix this morning."

"What was her flight number?" the attendant asked.

I looked at my notes, and gave her the number.

"Sir that flight arrived in Miami thirty minutes ago," she said, now looking at me like I was a moron.

"Shit," I said softly. I turned and ran out of the terminal and toward the parking garage. The Miami airport was at least an hour away. I had to get word to the Delta people that I was on my way. Good Grief! why didn't I ask the lady at the Fort Lauderdale gate to contact Miami to let them know what was going on. I was frazzled. There were no cell phones in those days, so I made a quick pit stop at a pay phone and called Sharon. Fortunately, she was home. I explained my mistake and asked her to contact Delta and let them know that I had gone to the wrong airport and that I was on my way.

I have no idea how I could have made such a stupid mistake, but all I could do now was get to Miami as fast as I could. What would everybody think? Good Grief! How could I be such an idiot? When I finally arrived, I was directed to the Delta's Sky Club. There was Alexa, safe and sound, and apparently not too worried about my failure to show up on time.

I was so embarrassed. The Delta people, regardless of what they might have actually thought, didn't treat me like a father who had tried to abandon his daughter. Alexa was old enough to see some humor in the mistake, and was probably enjoying my apparent duress over the matter. She seemed unfazed by the incident, although I could not help but me feel like maybe she expected this sort of thing from her father.

"Hi Dad," she said simply. She was smiling with a look that made me think that she knew I would eventually find her. I think that the only person scarred for life by this whole incident was me.

# Chapter 54

Unlike many of my classmates, I applied for a position at only one company upon graduation. IBM and Motorola had big divisions in the Fort Lauderdale area, and most graduates wanted a position with one of those firms. Not me. I wanted to work for Gould's Computer Systems Division. They had a cutting edge data communications group and that's what I wanted to get involved in.

Now, lest anyone think that this laser-focused goal was the result of careful research and analysis, and a carefully considered match for my skills and course work, let me set the record straight. Just before graduation, I met a guy in a bar who worked at Gould. During our casual conversation, I mentioned that I had taken a course in communication systems, and as part of that course I had to design a keyboard that was more efficient and ergonomically friendly than the standard QUERTY keyboards. I can assure you that my design was never picked up by any of the major computer manufacturers, but I found the course particularly interesting.

The stranger at the bar told me that Gould had a new communications program and were looking for people to staff the group. That's all it took for me. I decided then and there that I would join this group, and so I submitted my resume. I was single minded on this, and just assumed that I would get the job, despite the fact that I knew nothing of any consequence about data communications.

A few days before graduation I received a letter asking me to come in to Gould for an interview. Although, as I said, I assumed that I would get this job, I was surprised to actually get the formal invitation. I had never applied for a professional position before, and was only vaguely familiar with the process. I was very excited about the interview and Sharon was confident that I would get the job. How could they not want me on their team, she assured me as she extolled the abilities she thought I possessed.

I bought a new suit for the occasion. When I arrived at the Gould Development Center, I must have appeared like a hick visiting New York City for the first time. The place was huge and the lobby was decorated in a very modern and slick corporate style. I introduced myself at the reception desk. I was required to sign a log book, given a temporary badge of identification, and told to take a seat.

The person who came down to escort me was the hiring manager, Joe Tritt. He was a large man, probably in his late twenties or early thirties, essentially the same age as I was. I could tell he was a little surprised to see that I wasn't a kid. As we walked through the lower level hallway, he took a detour through the development testing lab. I was blown away. The room covered one half of the entire first floor, and it was filled to the gills with computers, testing equipment, and cables. There was a cacophony of sound filling the space and lots of people working on electronic equipment. It was very impressive.

The interview was no big deal. Joe asked me a bunch of technical questions that I didn't know the answers to, so he asked me about my course work and my background in the military and restaurant business. I judiciously avoided mentioning my roustabout experience. I interviewed with a couple other people, and then I was escorted out. I really had no sense of how I did, but hoped that I would get to work in a place like Gould.

Two weeks later I got an acceptance letter. I was very excited, but quite concerned by the starting salary of $23,000. That was double the money that I ever made at any job. I wondered what in the heck they wanted me to do for such a large sum. I mean, I didn't really know how to do anything yet. I was so concerned that I called Joe Tritt the next day and asked him if perhaps they mistakenly thought I was more qualified than I actually was.

"That's the starting salary Gould gives for all new college grads," he laughed. "Don't worry, you'll earn it."

"Oh," is all I could say. "Damn," I thought. I had a hard time wrapping my head around that kind of money.

My first assignment was to take over the development of an X.25 Wide Area Network protocol implementation on a Zilog Z80 microprocessor using that chip's proprietary assembly language. I was told that I was to design and code a Packet Layer protocol state machine on this microprocessor. So, perhaps $23,000 wasn't so much after all. I knew a little about X.25 and wide area networks, but not enough to know where to even begin with my assignment. The guy who was working on the project before me had left the company. Probably a wise man.

I did research, studied and asked anybody who would pay attention to my questions about the technologies related to my assignment. I ultimately memorized the X.25 Packet Layer Protocol specification, an accomplishment that eventually landed me in Vienna, Austria over Christmas the following year.

I sweated blood trying to figure out how to code a state machine in assembly language. That seemed like trying to build the Empire State Building out of matchsticks. Unlike modern, "high-level" programming languages, assembly language has a strong correspondence between the language and the machine code instructions. In other words, it requires the programmer to create many of the constructs that high-level languages take care of as built-in features such as classes, objects, abstraction, and inheritance.

Despite the stress of this brain-busting work, I felt like I was in my element. However, I discovered within the first year at Gould that I was not a gifted programmer and that I was not going to excel at software programming. I was a good designer and a natural leader, so I was soon coordinating work between hardware, software, testing and documentation groups. I was organizing review sessions to ensure that everybody stayed on the same path. Joe Tritt was reassigned one year after I started, and to my utter amazement, I was asked to assume the Data Communication Software Group manager's position. Of course, I humbly accepted.

It shouldn't have been a surprise really. Much like the military, the computer business seemed to be populated mostly by kids. They came right out of college at 21 or 22 years of age. They were mostly quite talented, some were brilliant, but few had any clue about the basics of managing anything. For me, managing these people was simple and I could relate to their geekiness which was a huge asset.

# Chapter 55

This is the point in most stories where the hero would finally buckle down and focus on managing a successful career for the rest of his days, "and he lived happily ever after". That would not be me, however. To be sure, the first few years at Gould were great. I worked hard to get where I was and I felt that I deserved everything that I had achieved. I was making good money and getting good raises every year. I was in charge of a leading-edge technology development team, and I knew that I had finally found my place in life. I was, however, not quite done with giving in to my impulses to pursue other, more fun, more adventurous interests.

As intense and stressful as my job was, and although I was still training six days a week at the gym, it felt like I had spare time. There were no more college classes, no more studying, and no more working nights. Plus, now I had money. I was so used to being poor that my new income situation made it feel like I could do things that I had only been able to daydream about in the past.

My experience at the boat yard had given me the "boat bug". I was especially enchanted with the notion of owning a sailboat. It was such a romantic daydream for me, sitting on the boat after a day of sailing, sipping wine with my sweetheart, watching the sunset. Yes, I thought that I would have to look into the possibility. Meanwhile, I thought that I should get a little boating experience by canoeing. I can't explain why I felt that I needed to start canoeing, but then I can't explain why I have done many of the things that I have done in my life. Maybe it was something like how Forest Gump just decided he needed to start running one day.

I had never canoed, ever, but I didn't think it would be so hard. Certainly not as hard as sailing, with all of those ropes and booms and stuff. I decided to try things out by renting a canoe and doing a weekend trip on one of the many rivers in Florida. Sharon was game, so off we went. The first trip was on the Peace River. It is located in the southwester portion of Florida, so it was relatively close and it was, well, peaceful. A good river to figure things out. That trip was quite enjoyable, so we started organizing more trips on different rivers throughout Florida.

There are a lot of rivers in Florida. It wasn't hard to find a river that offered something new and interesting each time we went. Some of the rivers even had rapids, like the Suwannee and the Hillsborough. They were only class 1 and class 2, but it was fun in a canoe. My favorite rivers though were those in and around the Everglades. I became very familiar with many of these and started offering to take people from work and their visitors on trips to these spots. I learned where to look for alligators and perfected the act of sneaking up on one to grab its tail. This would always result in a dramatic escape by the startled animal, which would in turn elicit screams of terror from the people I was guiding. It was great fun.

There was one river that I really wanted to travel, called the Turner River. It is located within the Big Cypress National Preserve within the Everglades, but it was difficult to locate. I had tried finding the northern entrance to the river once before but ended up on a different tributary. The Everglades, itself, is considered a giant river. In fact, it is a gigantic body of water flowing from north to south, with hundreds of tributaries.

Descriptions of the Turner River were included in various published guides as very exotic and beautiful, but it was like finding a needle in a haystack. At least it was in those days. I am told that in current times the river is crowded with multiple guided tours, but in those days there was nobody there. Nobody. Of course, we decided to do this trip at the end of summer, which I supposed in retrospect was not the ideal time.

I decided that I was going to find and travel the Turner River no matter what. I wouldn't turn back until I found it. I elected to take my sister's boyfriend, Randy, as my canoe mate, since I knew that this river had a reputation for being somewhat challenging. If somebody was going to get eaten by an alligator I would rather it be him than Sharon.

We set out early one Saturday morning. I used three different published guides to locate the entrance to the river. Each one offered some tricks and clues for finding it. The problem with the entrance to the Turner River is that it looked pretty much like every other little opening in the vast Everglades swamp. We knew approximately where it was, off the Tamiami Trail, near the Turner River Bridge, so we launched our canoe there.

We planned to take up to three days for this trip, and had provisioned ourselves accordingly. The plan was to find the mouth of the river, travel its 8.5 mile length to Chololoskee Island, and camp there for the night. Sharon would pick us up when we called to say we made it. The extra day was to give us extra cushion in case we had any trouble finding the mouth. I knew that we could enter the river at Chololskee and paddle upstream, but I thought that was too easy. I wanted to find the elusive northern entrance.

As luck would have it, we found the entrance without as much effort as I thought. I knew from one of the guide books that the entrance was deceptive because it was essentially a mangrove tunnel. This tunnel was quite narrow in some spots, and often so low that we had to duck to pass through. Since this part of the river was rarely traveled, spiders had the opportunity to build their webs across the tunnel. Think of the Indiana Jones movie, in the scene where he and his sidekick are in the cave and pass through thick walls of webs, ultimately getting covered with spiders.

Randy started stomping the bottom of the canoe.

"What are you doing?" I asked.

"There's a couple of spiders up here," he replied with apparent alarm in his voice.

I looked down. I hadn't noticed them before, but there were a lot of spiders on the bottom of the boat. Since Randy was in the front, he wasn't seeing most of them.

"I've got news for you," I said in a falsely calm voice. "There are lots more spiders back here. You've got a couple on your back too."

He turned around wide-eyed, rocking the canoe violently. Now, I can handle just about anything, but spiders are at the very top of my list of things that I don't deal with very well. Apparently, Randy was of like mind.

"Let's stop here and get rid of these guys," I suggested in a voice that was in a higher pitch than I'd like to admit.

There was an exaggerated flurry of stomping and, as I recall, cussing. Once the immediate threat was taken care of, we ultimately decided to roll down our sleeves, button the top button of our shirts, and wrap duct tape around our necks, wrists, and ankles. As we continued our journey in this creepy mangrove tunnel, we spent considerable time brushing spiders off of our clothes and stomping them in the bottom of the canoe. I'm sure that Indiana Jones would have shook his head in disgust.

The tunnel widened after several hundred yards, providing welcome relief from the arachnid horror chamber. The open area provided glimpses of the many birds that inhabit the Everglades, as well as exotic flowers. It was quite beautiful and quickly took our minds off the spider encounter. There were two more mangrove tunnels to pass through, but fortunately sans spiders. These other tunnels were separated by another beautiful open area, where we could see alligators along the banks or swimming in the open water. Everything was so pristine and primitive. I half expected to see a dinosaur emerge from one of the hardwood hammocks that lined the shore.

We found a large, prehistoric shell mound, which I knew were left by the Calusa Indians several thousand years before. We decided to take a closer look at one of these mounds. We also wanted to stretch our legs and just see if there was anything we might be missing from our vantage point on the river. We pulled up onto the shore and got out.

"Oh man, it feels good to get the kinks out of my legs," I said.

"That's for sure," Randy replied.

After just a moment, "Do you hear that?" I asked.

"Hear what?" Randy asked.

"It's a high-pitched whine," I said.

About that same moment, we both caught sight of a dark cloud moving toward us through the surrounding trees. It was slow, but relentless and had a surreal, almost ghost-like quality to it.

"Oh my God!" I yelped in earnest terror. "It's mosquitoes, millions of them."

We dashed for the canoe, and shoved off as quickly as we could manage, but they were on us. Intermittently swatting and paddling, and I vaguely recall screaming, we headed for the open water in the middle of the river so that we could get into the sunlight and some breeze. That seemed to discourage them, but the damage was done. Any exposed skin was covered with mosquito bites. So far, this adventure was fraught with more discomfort than I had bargained for. Did I mention that it was really hot and humid? I hoped it would get less perilous as we moved downstream.

The river ultimately opened up in a wide expanse of water on both sides. The journey did get easier and we were enjoying the sights and relatively leisurely rowing. As we neared the mouth of the river, however, we saw areas in the water where something was thrashing wildly.

"What the heck is that?" Randy asked, pointing to the commotion.

"I don't know for sure, but it sure looks big," I offered. "Maybe it's alligators." I could see four of these unidentified things thrashing about, each in a different spot.

The tide was moving out, effecting the depth of the river's mouth. This is why it required so little effort to paddle this part of the river. The downstream flow of the river, combined with the lowering tide created a fast moving current in our favor, but it also seemed to be exposing shoals at the river's mouth. These shoals where directly ahead in our current path.

We stopped paddling, but were moving inextricably closer to the commotion by the river's current. I suddenly recognized what this new denizen of the river was.

"Shit!" I yelled. "Those are bull sharks!"

The sharks were getting beached on these shoals and working frantically to get themselves off to deeper water. I was able to tell they were bull sharks because we passed by very closely to a couple of them, and I knew that bull sharks frequented Florida coastal waters and that they had a predilection for shallow, brackish waters.

We couldn't stop or back up, so we had to aggressively paddle our way through this new terror in order to avoid crashing right into them.

"Hurry! Paddle to the right," I commanded. "Now over to the left!" Randy was yelling out similar directions simultaneously.

We passed by these shark infested waters without any damage, other than to our nerves, and found ourselves at the river's end. Chokoloskee Island lay about three quarters of mile ahead, across open water. Good Grief! I thought. There couldn't be much else that Mother Nature could throw at us. We were almost at our journey's end.

We had been so preoccupied with the sharks that we did not notice the thunderstorm coming upon us very quickly from behind. We were alerted to it by a sudden flash of lightening, followed by an explosive clap of thunder.

"Good God!" we both exclaimed, reflexively ducking.

"You gotta be kidding," I lamented. We looked at each other for a moment with an expression of "now what the hell do we do?"

We felt very exposed there at the mouth of the river, but heading out into the open water was even more so. We were between the proverbial rock and a hard spot. After a quick discussion of our options, we decided to make a run for it. If we were going to get struck by lightning, it might as well be in the process of trying to save our asses rather than just sitting there hoping for the best.

The fast moving storm, with its attendant strong wind, was making the water out in the bay very choppy. Definitely not an ideal condition for canoes. The paddling was now extremely challenging, but we put our backs into it. A couple of blinding strikes of lightening, followed immediately by deafening crashes of thunder, and shameless screams of terror, motivated us to redouble our efforts. It was kind of like those situations you hear about where a woman lifts a car off of her child. We were paddling like men possessed.

We were still a hundred yards from shore when the heavens opened up. It came down in buckets. In Florida they call these storms "gator gushers".

"You've got to be shitting me," I bellowed, looking skyward. This was directed to God, Himself.

The canoe started quickly filling with water. I told Randy that I was going to have to start bailing, but that he should continue to paddle. I had to shout to be heard over the roar of the rain and wind. I used my official Indiana Jones, wool felt fedora hat as a bucket. Yes, I actually bought an Indiana Jones hat after I saw the first movie, which had come out just before this canoe trip from Hell.

We finally reached the shore, alive. We realized that any accommodations we might avail ourselves of were on the other side of the island. Fortunately, it was a small island, and we pressed on through the storm, around the southern end to a little marina.

We were soaked, as was all our gear. In fact, soaked doesn't adequately describe how thoroughly wet we and all of our belongings were. By the time we dragged the water filled canoe with its water logged cargo onto the shore, we were too exhausted to get out of the storm. What the hell, I thought. We can't get any wetter, and if I get struck by lightning after all this day had thrown at us, I didn't care. At least my misery would be over.

The storm finally stopped as suddenly as it started. We were still sitting there by the canoe. A few people came by to take a cautious look at us. The marina's facilities included a small motel. We decided that getting a room was a better option than pitching a wet tent and sleeping in soggy sleeping bags. I didn't want to take this whole adventure thing to that level of extreme.

Sharon and my sister picked us up the next day. We were still wet.

# Chapter 56

Having survived the Turner River adventure together, Randy and I became sort of partners-in-crime, and shared other canoeing adventures. One day I shared my dream about owning a sailboat with him. He quickly agreed that having a sailboat would be a most excellent thing, and we conspired to find one that we could afford. Having a partner in such an investment would make the odds of actually getting one more likely.

We found a 25 foot MacGregor Venture that was about the right balance between what we could afford and what we thought was the minimum acceptable vessel. It was a masthead rigged sloop with a small cabin. It had a tiller rather than a wheel to steer the boat, and the mast was deck-stepped, so that it could be taken down for transporting the boat by trailer. The boat came with a 3.5 horsepower outboard engine, called a Seahorse that looked like it might have been the first engine ever invented. The boat also came with all the necessary rigging, including a mainsail and a jib.

We found a private dock to rent just south of the Lighthouse Point inlet, which was perfect. The final negotiations were completed and the big day came for us to take possession and bring the boat to its new home. The boat was currently located on one of the many canals off the Intracoastal Waterway, just north of the 17th Street Causeway drawbridge in Fort Lauderdale. That location would be convenient since access to the Atlantic Ocean was just past that bridge, through the Port Everglades inlet.

While many, if not most of the things that I've attempted to do in my life have been done without a lot of previous knowledge or experience in the new interest, I did know a little about boating. I was familiar with the local Intracoastal Waterway, and many of its canals. I knew how to operate a boat with an engine, how to dock and cast off, and the basic rules of using a VHF radio and vessel right-of-way. I had the presence of mind to acquire and read a book on the basics of sailing. I believe that is was called, *Sailing for Dummies.*

On the big day that we were to take possession of our new boat, I asked Randy if he knew anything about sailing. He did not.

"No problem," I said confidently. "I know what we need to do. I'll need your help with the lines and such, but I'll tell you what to do." I exuded confidence. It didn't seem that complicated, at least not as it was described in the book.

"Great," he replied. We were both excited to take our maiden voyage.

Our first little conundrum was figuring out how to attach the sails. They had been stored in a bag, in a locker at the bow of the boat. We got them out and spread them out on the dock.

"Damn, these things are big," Randy observed.

"Yeah," I was trying to make heads from tails of these things. After careful study, I determined which one was the mainsail and which was the jib. Getting them attached to the boat, was considerably more difficult, but after some trial and error, we got them rigged.

The next task was to attach lines to the sails. Well, how hard could that be? We pulled all of the lines we could find in the boat and arranged them on the dock. After some further study, we realized that the lines that raised and lowered the sails were both already attached to the mast. The lines that control the mainsail boom were also already rigged. So, the only lines left had to be the docking lines and the one used to control the jib. A few glances at the pictures in Sailing for Dummies confirmed what we needed to do.

We packed everything up, including an ample supply of beer, and reviewed our plan with each other. We would motor from the dock, out into the Intracoastal Waterway, through the 17th Street bascule bridge, and out through the inlet into the Atlantic Ocean, where we would raise our sails and head north.

We turned our attention to the odd looking little outboard engine at the stern of the boat. This thing didn't look like much of an engine. It was quite small and all of its guts were exposed. It looked like the kind of thing one might see on a small bass boat, but it was what we had, so there was nothing for it but to get it started up. It took some effort, but we did eventually get it running. I hoped this damned thing would get us out to the ocean, but frankly I was skeptical. We found a single oar in the boat, and I wondered if that was a standard piece of equipment on a sailboat. It provided me a slender thread of reassurance, much like a life preserver would on a sinking vessel.

In our enthusiasm to get started, we cast caution to the wind and shoved off. We reached the general area of the 17th Street Bridge without incident, but there were lots of boats on the Intracoastal that day and the water was choppy from motorboat wakes. As we waited for the bridge to open up, allowing the big motorboats and the sailboats to pass through, a particularly large wake hit the side of our boat and washed over our little engine. It died.

"Shit," I said. It seems that I say that a lot when I'm engaged in my adventures.

We tried to restart the engine, but it would not cooperate. We were drifting and heading for a shallow area off to one side of the basin.

"Keep trying to start it," I said. "I'll get that paddle and try to keep us from getting grounded or getting out into the path of other boats."

While our sailboat was not very large and not very heavy, trying to use a paddle to propel and maneuver it in those conditions was, well I can't think of anything absurd enough to compare the futility of it. Fortunately, we drifted toward the shallows, and not into the main boat traffic. I could see the bottom, so I eventually jumped overboard with a docking line and held the boat from getting into further trouble.

I was going through a number of emergency contingencies in my head, when I heard that Randy finally got the engine running.

"I took the sparkplug out and dried it off," he said. "That seems to have worked."

"You're like a mechanical genius," I praised lavishly.

I decided that snide remarks denigrating the stupid engine would not improve our situation, so I merely asked for assistance in getting back in the boat. Since we had not yet acquired a boarding ladder, not having any inkling that we might ever need one, getting back into the boat was an extraordinarily difficult feat. I eventually did make it back in the cockpit, soaking wet and exhausted from the effort.

The bridge had long since closed, so we had to wait for the next opening. We carefully plotted how to avoid getting swamped again, laying off in a semi-protected area, bow pointed in the general direction of the big boat wakes, waiting until the last moment when we would make a dash for the open bridge.

When the bridge opened, we executed our plan flawlessly and arranged our timing such that we were the last boat to pass under the bridge. Unfortunately, our little engine didn't propel us very fast, so we found ourselves the object of much abuse from impatient automobile drivers waiting for the bridge to close so that they could continue on their way. The bridge tender was also blasting his horn at us and yelling from his tower for us to move it. To add insult to injury, another large motor yacht, possibly named the *Queen Huge*, had come up behind us and was leaning on its horns as well.

We were humiliated and mortified, but we finally got through the bridge and made our way out the inlet. We ultimately made it out into the open ocean. Now we could sail. We stopped the engine and pulled it up out of the water. We eventually figured out how to raise the mainsail and get it situated so that it was actually powering the boat.

It was a merciful act of God that the wind was coming out of the southeast, which made the sail to the north a fairly straightforward undertaking. Given our total lack of sailing experience, it also made getting the jib up an exceptionally dangerous task. We finally applied a little common sense, turned the boat up into the wind, raised the jib, secured the port sheet, and eased her back down wind in what might perhaps be the most painful jibe in the history of sailing. It was time for a beer, perhaps one of the most important items of survival gear on any boat.

After careful examination of our sailing guide, and a little cautious practice, we mastered the port and starboard jibes necessary to get us to the Lighthouse Point inlet. Getting the sails down once we were at the entrance to the inlet was much less traumatic than putting them up. The boat traffic at the inlet bascule bridge was also much less chaotic. The little engine started, and we motored to our new home dock without further incident.

The whole trip, from the time we left our houses to the time we got back home was close to eighteen hours. We had estimated six hours, tops, and had advised Sharon and my sister accordingly. Upon our arrival we discovered that they were very close to calling the Coast Guard to alert them that we were apparently lost at sea. We did not get the warm welcome that we felt we deserved after such a harrowing voyage. How did society function before there were cell phones?

We decided to call the sailboat the Ghost, after Wolf Larsen's seal-hunting boat from the Jack London novel, *The*

*Sea-Wolf.* I associated myself with Wolf Larsen's rough, tough character since my name was also Wolf. I sailed the Ghost every chance I got. I actually learned to sail, and within a few months I was a pretty damn good sailor. After a while, I found ways to work on other sailboats, both larger and smaller than mine, every opportunity I could find. I acquired and studied the U.S. Coast Guard's *Boating Skills and Seamanship,* and *The Annapolis Book of Seamanship.* I studied navigation charts of the Florida coast, the Keys, and the Bahamas.

# Chapter 57

My sister broke up with Randy, so we decided that it was time to sell the Ghost since the partnership had become an awkward social situation. I wasn't very upset about losing the boat. I was ready for something more sophisticated and something I could own by myself. I was ready to start cruising, and that required a vessel that was more seaworthy than the Ghost.

I eventually found a deal that I thought was really great. The boat ad indicated that three Swedish guys had sailed their Albin Vega 27 to the United States and now needed to sell the boat quickly and get back to Sweden. I contacted one of the guys and discovered that they were in the midst of completing a circumnavigation when one of the companions was notified that the girlfriend he left behind was pregnant. He was expected to return immediately. Since the other two shipmates didn't want to go on without the soon-to-be papa, they were motivated to sell the boat quickly, and I bought it.

An Albin Vega 27 is probably not the ideal boat for Florida waters because it was actually designed for blue water sailing in the North Atlantic. The boat has a fixed fin keel with a 3.76 foot draft, not a particularly great configuration for Florida waters known for their numerous shoals and reefs. The relatively short mast, resulting in reduced sail area, while excellent for blue water sailing provides less performance in the light airs that are typical in Florida waters. All in all, however, this boat is considered an excellent vessel, well designed and affordable.

I loved it. I thought it had very sexy lines and it looked like I thought a sailboat should look. It was much more sophisticated than the Venture. It was powered by an inboard 10 horsepower Volvo diesel engine, which unfortunately still made it underpowered in many situations. Seems I was destined to have boats that had too small an engine. There were lots of things to like about the boat though. Down below, it was compact but designed to accommodate two for ocean crossing voyages. It also had a complete inventory of sails to deal with every kind of weather and sailing condition.

I decided to call my new boat the Seawolf, in keeping with my affinity for Jack London's seafaring tale. I had a blue canvas Bimini top added, an essential accessory for sailing in South Florida and the Keys. This accentuated the blue canvas mainsail cover, dodger, and cockpit panels. Since Albin Vegas were very uncommon in and around Florida, I delighted in bringing her in to new ports. She always turned heads.

I took many a cruise on the Seawolf. I especially loved sailing down to and all around the Keys. Sharon and I once sailed to the Dry Tortugas at Easter time. The trip out was great, taking about five hours. We anchored there overnight, visiting Fort Jefferson and snorkeling the underwater trail around the fort. We pulled anchor early in the morning the day before Easter, planning to be back to our Key West dock well before dark.

There was a brisk wind from the southeast when we started, but the wind shifted to the east and freshened up as the day wore on. I had to change my tacking strategy to accommodate this shift in the wind. I found myself beating into a 25 knot wind. I changed my foresail to a smaller storm jib. Despite my efforts, we were not making very good progress toward Key West. I also realized that in order to avoid the myriad of tiny islands between the Tortugas and Key West I had to sail further north than I had expected. It was a crystal clear day, but the wind continued to intensify and I realized that we were not going to make landfall before sunset.

The Seawolf had a tiller for steering, and while I liked the control this gave, it could be tiring in rough weather. I eventually put on gloves that I kept in the boat for long runs. My hands were starting to get sore. Sharon tried to spell me at the helm but told me that it was just too much for her. I sent her below to get some drinking water and granola bars to keep in the cockpit. I knew that this might be a long night.

As the day began to wane, I decided to venture further north to ensure that I didn't accidently run up on a dark island or shoal area. Checking my charts, I knew I would be relatively safe using this strategy. Unfortunately, this took us further away from Key West than a straight line would. As darkness fell, I started the engine, hoping to get some extra forward power, but I knew that in this kind of sea the little 10 hp diesel wouldn't do us much good. I had Sharon turn on our running lights and notify the Coast Guard of our situation and estimated position. I could not leave the tiller.

The night wore on and the wind did not diminish. Every muscle in my body was aching and I had to urinate really badly. We were out in open water, far enough north that the seas were kicking up to four and five feet. This was wreaking havoc on the boat since we were beating into the wind. I tried every trick that I knew to reach a balance between the physical realities of heading upwind and making as much headway as I could. I eventually realized that I would just have to relieve myself where I was and I told Sharon that I was going to do this. She began to cry.

"We're going to run into something or sink," she said. "Even if we survive until dawn, where will we be?"

I told her I needed her to be strong and not panic. "I'm stressed out enough for both of us. I'm doing everything I can to get us to Key West. Try not to worry. I'll get us there." I was not as confident as I was trying to sound.

We sailed like this all night. The wind began to lighten and shift back to the southeast just before dawn. Just as the sun was rising, I asked Sharon to take the helm.

"It's much better now," I told her. "You should be able to handle it just fine. I have to contact the Coast Guard to see if I can determine where we are." I could see no land on any point of the horizon.

I called the Coast Guard on channel 16. They switched me to channel 68. I told them what had happened and asked if they had some way to locate me and tell me where I was in relation to Key West. They told me that they could not. I was in no mood to hear that answer.

"There must be some way to locate my position," I said insistently. "No, I don't have a locator beacon. I only have this VHS radio." This was a time before everybody had a GPS locator by virtue of having a cell phone. They told me to stand by.

I waited, sitting on the floor of the cockpit, with my legs hanging down in the cabin. I was beat. I hoped that I could stay awake until this was over.

"Seawolf, Seawolf, Seawolf, this Florida Marine Patrol," came over the radio.

"Florida Marine Patrol, this is Seawolf," I replied.

"We have a fix on what we think is you. You are about eight miles north northwest of Key West" was the response. "Do you have auxiliary power?"

"This is Seawolf. Yes, I have auxiliary power and my sails are in good shape," I replied.

"Set your course for southwest until you see land. You should be able to find your way in then," came the instruction.

"Roger. Head southwest for about six or seven miles. Thank you. Thank you very much," I said in a shaking voice. "Seawolf out."

Sharon heard the exchange and began crying again, this time from relief. So did I, but my emotion was influenced by utter exhaustion. I took over the helm again and adjusted our course. I knew that the Seawolf was capable of 13 knots in ideal conditions, but I estimated that we were probably only doing seven. Sure enough, in less than an hour I could see land. When I got close enough to figure out where I was more precisely, I tacked northeast until I knew that I could make a straight tack into the protective waters of Key West and its surrounding islands. We pulled down all sails and motored into the marina and tied up to our dock.

I popped open a couple of beers and we drank to survival. I know it wasn't really that close a call, but it sure felt like it at the time. If nothing else, it was one hell of a seventy mile trip. I changed my pants, and told Sharon that we should go have Easter morning breakfast at the Baguette, a nice little restaurant on Duval Street, close to our dock. She readily agreed.

We ordered breakfast and a glass of wine. When our breakfast arrived I was passed dead out at the table. With some effort, Sharon managed to rouse me and I finished what seemed like one of the best meals of my life.

# Part IV

## The Professional

*Then I grew older*
*I got some grey*
*I work all day*
*Not much time for pretending*

# Chapter 58

It was dark now, and the old man was still sitting at his desk working on his stories. The only light on the entire second floor was the little brass desk lamp that hung over his laptop. He was just finishing that part of the book which described his "pirate days". He realized, however, that there was a lot of overlap between the crazy stuff he did in those days and the part of his life that was very productive. He also knew that he would have to deal with his third divorce before moving on to the mature years, and this distressed him.

"Are you still up there?" he heard his wife call from downstairs.

He looked at his watch. Good Grief! It was later than he realized. "Yes, I'm up here. I'll be down in just a minute."

"We should be doing something about dinner," she added.

"Yes, I know. I'll be right there," he confirmed. He realized that she expected him to get to work on preparing the evening meal. He did a lot of the cooking in their home. He still liked to cook, and was still damn good at it in his own humble opinion. His wife was a good cook too, but didn't mind letting him deal with all the preparations that typically went along with the kind of food they prepared at dinner time. They ate well to be sure.

He sat there at his desk a while longer. All of this remembering of the past got him reflecting on who he was, the kind of person he was. He knew that in most ways he was quite different now than he was all those years ago, but he had to admit that he still struggled with some aspects of his personality and character.

He felt that he was, and always had been, a relatively good person, but he also knew that he wasn't always good. He sincerely wanted to be a good man, a good friend, a good husband and father. He had been very fortunate to have been loved by so many beautiful women, sweet gentle women. He had genuinely loved them too, but ultimately he had been the cause of those relationships falling apart. This made him think about his current wife and their relationship, which had lasted longer than all the others put together.

He was still content with his marriage, although the nature of that relationship had changed over time. The red hot passion had inevitably burned to a simmer, but their friendship had grown and strengthened. They were comfortable with each other, he thought, and their love had grown into something deeper than passion. Of course, they had to work out problems over the years, some of them monumental problems, but they had stayed together. Writing this book made him think about that sort of thing.

"Are you coming down?" she called.

He looked up and laughed softly. He had lost track of time again. "Yes Sweetheart, sorry," he said. "I'm on my way." He shut off his computer and turned off his light. It was very dark upstairs.

"Here I am, my Dear," he said as he emerged on the balcony that overlooked the living room. "Do you have any thoughts on what you'd like for dinner?" He was now ready to switch all his focus to wine and dinner, in that order.

When they went to bed that night and turned off the lights, he became aware of that odd sound they had been hearing. One of the peculiar things about the sound was that, once you let it intrude into your consciousness, it seemed to grow louder. Perhaps louder was not exactly the right term. Maybe it was just more insistent.

"Do you hear that weird sound?" he asked his wife.

After a moment, "Yes, it seems louder tonight," she said.

They both lay there quietly. When there was no other sound, the unidentified sub-sonic sound seemed to grow in intensity, until it became distracting.

"I think that I'm going to spend some time tomorrow trying to see if I can narrow down where it's coming from," he said finally. "We don't hear it when we're on the other side of the mountain, so I guess we can assume that it's coming from somewhere down here in our canyon. Maybe if I walk up and down the canyon, I can discern a change in the tone that might help indicate where it's coming from, although it doesn't really seem directional."

"OK," she replied, sounding less interested than he was.

The next morning, after he completed his normal ranch chores, he went upstairs to his "man cave" with his coffee and sat down to practice his music. He had recently composed a couple new songs and needed to keep working on them before he would attempt to perform them in front of anybody.

He had composed several pieces of music in recent years. He had written a love song to his wife about how they met and what she meant to him. He thought it was a good song, but he had added a new verse and needed to keep practicing it. He also just finished writing a song about life as a metaphoric journey down a road, which he knew was inspired by his retirement and all the reflection that was a result of writing his book.

He drank his coffee in between songs. When the coffee was gone, he wrapped up his music practice and was about to shift his attention to writing when he remembered that he wanted to see if he could pinpoint that odd sound. No sense putting it off, he thought. He'd do it straight away.

He went outside and considered how he would approach this task. He knew that he could hear the sound at the eastern end of the canyon because that's the direction that one had to travel from in order to get to their place, which was the last property before the open space preserve that bordered the western edge of their property. Their ranch covered fifty acres, nestled between two mountains that formed the canyon. The two mountains met about a mile to the east forming a wide box canyon.

He wondered if the box canyon itself was creating some audio-phenomenon. There was at least one such phenomenon in the canyon that he had discovered some years earlier. When hikers were at a particular place on the park trail, on the mountain above the ranch, he could hear them talking as if they were located in his barn at the bottom of the canyon. On several occasions he had gone searching for people he presumed were hiding in his barn before he made the connection with the mountain.

He headed west, toward the park. The sound was quite faint this morning. That would probably make it more difficult to determine any possible direction of the source. He walked about a quarter mile from the edge of his property line, into the park, when he realized that the sound had definitely stopped. He made a mental note of where he was, turned around and headed back. Within a few yards, he picked up the faint sound again. Okay, it was almost certainly coming from someplace in the canyon.

When he got back to his house, he decided to walk south. This took him past his barn, through the riparian forest that ran through his property, and up the north slope of Black Horse Mountain. It became evident that the sound faded the farther south he went. He climbed about halfway up the mountain slope, where the sound remained faintly consistent. He didn't have the energy to climb all the way to the top and over the crest to determine if the sound disappeared, but he thought that it probably would. If he discovered that the sound didn't increase on the other side of the canyon, the north side, he could always come back to this side for further exploration.

The mountain on the north side of the canyon was not on his property, and he was not sure how his neighbor would feel about him snooping around over there. He was also not sure that he wanted to advise his neighbor about what he was doing. He didn't really want anybody else involved in this little detective work, at least not yet. He wanted to try to figure it out for himself first. The sound was still faint and it was starting to get hot, so he decided to put off the search until later. Maybe the sound intensity would improve later on, in the cooler evening hours.

He headed back to the house and went up to his "man cave". He sat down and began to think about how he was going to write about screwing up another marriage. He was considering the notion of fabricating some event that made him look like less of an asshole. It was a fictional story, right? He supposed that he would just have to keep things relatively honest.

# Chapter 59

The dynamics of my life were changing. My so-called pirate phase was waning, getting squeezed out by the grownup responsibilities that I couldn't avoid. Sharon did not pass the CPA exam, despite all of her preparation. She took a position with the IRS, working on high profile individuals and corporations. She became consumed with the job. I became more focused on my job as well. Gould was involved with some amazing projects, many of which required the participation of my data communications team. These projects, while interesting and exciting, were often quite stressful.

The girls were growing up. Before I knew it, they were teenagers and had morphed into people whose personalities were hard to recognize or understand. What happened to the little girls who loved being around their parents? My daughter and her mother were having issues out in Phoenix, and it was decided to have Alexa come live with me. Now we had three teenage daughters to raise, and that was a challenge that I really had no clue about managing.

All three girls were now in high school, with all of the social pressures and temptations that go along with that phase of life. They were pushing for more independence. We had to deal with them driving now. I remembered how important having a driver's license was when I was that age, so I tried to balance all the conflicting feelings I had about this. Apparently, schools stopped providing Driver's Ed, so I felt that I had to teach them to drive. That was a terrifying experience.

The girls also wanted to dress to express their individuality during this time, which I found ironic. They essentially wanted to look like everybody else, who were all trying to look unique. This was the time when celebrities like Madonna and Lindy Looper, or whatever her name was, were setting styles that teenage girls wanted to emulate. I got it. I understood. I had tried to look like a Beatle when I was that age, so I was relatively calm about the way they dressed, or tried to dress. Sharon was not as liberal.

One day, the girls came down from their rooms, ready to go to school. They were all decked out in an odd collection of clothing, lots of makeup, and very unusual hair styles. I happened to be at the foot of the stairs as they all trooped down that morning. I looked up and did a double take.

"Well, are you girls going to the circus today," I chortled. Though they looked outlandish, I thought they looked cute. They stopped at the bottom steps and looked unsure but mildly defiant. "Does the school allow students to dress like this?"

"Oh, yeah," came a unified, predictable assurance.

Just then Sharon emerged from our bedroom, which was at the bottom of the staircase. She shrieked. I mean she actually shrieked.

"Oh no you don't," she said. She clearly was not going to be as flexible on this issue as I was prepared to be. I realized, however, that I had better stay out of it, so I slunk away toward the kitchen.

A lot of yelling and debating followed, which I tried to ignore. Sharon won that battle, but ultimately lost the war. Daughters, I soon discovered, will find very inventive ways to do what they want to do. They can be quite devious in their methods. Over the next couple of years, many battles were fought over clothes, makeup, boys, social activities, access to cars, and on and on. All of this was stressful, of course, and took its toll on personal relationships.

I was, however, very lucky to have my daughter, Alexa, living with me during this time. We really didn't know each other well and she was growing up fast. I thought she was kind of a chip off the old block. She was smart and fairly well grounded, but had a bit of a free-spirit side to her. When she was fifteen she wrote a letter to me. In this letter she said that when she first moved to Florida to live with me, she was afraid of me and didn't feel she could really talk to me, but now that she'd been with me a while she was feeling different about things.

She wrote that she now felt closer to me and was glad to have the chance to be raised by me. She went on to say that she knew she wasn't perfect, but that she tried hard to meet my expectations because she wanted me to be proud of her. She finished by telling me that she thought I was doing a good job as her dad. I still have that letter.

I continued to train for bodybuilding contests, which consumed most of any free time I had. There was less time now for playing pirate on my beautiful Seawolf. I was also traveling more for my work, and that added to the strain on just about everything in my personal life. Yes, the times, they were a changing.

I had been a geek in my early life, kind of an egghead, and no good at sports. Then I entered the Air Force, became a warrior, developed a Billy-badass attitude, got buff, and lived like a pirate. Now I was going back the other way, focused on intellectual pursuits and trying to be a good family man. Not that I'm complaining. This was a good path for me.

I actually used to think about how I would know when I became a man, a man in the sense of being mature and responsible. I used my father as my standard. When Sharon threw a huge party for me on my fortieth birthday, I stopped to reflect on my progress. The birthday party invitations were titled, "A Pirate Looks at Forty". I didn't think that I had reached my ideal manhood goal yet, but I thought I was making progress.

Most of my time was consumed with work, and this was a positive thing. The data communications team at Gould was growing and I was now managing the hardware and software development of cutting edge inter-computer communication solutions. In addition to research projects, our team was working on several major applications for large customers.

In fact, this was a very exciting time in the computer technology industry. The Internet and World Wide Web did not exist yet, but most computer companies were involved in laying down the foundation for that future. The computing world was dominated by mainframes, but companies like ours were developing new technologies that provided powerful computing capabilities in systems that were much smaller, less expensive, and often more capable in specialized applications such as real-time computing.

Gould operated a computer science research center at their headquarters in Schaumburg, Illinois, just outside of Chicago. Some of the research scientists there were working on an early version of data communications protocols called the Transmission Control Protocol, or TCP, and Internet Protocol, or IP. These were to become two of the main protocols in what is now the Internet protocol suite. My team in Fort Lauderdale had developed a related data protocol called the User Datagram Protocol, or UDP, which we considered to be more appropriate for the real-time applications that ran on Gould's SEL super-mini computers.

Prior to the Internet's existence, the computing world was largely segregated into many commercial, academic, and military networks. One of the main commercial network solutions was sponsored by IBM and was called the Systems Network Architecture, SNA. The primary precursor for the Internet, however, was the ARPANET, which was funded by the U.S. government. By the mid-1980s, worldwide participation in the development of network technologies began in earnest.

I was participating in, on behalf of Gould, several national committees that were involved in establishing internetworking protocol standards. Some of these organizations were actually competing, so we found it necessary to be involved in every serious program to ensure that our interests were considered and allow us to keep up with the evolving developments. As a consequence, my team had to work on two different sets of communication protocols, one from the International Standards Organization, called Open System Interconnection protocols, and one from the National Science Foundation, which was funding work on its NFS Network. Although the protocols were quite similar, they differed in the details and were not compatible.

My team was particularly interested in keeping up with TCP/IP and Ethernet, as these were the basic communication protocols that allowed inter computer communication and were the protocols that other major commercial system developers were focused on, including our competitors. I was sent to our research center to investigate the work that was being conducted on TCP/IP. There I met Reggie. He was the scientist in charge of this project.

Reggie and his team developed data communication protocols in a high-level programming language, call LISP, which was often used for artificial intelligence research. Gould real-time computers used the programming language FORTRAN, so my mission was to determine if Reggie and his team had made enough progress on the research version to allow my team to use its design to program the same functions in FORTRAN. Otherwise, my team would have to start from scratch. The research version was, in fact, fully functional. It was decided that Reggie would move to Fort Lauderdale and work with us to expedite the development of a commercial version of TCP/IP.

Reggie was from Malaysia and educated in England. He had not been in the United States very long, but was quite eager to leave the winters of Chicago for the balmy weather of South Florida. I volunteered to drive down from Chicago with him. He was concerned about driving such a long distance, through several southern states. He was dark-skinned and thought that he might run into trouble in the South. I told him that I didn't think that he had to worry, but that I was delighted to go on a road trip with him on the company's nickel.

It was, indeed, a memorable trip. I got to know Reggie and had fun acquainting him with places and customs of the United States along our journey. I convinced him to take some back roads in order to give him a chance to really see America. While driving through Georgia, deep in the pines, I stopped for gas at a remote station that also apparently served as the area's gathering place for local citizens. It only resembled a gas station in that there were a couple of gasoline pumps in front of an old ramshackle building.

Several large old trucks were parked off to one side. There was no pavement at this establishment, only gravel. The front of the building sported a covered porch, which provided a variety of rickety old chairs, many of which were occupied by gentlemen garbed in denim coveralls. One of these men wore no shirt under his coveralls, exposing a large, hairy set of shoulders and arms. What really set this scene off was the young, attractive woman in cutoff jeans and a sleeveless T-shirt. It was a scene right out of *Li'l Abner*. The only thing missing was banjo music.

It was the young woman who approached the car to ask us what we needed. The men on the porch just sat there and looked on.

"Whatcha need mister?" Daisy Mae asked in a deep southern drawl.

"Fill it up please," I said. "Do you have any sodas inside?"

"Sure do," she said cheerfully.

"Come on," I said to Reggie, "let's see what they've got."

He wouldn't move. He told me to go ahead. I asked him if he didn't want to stretch his legs, but he looked quite distressed. I leaned over toward him and asked if something was the matter. He told me that he didn't feel safe here. I shrugged my shoulders and headed for the building.

I said howdy as I passed the guys on the front porch, and they nodded back. The inside reminded me of the old Dixon Road store that we used to go to when we were kids and had a dime to spend. I came back out with my purchases, paid the attractive young woman, and started the car.

"You see," I said to Reggie. "No trouble here. I hit the jackpot inside this place." I opened my brown paper bag. "Let me introduce you to a true American delicacy, RC Cola and a Moon Pie." I was smiling triumphantly. He looked at the goods suspiciously, then cast a cautious look back up to the porch to be sure nobody was coming to drag him out of the car.

I left the station and headed for the Freeway. I thought that Reggie had had enough back country Americana for one trip. As we drove, he took a tentative bite from one of the Moon Pies. I could tell that his tastes were probably not quite as proletariat as mine. He asked me if people ate the whole thing in one sitting. I laughed and told him he didn't have to eat it.

# Chapter 60

Reggie and I made a great team. He was a very smart guy and we started making progress on our project very quickly. There was another person on the communications team that I became heavily dependent upon to get tough programming assignments done, Maximus. I hired him right out of college. Most of the people on our team were smart, but Maximus was really smart. He was the kind of guy who could rattle off details about things that you didn't think that anybody would know, right out of the clear blue sky. Once at a party, a group of us were talking about the planets in our solar system, specifically those closest to the sun. Somebody wondered out loud about the difference in the distance from the sun between Earth and Venus.

Mark who was not directly involved in the conversation, but standing close by, turned and said, "Well, Venus is 67.24 million miles from the Sun, while the Earth is 92.96 million miles, which would put Venus 25.72 million miles closer. Venus is also the hottest planet in our solar system, even hotter than Mercury due to the greenhouse effect caused by the perpetual cloud cover."

He said this nonchalantly with a perfectly straight face. We all stared at him. Who in the hell would know that kind of thing off the top of their head?

He was also funny and had a goofy sense of humor similar to mine. As soon as he realized that he had said something that the rest of us thought was incredibly nerdy or silly he would laugh with the kind of laugh that includes a snort, which I thought was pretty funny in and of itself. He became an integral part of our core development team.

One of the first major projects that my team worked on to demonstrate that Gould's super-mini computers could communicate with other computer systems was a program called Manufacturing Automation Protocol, or MAP. This was essentially a standard manufacturing protocol, promoted and used by General Motors and Boeing, to facilitate the interconnection of devices from different manufacturers. By 1985, GM was using over 2000 programmable devices, including robots, in their manufacturing plants.

MAP was adopted as the IEEE 802.4, token bus standard, one of several competing network protocol efforts underway during that period. Several technical changes that were required after the initial issue of MAP in 1982, however, made it difficult for all participating vendors to remain compatible. A very large, highly publicized demonstration of MAP at the 1985 Computer Dealers' Exhibition, called COMDEX, was organized. This turned out to be a good example of how difficult it was to get a whole bunch of computing systems made by competing vendors to talk to each other.

Several members of my communications team went to that COMDEX show in 1985 to set up and configure our new Gould SEL 32/67 supermini computer as part of the highly anticipated MAP demonstration. All of the big computer companies were involved in this demonstration, including IBM, Allen Bradley, Burroughs, Sperry Rand, and Digital Equipment. General Motors created a miniature auto manufacturing model that was connected to a computer from each one of the demonstration participants via the MAP network. Each computer was responsible for one of the half dozen simulated manufacturing processes in the model.

The demonstration required an input terminal be positioned next to the elaborate model, enabling the human selection of a set of options for building a toy car. These options were transmitted to the computers attached to the MAP network. Visitors to the

MAP booth would be allowed to "build" a toy car to their specification by selecting options from a predefined list appearing on the input terminal. So, you could build a red truck, for example, or a blue sedan. The manufacturing model was very impressive, covering the space of a large dining table, and containing several little robotic doodads that ultimately built the toy, which you got to take with you as a souvenir.

The manufacturing model stood in the middle of a very large booth. General Motors got most of the limelight, but all of the participating computer manufacturers also had their corporate logos hanging in the booth above their individual computer systems. It was damned impressive, and on opening day there were a lot of reporters and dignitaries attending the inaugural demonstration. Hordes of conference attendees crowded around the booth.

My team and I had stayed up all night trying to get things working correctly, as did many of the teams from the other computer companies. There were problems with the networking communications. Generally, everything worked pretty well, but occasionally a network token got dropped and that meant that some instruction would not get executed. This would be hugely embarrassing for everybody participating, so we tried very hard to figure out the source of the problem. Unfortunately, we didn't succeed in figuring things out by the time the demonstration was to begin.

Although the Gould computer, as far as we could determine, was not the source of the problem, we knew that it was possible to engineer a band-aid fix. Our superspy monitoring equipment was capable of generating a "fake" instruction on the network, assuming that we knew what instruction was missing. This "fix" required human intervention, involving somebody standing near the input terminal to physically see what was being typed in as the set of options. Another person, literally behind the curtain next to our equipment, had to artificially generate the missing packet of data.

To implement this clandestine operation, we worked out a predefined, fake set of data packets which we could generate with the push of a button, but the ruse required GM to allow us to stand next to the terminal and provide some kind of signal to the man behind the curtain. I advised the GM manager in charge of the booth of the problem and our suggested solution. He was very unhappy. I had to keep reminding him that it was not the Gould computer causing the problem and that I could prove that to him. But, he was understandably in panic mode. We were running out of time.

A lot of strings had to be pulled to get me in the correct position, since this is where all the VIPs would be standing. I was a nervous wreck. We had been up all night, so we were running on adrenalin and nervous energy. Maximus was designated as the man behind the curtain at the monitoring controls. Another colleague was with Maximus, peeping out of a small crack in the curtain, watching for my signals. We had worked out a set of what we thought were clever hand signals involving me touching my head in specific places and in specific ways to communicate what needed to be done.

I watched what a user typed into the terminal as their unique selections for the toy car, then watched the model to make sure everything kept moving as expected. Fortunately, there were not a lot of options so it was not too difficult to remember the signals.

The way a problem manifested itself was that the model simply stalled if an instruction got dropped. If the model stopped for more than a few seconds, I would give the appropriate signal, and the predefined data packet would be launched from our diagnostic equipment, and things would start moving again. It was also fortunate that the problem did not happen too often. The biggest challenge was trying to maintain my strategic position at the model.

I think it was a miracle that we got through the day without any catastrophic failures, but at the end of that first day the GM people and all the visitors to the booth were happy. We all went to our hotel rooms and collapsed, missing the big happy hour party and dinner that evening.

Despite our heroic efforts to cover up what was only a temporary setback in the MAP protocol capabilities, that network standard fell out of favor and was ultimately replaced by the now ubiquitous IEEE 802.3, Ethernet standard. Fortunately, our Gould data communication team was already working diligently on this standard, as well as several of the communication protocols that operate on top of it.

# Chapter 61

The 1980s and early 1990s were a time of tremendous advancement in computer network technology, but there was so much competing effort among competing vendors that a significant amount of time, energy, and other resources were ultimately wasted. Despite national and international committees being established for trying to keep all of the innovation and input managed, there was still chaos. Large computer firms, government entities, and other groups were all trying to put their stake in the ground for competitive advantage or selfish interest. In addition to all of the conflicting work going on to develop "standard" networking solutions, operating systems were also evolving.

There was a mighty struggle for dominance in operating systems on several fronts, but the one that was affecting us at Gould the most was what was often referred to as the "Unix Wars". Mainframe manufacturers invested heavily in their own proprietary operating systems, while the emerging PC market, requiring something considerably less complex, invested in a totally different direction. Unix was of interest to Gould engineers because it was more flexible and portable than other alternatives. By the mid-1980s it had been rewritten from the original assembler language, to the high-level C programming language, and that allowed any system that supported C to use it.

There were several versions of Unix emerging during this time, but all were essentially based on either the original AT&T, System V version or the newer Berkley Software Distribution, or BSD version. Gould's supermini computers were real-time systems, requiring fundamental differences in the operating system that Unix, in its different forms, did not support. Gould engineers began developing a real-time version of Unix, which they called UTX. Since the "Unix Wars" were still ongoing, our senior management decided to our engineers develop a dual universe system that contained many of the features of both BSD and System V.

All of this innovation and lack of solid standards lead to the need for continuous changes in all aspects of software and hardware engineering. For my communications team it was necessary to rewrite much of our software from FORTRAN to the new C programming language. Our communication hardware also required redesign. Both of these tasks were complicated by the evolving designs in the core real-time operating system and system bus components. At the same time, we were defining innovations in configuration utilities, documentation, and quality assurance testing. Despite the resulting stress, it was a crazy, heady, insanely fun time.

Most of the members of our data communications team were involved in some kind of sports. One young woman was a competitive water skier. Several of the team competed in 3K and 5K races. Just about everybody on the team played in the local golf league and softball league. Most of us hung out after work and partied. We eventually arranged to outfit ourselves in corny satin sports jackets. They were black with a green dragon holding two crossed lightning bolts on the back of the jacket. Across the top, arching over the dragon, were the words "Comm Jocks". We all wore them when we attended functions or parties together. Of course, we took a lot of ribbing over this, but it was part of the fun.

The projects that we were involved in were quite amazing. We worked with Siemens on the development of the national power grid control system for Singapore. Gould controlled 75% of the commercial flight simulation business, and our communications team was involved in several of these projects. My team worked with the Jet Propulsion Lab in Pasadena on the range and telemetry subsystem communications supporting the prestigious Hubble Space Telescope program.

Just as things were getting interesting, however, business took a downturn and an odd business transaction occurred. In 1988, Gould was purchased by a Japanese firm, Nippon Mining. Gould's Computer Systems Division, the place where we worked in Fort Lauderdale, provided key components of national defense projects, and foreign companies were not allowed to own control of such companies. So another company, called Encore, bought the Computer Systems Division from Nippon Mining. While Encore was already focused on real-time computing, the transaction threw most of us into a tailspin of confusion. Layoffs began shortly thereafter, and morale plummeted.

# Chapter 62

I seem to have a propensity for getting myself into multiple disasters at the same time. It was during all of this professional turmoil that Sharon and I split up. I had developed a close relationship with a young woman in another department at Gould during the previous year. This young woman was living with a guy, so our relationship was relatively casual. Nevertheless, I was misbehaving and Sharon found out.

The breakup was traumatic, especially for Sharon. I came home one evening to find all my belongings out on the sidewalk in front of our townhouse. She had always been very gentle and vulnerable emotionally, the kind of woman you feel compelled to prove to that not all men are assholes. I had let her down and I felt very badly about it.

I discovered that, after the breakup, she was having me followed. On the occasions when I would need to see her about some detail or another, she would surprise me by describing my comings and goings, where I had been, and who I had been with. I couldn't figure out how she knew so much about what I was doing. At first I suspected that somebody at work or one of my friends must be keeping her up to date, but there were a few accounts that I was sure no mutual acquaintance knew about.

I finally got to the bottom of caper, discovering that there was an actual investigator keeping tabs on me. I was furious. This person was also keeping tabs on a couple of my friends, and when I told them about it, which I felt obligated to do, they were shocked and none too happy about it. I asked Sharon why she would do such a thing, what had she hoped to achieve. She told me she wanted more reasons to hate me. That hit home pretty hard and I felt very sad for her and ashamed of myself.

It was time to move on again, but I damn sure wasn't going back to Alaska to do more penance. I knew that I needed to turn over some new leaves, but also felt strongly obligated to press forward with my career. I felt like I had something worthwhile to give to the high tech industry and just needed to find a new home for my talents. Fortunately there were lots of opportunities at that time.

I had made a choice a couple of years into my tenure at Gould that would ultimately shape and define my professional future. I discovered that I was not a particularly good programmer. In fact, programming didn't really interest me. I did enjoy design work and using my knowledge of programming to manage software and system programs, projects, and people toward achieving a designated goal. I had also developed a keen sense for figuring out how to apply technology to solve specific problems. So, I decided to cultivate my capabilities as a manager and pursue opportunities in that direction.

I found a position in Cincinnati, Ohio, that seemed to be the right next step for me. Intercomputer Communication Corporation, or ICC, was looking for somebody to help them manage their growing business. They developed solutions for PC to mainframe inter-connectivity. Their products allowed a user on a PC to access a terminal, which in turn has access to legacy applications, typically on a mainframe. The PC has the ability to present the data from the terminal in a different user interface architecture, such as a graphic interface.

This sort of emulation technology was becoming very popular as the world was migrating from dominate mainframe applications to distributed systems using newer technologies. ICC focused on Unisys emulation. To accomplish this technical marvel, one of several different data communication protocols could be used, and the ICC products included a line of data communication technologies, which of course was what I had spent the last nine years doing in Fort Lauderdale.

I was hired as ICC's engineering manager of what they called the A/V Division, which focused on products for the Unisys A, V, and B series computers. I was pleased to have the opportunity to learn more about these new technologies as well as the kinds of business applications that they served.

Moving back to Ohio would coincidentally provide some personal benefits. I would be much closer to where my parents lived. I thought of my parents as the best examples in my life of good people, and I thought that this move might just be the thing to get me re-centered. My sister, Daisy, was in the Air Force and currently serving as a Load Master supporting the Gulf War effort. She was due to come home about the time I would be arriving in Ohio. I had not seen her in many years and it would be good to get reacquainted.

# Chapter 63

About this same time, one of the most amazing things in my life happened to me. It all started with a sailing event. I was still very much into sailing, and when the 1989-1990 Whitbread Round the World Race announced that one of the race's six legs would begin in Fort Lauderdale, I was determined to be there to witness the historic event. The racing yachts would arrive over an extended period beginning in early April. The largest yachts would berth at the Pier 66 Resort and Marina. Several receptions where planned and I determined to attend at least one of them.

My friend, Maximus, had recently broken up with his girlfriend. Hewanted to try to meet somebody new, but was unsure of his skills at meeting women. I told him that maybe I could help in some way, but insisted that the only way to meet somebody was to go places where women were likely to be.

"There are essentially three places where you can meet women," I lectured. "Church, work, or bars. Of course, you can get introduced to a woman by your family or your friends too. I'm guessing that you don't go to church, and you don't seem to be having any luck at work." His former girlfriend worked with us at Gould, so the prospects of another woman from work taking her place were pretty limited.

"Yeah," he admitted. "I guess you're right, but I don't want to just hang out in bars. I don't know how to approach a woman in that setting."

"Yes, that is difficult," I said sagely. "I think that all the women in bars are by default suspicious of any guy who tries to talk to them. I don't blame them. The assholes of the world have already ruined things for the rest of us." I was being a little lenient on myself and my own record of disappointing women.

"So, what do you suggest?" he asked.

"Well, there is a big event happening this weekend at Pier 66," I said. "There will be tons of people there. It's the Whitbread Round the World Race, and they are stopping here in the U.S., in Fort Lauderdale, for the first time ever. It's a really big deal, so I think we should go. I bet there will be lots of women there."

It was agreed. We would go there on Saturday and try to get in. I had heard that it would be a zoo, but I really wanted to be part of the scene.

When we arrived, it was indeed a zoo. There were hundreds people crammed into the large ball room at the Pier 66 conference center. The event was being sponsored by Beefeaters Gin, and those guys that are on the label, the Yeomen Warders who guard the Tower of London, were walking around in their costumes with those long ax looking things. Pretty cool. The electricity in the place was palpable.

We made our way to one of the bars with great difficulty. I ordered us a couple glasses of wine and we tried to act casual, taking it all in. It was amazing. So many beautiful people in one place. I assured Maximus that we would find somebody he thought was interesting and that I would coach him in introducing himself. I told him that since we were together, he wouldn't seem like a lone wolf, and since he was a good looking, polite, professional young man, he was sure to be interesting to one of these ladies.

Then I saw her. She was standing near the bar, several yards away, looking around at the crowd. She was stunning, she was like a movie star. She made everybody else in the room diminish until all I saw was her. I didn't say anything to Maximus. I was mesmerized, and in fact, I forgot all about Maximus.

As I watched her, I could see that she was drinking a glass of wine, but clearly didn't think much of it. She was making subtle little faces each time she took a sip. I don't know what came over me, but I started walking toward her. She was clearly way out of my league. I would be a mere speck of dust to her, but I didn't care, I wanted to speak to her. I left Maximus on his own.

"Hello," I said, wide-eyed. "I noticed that you don't seem to approve of the wine you're drinking. I have some experience with wine. Perhaps I could recommend something more to your liking."

She looked at me with an expression that said, "Why is this speck of dust speaking to me?" I was standing there in front of her in the classic but pathetic male stance, with shoulders back, stomach tucked in, trying to look suave and masculine, but casual. She turned to the bartender who had just stepped up, apparently noticing that this goddess wanted something.

"Give me a Stoli Martini on the rocks with extra olives," she said, pushing her wine away as though it was full of something akin to a purulent discharge.

"Well, that's another way to go," I said, undaunted and laughing my goofy laugh. Since I had her captive while she waited for her drink, I decided to introduce myself.

"My name is Wolf," I said with a very slight bow. "I have a sailboat and wanted to be here to be part of this historic event. Are you a sailing enthusiast?"

"No," she said simply. She had all of her feminine defenses up, and though I knew this would all end in rejection and abject humiliation, I was compelled to press on.

"Are you familiar with the Whitbread Round the World Race?" I asked. Maybe I was pressing the sailing thing too hard, but I didn't have anything else to try to connect with at that moment.

"Not really," she said, finally looking at me with a hint of mild curiosity. "I'm here with my girlfriends. They wanted to come see what was happening. We're going to the Branding Iron after this."

"Oh, the Branding Iron," I said, apparently revealing that I had no idea what or where that was.

"It's a country western bar out in Davie," she said. "We go there to dance." She looked at me as though she was thinking, that I probably couldn't even walk normally let alone dance. She took a sip of her martini, which had just been delivered. Just watching her take that sip made me feel all quivery inside.

I didn't offer to pay for her drink. I thought that was too obvious. All guys offer to pay for a girl's drinks, as though that might be the quickest way to her heart, or more likely her bed. I was trying not to look too much like a puppy groveling for her attention, and hoping that hormones weren't oozing off my body and pooling on the floor around me.

She was petite, probably just over five feet, I thought. She had gobs of thick, long, curly blond hair that hung down past the middle of her back. She wore it pushed back to reveal a beautiful face, with big eyes that seemed to change color with her movements. She wore a white shirt with the collar pulled up on her slender neck, and unbuttoned enough to reveal a colorful neckless and a very attractive view of her cleavage. She wore tight red pants that matched her bright red lipstick, finger and toenail polish. All of that splendor stood there on top of very fashionable high heeled sandals.

I guess I was just standing there gawking, trying desperately to look at her face and not shift my eyes to her breasts. When I heard her asking me if I was a fan of country western music. I snapped out of my temporary daze.

"Oh, well, I guess I don't listen to a lot of country music," I said weakly, "but I like all kinds of music." That reminded me that I actually had two tickets to a chamber ensemble concert that Sunday. "In fact, I have tickets to the upcoming Fort Lauderdale Chamber Ensemble." I guess I thought this might impress her.

She suddenly said, "My name is Chase," and held out her hand.

I took her hand and shook it in a firm manner. Her hand was small and soft. "Well, it is very nice to meet you Chase."

"Wolf is an unusual name," she returned.

"Yes, I guess it is," I said sheepishly. "My brothers are named Bear and Tiger, so it's kind of a family oddity. We're all pretty normal though."

She smiled at this, but then she was looking past me and over my left shoulder, then back at me. I thought, "oh no, her boyfriend or husband just walked up behind me." I turned around to see what she was looking at and saw Maximus standing there, dutifully, observing what I suppose he thought was a lesson in how to meet women. Actually, I had forgotten all about him.

"Oh, that's Maximus," I said dismissively, in way that Tarzan might introduce Cheetah, "me Tarzan, him Cheetah".

Chase smiled and shook his hand. "What do you do for a living," I heard Maximus ask.

"I'm a teacher," she offered. "I teach art at the high school in Davie."

"Wow," I thought. They didn't have teachers who looked like this when I was in high school, but then I suddenly remembered that the art teacher at my high school was probably the best looking teacher. Maybe it was a requirement for employment to teach art.

Both Maximus and I described what we did for a living, which is not easy to do. Most people glaze over when I try to explain my job. Over the years, I've learned to say something simple, like "I work on computers". That usually satisfies whoever is asking, but I thought I could detect a faint degree of interest in Chase's expression. For good measure I added that I had planned to study art at Ohio State University, but that financial circumstances ultimately compelled me to enter the Air Force instead.

Since, Chase was art teacher, I thought that she might appreciate classical music. So, I asked her if she would be interested in attending that chamber recital with me on Sunday. I told her the time and place it was to be held. For effect, I pulled the tickets out of my shirt pocket. She hesitated, and I braced myself for the big rejection, but she finally said, "Perhaps."

"Why don't you call me tomorrow afternoon, and I let you know if I can go. She got a scrap of paper and a pen from her purse, and wrote down her telephone number. She gave me another penetrating, critical look, as though to finally determine whether or not I was an ax murder, or even worthy of her attention, then she handed me the paper. She took another sip of her martini and seemed to be studying me as though I might be someone with slightly elevated possibilities. I straightened myself just a little bit more, hoping that I would not sprain something in the effort.

We continued to chat, when her girlfriends came upon us in a whirlwind of feminine chatter. Chase introduced us. The other women looked Maximus and I up and down in a mixture of unabashed flirtation and unvarnished suspicion. Chase urged the girlfriends to move on to the Branding Iron, which gained immediate acceptance. They all said goodbye, and they were gone.

I stood there collecting myself for a moment.

"That was really great," I heard Maximus saying. "I see what you were trying to tell me about how to talk to women."

"Huh?" I said absent mindedly. "Oh, yeah, but this was different. I wasn't expecting to run into somebody like her." He looked at me quizzically. "Never mind. Looks like I might get to see her again on Sunday." The rest of the evening went by in kind of a blur.

# Chapter 64

The next afternoon, Saturday, I nervously called Chase's number. She didn't answer, so I left a message. I suspected that she might be monitoring her calls and when she heard it was me, decided not to bother telling me that she didn't want to go to the concert. Well, nothing ventured, nothing gained. A couple hours later, however, she called me back and told me that she could go. She wanted to meet me at the venue rather than have me pick her up at her home. I told her that would be fine and that I looked forward to seeing her again.

She met me as planned and we went into the hall to enjoy the music. Unfortunately, the air conditioning was not working that afternoon, and it became quite unbearable inside. I felt bad for the musicians, who must be melting up on the stage. I finally leaned over and quietly asked Chase if she wanted to leave early due to the heat. She agreed that this was a good idea.

It was still quite early in the afternoon, and we were close to one of the chic areas of Fort Lauderdale known as Las Olas. I suggested that we walk to a restaurant there for some lunch and a drink. Again, she agreed that this was an excellent idea. We had a very pleasant time and got to know each other a little better. Before we parted, I asked her if she would consider going for a short ride on my sailboat for some lunch at one of the local anchorages that I knew. I assured her that we wouldn't go sailing, just a cruise on the Intercoastal. She accepted.

I thought that next week would never end. I wanted to see her again, but I didn't want to seem like I was too eager. I called her on Friday to confirm our boating date. This time she gave me her address and asked me to pick her up at the appointed time. I suggested that she wear flat, rubber soled shoes that would be appropriate for a boat, and told her I was preparing a lunch for us. I was looking forward to the soiree.

She told me that her friends had all been surprised the night that she gave me her phone number. Apparently there was a rule that they all agreed to: don't give out your phone number to guys in bars. She said that she thought I was okay, but that she had given her girlfriends all of my information in case she didn't return from our boating trip. I wondered what kind of guys she had met in the past.

The big day finally arrived and we departed the dock, heading for a little spot that I thought would be perfect for our lunch. It was a small cove just south of the Las Olas Bridge, where the shore was actually a little park, called Merle Fogg. It was a short trip from the dock. I dropped my anchor, made sure it was hooked, and proceeded to the galley to fetch a cold bottle of chardonnay.

I was wearing white deck pants and a long-sleeve pink dress shirt, with the sleeves rolled up. Now lest you think that this was a bit feminine for a manly man such as myself, let me remind you that this was the time of Miami Vice and Don Johnson. I was in style, I assure you. Add sunglasses, and I thought that she would not be able to resist me. The Bimini top was up, so we had shade, a nice breeze blowing from the Atlantic Ocean a block away, and a bottle of wine, which I placed in an ice bucket in the cockpit. She looked devastating, dressed in shorts and a sexy little tank top, and all that glorious hair. Thank you Jesus, I was saying to myself.

After a glass of wine, I went below to prepare our lunch. I had made a curried chicken, cranberry, and walnut salad ahead of time. I served this on a large leaf of lettuce, along with a fresh croissant and some gruyere cheese. I kept linen napkins and some nice tableware on board, so I set up my portable table on the deck with these implements and presented my lunch with an exaggerated flourish. I poured another glass of wine to accompany our lunch and sat back to enjoy the afternoon. I could tell that Chase was duly impressed, and we had an excellent time getting to know each other a little bit better.

When it came time to weigh anchor and head for home, I could not get the engine to start. I had encountered this problem in the past, so I knew how to resolve it, but it required removing the deck cover at the bottom of the cockpit and getting down into the greasy engine compartment. I think that Chase thought this was some kind of trick, the old "we've run out of gas" routine. I assured her that I could get it fixed, but I'd have to ask her to get out of the cockpit and up on the roof of the cabin.

I knew that this would take some time. I had brought a bottle of champagne in case things got to a point where champagne would be called for. I sheepishly told her that I had some bubbly that she could sip while I was taking care of this problem. She accepted the offer with a cocked eyebrow, not sure yet how to size me up. After serving her the champagne, I unscrewed the deck floor. I decided to take off my pink shirt in an effort to minimize the damage to my cloths that was likely to occur down in that greasy engine compartment.

I didn't think about it at the time, but I suppose that Chase probably thought that I was showing off. I was muscular, ripped, and tan from a recent bodybuilding contest. I had not mentioned anything about that to her yet, so she was probably a little surprised at my appearance. She did tell me much later that when she saw what I looked like without my shirt, she decided that I might be worth getting to know a little better.

I got the engine started without getting much grease on my white pants. I put the deck back on, pulled the anchor, and headed toward the dock. I took her home and saw her to the door. She told me that she had a very good time and that she was impressed with the boat and the lunch. I didn't ask to come in or even try to kiss her. I didn't want to rush things for a number of reasons. I was still smarting from the breakup with Sharon. I knew that I would probably not be staying in Fort Lauderdale much longer due to the situation at Gould. I also just wanted to let this new relationship take a more deliberate course.

The next time I called her to ask her out on a date, she suggested that we go to a movie. That sounded good to me, so we arranged to get together the following Friday evening. She said she wanted to see the new movie called, *The Cook, the Thief, His Wife, and Her Lover*. I had never heard of it, but if that's what she wanted to see, then that's what we would go see. It was, without a doubt, the weirdest movie I had ever seen, and I found it disturbing. Chase said she thought it was interesting. I tried not to think about it.

That evening, when I took her home, she asked me if I'd like to come in. I did. She brought out a bottle of wine and asked me to open it, which I did. We sat on a very floral, burnt umber and light beige couch, which looked great with her South Florida décor. She had a pet dog, a red Doberman Pinscher, named Grinta. Grinta initially made me a little nervous because she was determined to sit right at my feet and stare at me. I eventually realized that she was, in fact, a very sweet dog.

We sat and talked and drank wine. I opened a second bottle. When two people meet and determine that they like each other, there seems to be no end to the things they want to know about each other. We talked for a long time. I loved just being with her. At one point, during a little lull in our conversation, I saw her looking at me in an inquisitive way.

"What are you thinking about right now?" she asked.

I looked at her for a moment. She was so beautiful. "I guess I was thinking about what it would be like to make love to you," it came out before I could even think about what I was saying. I could feel my face getting red. I tried to suppress an embarrassed laugh and looked down, away from her shocked expression. When I looked up again, she was smiling.

"Well, that's a pretty candid response," she said in a tone of voice that I wasn't sure how to interpret. "We'll see." She said, "We'll see." I felt like I had just been plugged into an electrical socket. I tried to act normal. As it turned out, I did spend the night that evening, and found myself beginning to fall helplessly in love.

Our relationship evolved quickly. Just to show how crazy I was for this girl, I came over one weekend and painted the outside of her whole house. I hate painting, but somehow it didn't seem that bad doing it for her.

On another occasion she asked me to go to the Branding Iron. I knew nothing about country music or country dancing, but I went willingly. That night was apparently "girls' night", and the place was featuring a bare chest contest as part of the night's entertainment. Chase urged me to sign up, so after several beers I did. It was embarrassing, since unlike a bodybuilding show, this was more like a striptease. There were five or six other guys up on the stage. I was the oldest by at least ten years. All the women in the place were hooting and screaming at the contestants. I was surprised when they announced that I won the contest. The prize was a bottle of cheap champagne. I think Chase was impressed, so I was on cloud nine.

It wasn't long after we met that I had to find new employment and got the job up in Cincinnati. When I told her what was going on with my career, she took the news with what seemed like passive acceptance. I wasn't sure how she really felt about this sudden change in my life and its impact on us as a couple. I was beside myself. I knew that the probability of a long distance relationship working out was slim. I told her that I wanted to continue to see her and that I hoped she felt the same. She said she did, but I knew this would be difficult.

The day that I had to leave for Cincinnati came too soon as far as my personal life was concerned. I told Chase that as soon as I got myself settled I hoped she could arrange to come up for a visit. It was a difficult goodbye, but off I went, to another chapter in my life.

# Chapter 65

Cincinnati is a great city. I was surprised by all that it has to offer. I found it to be very pedestrian, with lots of people on the downtown streets, coming and going to all sorts of activities. Life seemed so vibrant in that city, with all its museums, galleries, parks, theaters, and excellent restaurants. I ended up finding a little two bedroom house in the tiny old city of Deer Park, a little north of Cincinnati. It was one of those small, suburbia houses that were built just after World War II as part of the economic boom. The house was close to my new office, and I liked the old neighborhood where it was located.

I had a lot to learn at my new company. I had to learn about terminal emulation and about the Unisys systems that our products supported. Of course, I also had a new team to get to know and figure out how to lead. The people who developed the technology, who sold the products, and who provided all the support needed to make everything happen at this new company were like most people I had worked with in the past. They were all easy enough to get to know as individuals and groups. I liked them. As a manager, I'd like to think that I provided these people with the kind of leadership that made their professional life a little bit better, possibly more productive.

The senior management team was a mixed bag. Gerald, the man I directly reported to, was a good man, a straight shooter, and a very capable manager. The rest of the senior managers, however, did not provide me with a high degree of confidence, but the company was doing well. The senior managers did occasionally have their moments. The three founders had been together for several years and they were going through that awkward transition from being young, hell-raising entrepreneurs to more mature corporate managers. I think that they were finding this metamorphosis difficult. They hired a new CEO to help them with the transition just before I was brought on board.

Like most companies, ICC struggled with determining and then navigating the best course for success. This is what managing teams get paid to do, and it takes a team of talented people who are able to work well with each other to get it right. Working well together is the challenging part, due in large part to the fact that senior managers typically have large egos and alpha personalities. It takes a special kind of person to provide the vision, motivation and direction required to mold the senior managers into an effective, kickass team capable of taking a company to its highest potential. In my opinion, we still had some work to do in this department at ICC.

Sometimes the stress of dealing with senior management got to me. One evening, after a difficult day at the office, dealing with a few of these senior guys, I stood on my back porch with a large Jack Daniels Manhattan. I was fuming about one of the particularly aggravating events of that day.

"If I'd only ripped that asshole's head off and shit down his neck," I said out loud. This was a colorful metaphor that I learned during my military service, often used by assholes bullying some poor slob. This outburst was, of course, fueled by the Jack. While, this type of post-asshole therapy usually worked, on this particular evening it did not. I was stirred up.

I will admit that I have a low tolerance for people who act like assholes, and I would say that approximately half the world's population are assholes. I actually think that most of the people in the world would agree with that assessment. If you are not an asshole, you know that about half the people you run into are assholes. The people who are assholes typically won't admit that they are assholes, and ironically they think that everybody else is an asshole. So, we are essentially surrounded by assholes. They are the takers, the bullies, and the devious, self-centered, selfish people that make life less peaceful and comfortable than it should be. Unfortunately, it's pretty hard to get through a day without running into an asshole.

Assholes are not confined to any one group. Oh, no. An asshole can be a government worker or worker in the private sector. An asshole can be a cop, a fireman, a priest, a teacher, a plumber, a mechanic, an office worker or anything else. They can be young or old, male or female, any religion, any race, any nationality, any political persuasion. Those of us who are not assholes mostly just tolerate all of those people who are. Sure we get upset and angry, but we usually just suck it up and shake it off. We might complain about it to our friends or family, because an encounter with an asshole often upsets our whole day and we need to vent about it.

As my evening dragged on, stewing over this current encounter with assholes, I had an epiphany. What would happen if I behaved the same way as an asshole did when confronted by one? Could I even bring myself to consciously act like an asshole? A plan began to form in my mind. As the Jack Daniels coursed through my veins, my resolve strengthened.

The very next day I got my first opportunity to apply my theory. One of our senior executives loved to read books on self-improvement and new management techniques. It was kind of an inside joke around ICC that our management style would change about every 6 to 8 weeks to conform to the latest book this guy was reading. This executive was a very assertive man by nature, and loved to bully his management staff. He most recently had been reading a book that encouraged managers to keep subordinates "off balance". One of the techniques was to stand physically close to the other person when issuing directions, essentially invading their personal space. This was supposed to put them off balance so that you could assert whatever it was that you wanted to assert more effectively.

This executive called me to his office. As I entered the room, he got up from behind his desk and walked up to me, stopping approximately eight inches from my face. He started telling me what he wanted me to do about improving one of my projects. My immediate instinct was to back away from him since his closeness was extremely annoying, but I recognized this as a definite act of asshole-ism, so I steeled myself and retaliated.

I leaned in a little closer to him so that our noses were nearly touching, put my finger on his chest and, interrupting him, said in my most asshole-ish voice, "If you don't get out of my face, I'm going to kick your ass, right now, right here in this room." He immediately stepped back with an alarmed, embarrassed look on his face. He quickly stammered a summarization of the self-help book he was reading and that he was trying it out. I told him that the technique just pissed me off and made him look like an asshole.

We were on much better terms after that. The fact that I was a six foot two, 220 pound bodybuilder may have contributed some additional emphasis on the threat to kick his ass, but the point is that I put some reverse asshole on him and that caused him to changed his behavior. I felt like Spiderman must have felt when he first discovered that he had spidey powers!

Now, of course the average person has to apply some common sense to this counter-asshole stuff. I mean there are professional assholes out there – pathological monsters who will kill you or do serious bodily harm if you try to out asshole them. People should only use this "good asshole" technique on the run-of-the-mill assholes. Don't try to out asshole somebody who is exhibiting road rage, for example. You're likely to get run off the road or shot.

Generally though, I say that people should go out there and give it a try. The next time you go to the express lane at the grocery store, and there's somebody just ahead of you with half a cart of groceries and they have their checkbook in their hand, even though the sign clearly says "15 items or less, no checks", say to them, "Hey asshole! Can't you read? This is an express lane. " Then, yell at the checker, "Why the hell did you let this moron use this lane? Now all your customers with small orders have to stand here and wait for this asshole."

Sure, you're going to feel like an asshole, and everybody in the store is going to think you're an asshole, but the real asshole is going to get a piece of your mind right there in front of God and everybody. The real asshole will hopefully feel like a jerk, and everybody else will be secretly agreeing with you. You'll be able to go home and tell all your friends, "I was an asshole today, and I really told some other asshole off." Oh yeah, it will feel good. Pour yourself a glass of Jack Daniels and know that you have become a warrior for the good of mankind.

# Chapter 66

Chase arranged to come up for the initial visit to Cincinnati, and we had a great time. There was this little hole-in-the-wall, 1960s-era diner, called Chicken on the Run, which we visited a couple of times for dinner. There was definitely nothing fancy about this place. In fact, it was the antithesis of fancy, but the food was good. Burgers, fried chicken and chili were the main menu items. We could walk to it from my house, through the back yard and down a little alley, which made it even more fun.

During her visit, we made our own chili, which I called Buzzard's Breath. It contains ground beef, pork, and venison, as well as several different kinds of chilies. Two of the more unusual ingredients are tequila and cigar ashes. The ritual of making Buzzard's Breath chili includes drinking a shot of tequila and smoking a cigar, then pouring a healthy amount of the tequila into the chili and flicking the ashes into the pot as well. Sounds gross, but it's really good.

That first trip for Chase included an unpleasant surprise that I thought might dissuade her from ever considering Cincinnati as a place she might want to live. It happened to be the year and the exact month that the seventeen year cicada decided to emerge from their long underground existence. This is not a bug that most people can warm up to, being a large, black, winged creature with beady red eyes. They make a terrible racket as the males congregate to attract mates.

There were millions and millions of the bugs out and about upon Chase's arrival. They covered whole walls of some buildings. They were so many on some streets that cars would lose traction as if they were on ice. The bugs were so thick that it was difficult to get into or out of a car without one or more of the creatures getting inside. I tried to assure her that these things were not a normal part of the Cincinnati landscape.

Over the next several months, I would visit Chase down in Fort Lauderdale and she would come up to Cincinnati. She was completing her master's degree from Florida International University and teaching at the Davie high school, and I was very busy with my job. So it was challenging to arrange for visits that were frequent enough to keep the fires of passion burning. Despite this, we were growing closer, but the periods between visits seemed interminable.

Frequent phone calls were the principal way we kept the relationship going. On one of these calls Chase reminded me that she had completed her graduate degree program and that the school year was nearly over. She told me that she had given it a lot of thought and that she was ready to be married again. Now, there has been a considerable amount of spirited disagreement over the years about what was actually said and by whom, but from my recollection it sounded like I ought to be proposing if I wanted to keep her. On her next visit to Cincinnati I did just that, and she accepted.

We went to the County Clerk's Office to apply for our marriage license. Among other documents, we had to present our divorce papers from previous marriages. Chase had been married twice before, and I three times. When we placed the five bundles in front of the thin, elderly clerk, he looked at them for a moment, then looked up at us.

"My, my," he said, with a bit of twinkle in his eye, "We've had a bit of practice, haven't we?" We all laughed.

We were married in January on a cold, snowy winter day in Cincinnati. The wedding was not typical. For reasons that neither one of us can recall, we decided to have the ceremony in a Scottish Church, complete with bagpipes rather than the traditional organ. The bagpipes set off car alarms in the church's parking lot. Chase wore a beautiful, bright red wedding dress, and she looked like a movie star. The reception was at our new, much larger house, which we called Loge o' the Woods. I carried her over the threshold as snowball size snowflakes were coming down outside. We had a devil's food wedding cake with chocolate frosting. It all seemed perfect for who we were and where we were at that time in our lives.

# Chapter 67

My company began a vigorous effort to get themselves acquired by another company. This, understandably, makes most employees nervous. Since the company was doing quite well, it seemed very likely that a transaction would eventually occur. I tried not to think too much about it, and continued to do my part to maintain our technology development commitments.

Ultimately, ICC was acquired by a company, called DCA. They had similar, complimentary products, which made the merger look like a good idea, at least on paper. It is no secret that an alarming percentage of corporate mergers and acquisitions fail to meet financial expectations and ultimately fail altogether. The human toll on employees is significant, so the general angst that accompanies these transactions is well founded.

For me personally, the acquisition resulted in the elimination of my position. This is also quite common, so I wasn't really surprised. In fact, I had anticipated this possibility, and when I was required to go to the new company's headquarters in Georgia, I made a point to talk to as many senior managers as I could in order to determine their plans for the future. As a result, I learned that they had decided to form a new international division, with an initial focus on Asia.

I arranged to meet with the executive who was charged with bootstrapping and managing the new unit. He was one of the most disagreeable people that I ever ran into during my career. When I told him that my position was going to be eliminated, and that I would therefore be available, and that I had just the right experience for helping get the new business going, he was rudely skeptical. I frankly don't think he had a clear idea of what he was going to do or how he was going to do it, but I kept my opinions to myself and persisted.

During our discussions, this executive revealed that they planned to start in Japan and that they had a partner there lined up, a company called Softbank. I did my homework and discovered that Softbank was one of the largest public corporations in the world, involved in communications and related technologies. They were looking for an American company to work with them to develop a double byte character set for terminal emulation. At that time, American emulation products only supported single byte characters, which could not accommodate ideographic characters commonly used in Asia to represent language.

I really wanted to be part of this, but it didn't look like this executive was sold on me being the ideal resource. I recalled that my friend and colleague, Maximus, was raised in Japan and could speak and even write Japanese. Maximus had come up from Florida to attend at our wedding, and I knew that he was concerned about his position at Encore. I contacted him to see if he would be interested in a project like the one DCA was planning in Japan, and he was enthusiastic about the prospect. I shamelessly offered Maximus as a bonus resource if I were put in charge of managing this startup Asian effort. I got the job.

I actually knew nothing about double byte characters and less about ideographic languages, but ignorance about something I'm about to do had never stopped me before. With Maximus's help, I quickly boned up on the subject. I was a bit daunted by the fact that every Asian country seemed to have their own proprietary code set for enabling the display of their characters on computer screens. On the bright side, however, this situation would ensure that there was plenty of work to be done.

As I became more involved in this work I found that it was much more complex than just the challenges of managing the codification of Chinese, Japanese, and Korean characters. Like so many other things that were happening in the computer industry at this time, there were many competing efforts underway at the same time by companies like IBM, Apple, and Microsoft, not to mention the movement toward establishing a multi-byte standard, called Unicode, to facilitate the internationalization of software. The good news, at least at that time, was that all this turmoil kept us very busy.

# Chapter 68

Maximus did join the team, and our first effort was to establish an office in Tokyo. Over time we ultimately traveled to Korea, Hong Kong, Singapore, and Malaysia as well. We were invited to work with Microsoft in their language lab in Redmond, Washington. It was an exciting time professionally, but the best experiences actually involved food and drink.

One of the most memorable experiences happened one night after work in Tokyo. Maximus could speak perfect Japanese and knew more things about Tokyo than practically anybody. His Japanese was so good that Japanese people tended to forgot that they were talking to an American gaijin. On my first visit to Tokyo, Maximus took me to a place where we could have a drink at the end of the first day. This place was an izakaya. These were ubiquitous, casual places for after-work drinking. They traditionally have red paper lanterns in the front of the shops, and so they are more commonly called "red lanterns".

Maximus had previously described how most Japanese businessmen, referred to as "salarymen", go to these red lantern places after work to drink and eat for several hours before heading for the train station and home. He told me that a lot, maybe most of business deals get pounded out at these establishments. I was curious and wanted to see what they were like.

We entered a nearby red lantern and it was immediately obvious that we stuck out like a pair of sore thumbs. Both Maximus and I could not look any more gaijin, which is to say less Japanese, with our light brown hair, six foot plus height, and

Anglo faces. The place seemed inordinately quiet for a place where a lot of business was supposedly being conducted. The Japanese people are very polite, so they were studiously avoiding outright staring, but I could feel a disturbance in the Force.

We sat down and a young woman eventually approached our table to take our order, reluctantly I thought. She first provided us with two wet towels. Maximus explained that this was typical and that we were supposed to wipe our hands with them.

After cleaning our hands, Maximus simply said, "Two Sapporos please," in English, holding up two fingers.

The young woman bowed and walked away. I asked Maximus why he didn't order in Japanese. He said he wasn't comfortable doing that in that place. I shrugged my shoulders and we started discussing the day's activities. As we sat, drank our beer, and talked, the salarymen around us eventually began talking to each other again. We ordered another beer, and were already feeling the effects of the brew on our empty stomachs.

I casually looked around the place and noticed that many of the tables had bottles of what looked like whisky on them. The men at those tables were drinking the spirit in little glasses.

"I'd like to try Japanese whisky," I said to Maximus. "Could we order some?"

"This place has a bottle keep service," he replied. "The guys drinking whisky are drinking from their own bottles. They keep them here. I don't think that they have whiskey on the menu."

"Oh," I said. "There are bottle clubs back in the States too. Well, maybe at some point during my visit we could find a place where I could try it."

"They're talking about us," Maximus suddenly said in a very low voice, looking down at the table.

"What?" I said. "What do you mean?"

"Most of the guys in this place are talking about us, saying that we should not be in here," he elaborated. "They are referring to us in unflattering terms."

I laughed. "Why don't you say something to me in Japanese and see what kind of reaction that gets."

"No," he said emphatically, "That would be rude."

"Rude? Aren't they being rude?" I asked, still laughing. "Come on. You've got no balls if you don't say something in Japanese. Let's see. You could say that I will have to wait to try Japanese whisky until tomorrow night when we have dinner with the Softbank managers. That ought to catch them off guard."

He was reluctant, but the beer and my goading were breaking down his resistance. Suddenly, he started speaking to me in Japanese, just loud enough to be heard by others. He looked straight at me as he spoke. I knew practically no Japanese, but I did have a few expressions that I had memorized. I pulled one out of my hat that I thought would be appropriate for whatever he said.

"Oh, wakarimasu," I said as I nodded my head, which means "I understand". Then in English, "Well then, should we have another beer?"

The place went dead silent. Nobody looked up from their tables to look at us. They just sat there. It was all I could do to keep from bursting out with laughter, but I knew that the salarymen were very proud and I did not want to insult them. I just thought it was a good joke. The young woman hurried over to our table, clearly unsettled. Maximus ordered two more beers in his flawless Japanese.

The young woman came back to our table with the two beers, but she also had several of the small glasses of whisky on her tray and proceeded to place them on our table. She said something to Maximus in Japanese. He nodded his head, then looked out across the room. With a very serious look on his face, he lowered his head in a bow, and said, "Arigato gozaimasu." I knew that meant "thank you", so I followed suit.

I picked up one of the glasses, made a show of examining it, smelling its aroma, and took a sip. It tasted like Scotch, which I am not fond of, but I took a moment to savor its flavor and characteristics, then took another sip. I looked at Maximus and asked him how to say "good", in Japanese. I raised my glass toward the general direction of the room and said, "Totemo yo." That seemed to make everything alright. The room filled with lively conversation and everybody seemed in good spirits for the rest of the evening.

# Chapter 69

A couple of nights later, Mister Kishi asked Maximus and I to accompany him to dinner. Mister Kishi was the Softbank senior manager who was assigned to us as the business liaison to DCA. He was an older gentleman, who always reminded me of a character in the TV series, *Samurai*. He had a low, gravelly voice that reinforced that image of him. He was a very serious guy, but he seemed to enjoy working with us and wanted to show us around Tokyo.

Maximus told me that this invitation was special in that Mister Kishi needed to demonstrate his recognition of my status as an American manager and the importance of the joint venture that we were engaged in. I assured Maximus that I would be duly impressed no matter how the evening unfolded. It was, in fact, a night that I would not soon forget.

Mister Kishi picked us up at the hotel where I was staying. We took a taxi from there to the Shinjuku district where, according to Mister Kishi, the best restaurants in Tokyo were located. The taxi dropped us off in what seemed like an alley that might have been from a scene out of *Blade Runner*. I felt very much the foreigner in that place.

We entered a little yakitori bar. There was nothing fancy about the place, which surprised me a little considering the big build-up of the evening that Maximus painted. Mister Kishi directed us to a low bar that faced the charcoal braziers where the yakitori was prepared. The people working in the place seemed to know Mister Kishi and he spoke to them at some length. Of course, sake was served to us in short order and we toasted to the success of our business venture. Mister Kishi spoke quite a bit of English, but he often spoke in Japanese, asking Maximus to translate for me.

Yakitori is essentially chicken cut into small, bite-sized parts which are skewered and cooked on a small charcoal brazier using a special binchotan charcoal. During cooking, the meat is seasoned with a dipping sauce. It's also served with one or more sauces. The chicken can be just about any part of the chicken you can imagine. As we drank sake, we discussed business plans and plates of different yakitori were eventually served. We would each take a small portion of the skewered meat and put it on an individual, smaller plate set before each of us.

Mister Kishi was sitting on one side of Maximus and I on the other to facilitate the translation. Maximus told me later that this translating while eating and drinking wore him out mentally. This was the beginning of the evening, and I was focusing on the conversation, trying to play my part as the bigshot American manager representing our company. I was absent-mindedly eating whatever yakitori was put before me. It all looks pretty much the same when it arrives from the grill.

The yakitori that we were served was quite delicious. After three or four different versions had been consumed, accompanied by copious amounts of sake, yet another skewer was presented. Mister Kishi took the skewer and portioned out the meat. Maximus slid my plate over to me. I was engaged in a detailed conversation with Mister Kishi, in English, when I picked up the morsel on my plate with my chop sticks. While Mister Kishi was responding to my last statement, I put the food into my mouth and bit down on something that had the texture of a dry piece of shredded wheat and tasted like musty dirt.

I immediately stopped chewing, and looked down at Maximus's as yet untouched plate to see if I could identify what was in my mouth. Perhaps the expression on my face belied my distress. Mister Kishi stopped talking and Maximus looked over to see what was going on. I knew that it could be insulting to reject food that didn't appeal to you in many Asian countries, but there was no way that I was going to chew and swallow this thing that was in my mouth. I could see from Maximus's plate that it was a newly hatched, baby chicken. Maybe it wasn't even hatched for all I knew.

I was panicking, but I had to get it out of my mouth. With what I hoped was a look of apology, I picked up my little plate and let the little abomination drop out unceremoniously. I immediately began to apologize. I told them that I just could not eat this. Mister Kishi seemed not to be offended at all and laughed heartily. Maximus seemed to only then take notice of what had been served. He nonchalantly told me what it was called in Japanese then picked his portion up and ate it without any apparent reaction. His only comment was that it was a bit crunchy. Maximus was widely known to be able to eat just about anything, including the worm at the bottom of a bottle of Mescal.

We left the yakitori place shortly thereafter, with me still worrying that I had failed in some way at corporate diplomacy. I assumed that the evening dinner was over, and was surprised when we entered another eating establishment several doors down from the yakitori bar.

This new place was also quite small and dark, lacking any evidence of opulence. We were seated at a traditional Japanese table. This was a challenge for me since the table required one to sit on a cushion on the floor. Typically, people sat crossed legged at this kind of table, but I found that unbearably uncomfortable. I tried to put my long legs under the table, which Mister Kishi assured me would be okay, but that wasn't much better. I knew that I had to just deal with it.

Mister Kishi appeared to know the people at this restaurant quite well. He had a long conversation with a man whom I took to be the owner. I noticed that Maximus was making gestures and sounds of great surprise during the conversation, all in Japanese.

Finally, he turned to me and explained that Mister Kishi had asked the owner to provide us with a very rare ceremony that was supposed to increase our virility. I could see that Maximus was either impressed or alarmed or perhaps both. I merely nodded, trying to look appropriately impressed, and hoping it didn't involve another whole baby chicken.

I was told that this place specialized in eel and that this is what we would be served tonight. I had never eaten eel, and I was not very enthusiastic about the prospect. We were sitting next to a large tank where the snake-like creatures were swimming around, looking more like snakes than a fish. I didn't have much time to think about it. Two men came out of what must have been the kitchen and walked up to the tank. They had a very large wooden bowl, which they sat on the end of our table. At the same time, a woman brought a very small, ornate sake service to the table and carefully set a thimble-sized cup in front of each of us. Maximus explained that this sake would be very cold. This was a welcome distraction, but I had not yet made any connection with the mini sake set and what was about to happen.

It all happened so quickly. The two men pulled three eels from the tank and placed the writhing creatures in the large bowl. I backed up a couple of inches in reaction. While one man held one of the eels, the other man made a quick slit down its body. At the same time, the woman carefully poured the chilled sake into our tiny cups. The man with the knife then opened up the eel's body and plucked its heart out, placing it in one of the cups of sake. This process was done twice more until Mister Kishi, Maximus, and I all had a pumping eel heart bobbing around in our sake cups.

Mister Kishi ceremoniously raised his cup, saying something in Japanese that by its tone sounded very solemn. The restaurant owner and staff stood there in similar solemn witness to the spectacle. I found myself holding my little cup, wide-eyed and too shocked to do anything but follow suit. Suddenly, Mister

Kishi and Maximus knocked back the contents of their cups. Before I had time to think about it I drank mine in one gulp as well. Then it was done. I had a pumping eel heart inside me. Another cup of the cold sake was poured, which was also consumed with some kind of formal toast or incantation.

The bowl of eels was quickly removed from our table and the cold sake tokkuri, as I discovered the tiny sake set was called, was replaced by a larger vessel containing sake at room temperature. Mister Kishi poured this sake into our new, larger cups, which are called choko. Then Maximus poured sake into Mister Kishi's choko. I was becoming increasingly aware of the ritual and subtle protocol that Japanese considered important. Although I was not certain of the significance of all that had just happened, I had the presence of mind to know that I had been privileged to be part of something special, so I thanked Mister Kishi as formally as I knew how.

The eels meanwhile were grilled and ultimately served to us on a bed of rice. I was told that these were Japanese freshwater eels, called Unagi. Despite their unappealing look when they were writhing around on our table, having their hearts plucked out, the dish was quite delicious. The dinner was followed by more sake and more business discussion.

When we got up to leave, I wasn't sure my legs would unknot and work again, but I managed to walk out without falling down. We were all feeling quite nice at this point, thanks to the sake. We walked a couple of blocks down this same street that seemed almost surreal with all of its exotic lights, and sounds, and smells, and people. We stopped in front of another restaurant. Mister Kishi was saying something in Japanese to Maximus, who had a dubious expression on his face. We entered the place. More food?

Once again, Mister Kishi was greeted as a person who was well known and we were immediately seated at a table, despite the crowd that was apparently waiting to be seated. Maximus still had a funny look on his face, one that I recognized as the look he wore when he wasn't completely sold on something. Mister Kishi kept talking to Maximus in Japanese as if he was reassuring him or trying to convince him of something. Maximus was not translating. I was just incredulous that we were apparently going to eat again. I can't say that I was stuffed, but I certainly wasn't hungry.

A small bowl of edamame was placed on the table along with three large glasses of liquid, each covered with a lid. I looked at Maximus questioningly.

"It's sake," he explained.

"Why does it have a lid?" I asked.

"That's just the way they serve it here," he said with a wave of his hand.

I lifted the lid on my glass. Floating on the top of the clear liquid was what looked like a fish tail. I stared at it for a moment, and then looked up at Maximus, who seemed to be studiously avoiding my look.

"Is that I fish tail," I finally asked.

"Hai," Mister Kishi answered, then in English. "It is special sake to go with the sakana, anno, fish we are going to have."

"Oh, great," I said. I was contemplating how I was going to get through this large glass of sake, given the amount we had already consumed that evening. "Are you supposed to leave the fish tail in the glass, or take it out?"

"You can take it out," Maximus said.

Some time passed, and we continued to talk about business, but I was having a hard time concentrating through my increasing alcoholic haze. How in the hell did these Japanese businessmen manage to get business done after drinking all night?

At length, a woman brought a large platter to our table and set it in the middle. It was amazing. I knew it was fish, since that's what Mister Kishi said we were having, but I had never seen anything like it. It looked like a lace doily spread out on the plate. The raw white flesh was cut so thin that I could see through it. There was some shaved ginger and some other garnishes on the plate and little bowls of sauces off to the side. It was quite beautiful, perhaps the most beautiful dish I had ever seen.

A man, who I took to be the owner, came over to the table, as well as another man who I assumed was the chef. There was a great deal of exchange between these men and Mister Kishi, who was obviously expressing his admiration of the dish. Everybody suddenly looked at me. I tried to express my admiration as best I could in English. Mister Kishi gestured toward the dish for me to try it. I wasn't sure how to approach such a dish.

Maximus suddenly leaned forward and put his hand on the table. He looked grave. "I think you should know that this is fugu."

I looked at him, trying to comprehend what that meant. All I could muster was, "Ah. Well, it's wonderful. How does one eat it?"

"Fugu is from the Puffer Fish," he continued. "It can be fatal if it is not prepared exactly right."

"Ah," I said again, looking at the dish in a slightly more circumspect manner.

"It is okay," Mister Kishi quickly interjected. "Most experienced cook in Japan," motioning to one of the men standing next to our table. He said something in Japanese to the two men, who immediately started trying, I assume, to reassure me in Japanese that it was very safe.

Well, I had already spit out a baby bird and drank a pumping eel heart that evening, and I was by now quite shitfaced. Without much more thought on the matter I picked up a delicate, translucent piece of the sashimi with my chopsticks and put it in my mouth. It was delicious. It was more than delicious, it was absolutely wonderful. The expression on my face must have revealed my reaction. I took another piece and dipped it in a dark sauce. "Wonderful," I said.

They actually started clapping. Even people at other tables, who must have been taking in the scene were clapping. Mister Kishi helped himself to some of the fugu. Maximus finally tried some. None of us died, so I presume that chef knew what he was doing. I discovered later that the preparation of this dish was indeed very controlled by the Japanese government, but that people did die after eating fugu that was not properly prepared. I also found out later that this dish was amazingly expensive, that in fact, the eel dinner was also very expensive. Maximus told me later that the evening's fare probably set Mister Kishi back a couple thousand dollars or more.

After the fugu, Mister Kishi suggested that we go to a club that he belonged to. Maximus protested. He looked like he was about to drop. I told Mister Kishi that I thought I should probably go back to my hotel, as I was still trying to get used to the time change. In fact, I was blind drunk and it took all of my concentration to try to keep from doing something or saying something stupid or just passing out. Mister Kishi said that he understood and got us back to my hotel.

Unfortunately for Maximus, Mister Kish also belonged to a club in that hotel and he insisted that I accompany him there for a nightcap. This guy must have a lot of money, I thought, and he damn sure has more stamina than I do. I told him that I would have just one drink with him.

The club was yet another amazing place. It was what I would call an English hunt club atmosphere, with dark paneled walls, richly appointed furnishings, including plush leather chairs, a wall full of very expensive looking books, a large fireplace, and a remarkable bar. Mister Kishi gathered some glasses and a bottle of expensive Japanese whisky. He asked if I wanted ice, to which I said I did. Maximus seemed comatose and declined any further alcohol. He was no longer serving as an interpreter, so Mister Kishi and I managed some light conversation on our own.

Upon finishing my drink, I thanked Mister Kishi profusely for a magnificent evening, for being such a gracious host, and asked him to excuse Maximus and me, as we needed to get some sleep. He told me that he looked forward to working with me as I staggered out of the room. This international business thing is hard work I tell you.

# Chapter 70

Chase and I both liked living in Cincinnati. It was close enough to both our families that we could visit more frequently. We had developed very good friendships with many of the people there, and the city was just a fun place to live, with lots of diverse attractions.

Chase was in the process of trying out a couple of different paths for her personal and professional development. I think that she had mixed emotions about leaving her teaching career in Florida. She did a little substitute teaching in Cincinnati, but was more focused on trying her hand in the private sector. She got a position as an event coordinator with a local company, which seemed to suit her. She also volunteered as a docent at the Cincinnati Museum of Natural History, which was housed in the old Union Terminal. She took a particular liking to the care of a colony of Brown Bats that were part of the exhibit.

Things were going quite well with my new Asian projects, but then we got the news that DCA had been acquired by another company, a competitor. That meant only one thing as far as I was concerned. I was going to be out of a job again.

I contacted a former colleague from Gould, Jack Camp. He had been with Gould's government group, and I worked with him on a project that included placing special SEL real-time systems in the U.S. embassies around the world. During that project I had to visit NSA headquarters in Langley, Virginia, to work on a problem with the communications subsystem. During that visit, I was escorted to a little room containing only a chair next to a counter with a turnstile on which I was given a green bar printout of highly redacted code. It was so obscure that I was never able to do anything with it.

During this project, Jack and I got to know one another, and we kept in touch from time to time. As fate would have it, when I contacted him to see what he was up to and to tell him that I would probably need to look for a job soon, he told me that he had just negotiated a deal with a company out in San Diego, California, and was looking for somebody to help him sort things out there operationally.

I did some research on the company and found that it developed and sold data communication products to an impressive list of clients. However, I noticed that the products were pretty dated and that the communication protocols they had developed were mostly very specific to what I considered obscure applications such as radar tracking, command and control, battlefield communications, air traffic control, various military functions. The business was extremely profitable, enjoying an 80-plus percent profit margin, but it was clearly going to have to sunset most of their products in the not-to-distant future. I was sure I could help this company move into the future.

I signed on with Jack and the company in San Diego. Chase and I had mixed emotions about leaving Cincinnati and moving out to California, but we felt that it would ultimately be a good move. It would be yet another adventure. We had no trouble selling Loge o' the Woods. In fact, it sold a few days after we listed it.

After the moving company loaded the majority of our stuff, we packed up everything that we wanted to keep with us on our road trip, including my wine collection. We were about to head out west when the biggest winter storm to ever hit the Midwest happened on the very day we were scheduled to leave. The Interstates closed down due to ice and blizzard conditions. We stayed with friends until the roads opened, then got on the road, heading due south to warmer latitudes. We were getting out of the cold North just in time.

It took us three and a half days, to get to San Diego. From Cincinnati we headed for Memphis to pick up Interstate 40, then on to Little Rock to get on Interstate 30 to Dallas. Past Dallas, we used Interstate 20 to get to Interstate 10, then to Interstate 8 in Arizona. Interstate 8 took us right into San Diego. We were looking forward to living in a place where the weather was warm. As we crossed over the Cuyamaca Mountains, only 30 miles from the San Diego City line, it started to snow.

"What!" I exclaimed. "How can it be snowing? We're only 30 miles from San Diego." I wasn't considering that we were above 4000 feet in the mountain pass. The snow eventually turned into rain, and we entered our new home town in the midst of a torrential winter rainstorm.

I was excited to be out West. I loved the time that my family lived in New Mexico, and my previous time in California. I think that I must have been a cowboy in another life. Things just felt comfortable out here. I think that Chase was a little more apprehensive, but she was definitely being a good sport about the move.

We ended up in a little village called Ramona, in a non-incorporated, eastern part of San Diego County. That part of the county was generally referred to as the "back country" and it was just the kind of place I wanted to be. I felt renewed in this place. Our first home was in a large, master-planned community, just outside Ramona proper. It was considered an affluent resort complex that featured two equestrian centers, a golf course, tennis courts, and dining facilities. The vast majority of the home there were custom, so the community didn't look like a cookie-cutter development.

One of the main reasons we were drawn to this community was that the homes were a good value compared to those closer to San Diego. The majority of the lots were half an acre, and keeping horses was permitted. Although at the time we didn't plan on having horses, it just seemed like a cool option. One of the trade-offs was the drive into the greater San Diego area, which is where my new company was located. My commute was one hundred miles a day, round trip, but it didn't seem so bad since much of it was in the beautiful back country.

Once we got settled, I dug into my responsibilities at the new company. My initial job was to evaluate the condition of the company's product development and operations, determine what should be salvaged and what should be trimmed, and that included staff. Not the most comfortable role one could have. Chase started looking for teaching opportunities and did some substitute teaching. She seemed to be ready to get back into education.

Although we didn't know it at the time, we were on the cusp of a new beginning that was to be very different than we had ever imagined. Chase did restart her teaching career at the local high school in the art department, and I continued to progress in my career. The real new beginning though was in our life style.

# Part V

## The Grown-up Man

*But then I was a cowboy*
*I got a horse*
*And a hat of course*
*I ride off in the sunsets*

# Chapter 71

The old man had just finished his lunch and was back up in his room. He had just completed the part of the book that he had been dreading because it dealt with some things that he was not entirely comfortable with in retrospect. He wondered if any of his previous wives or female intimates would ever read the book. A wry smile formed on his face at the thought. He was assuming that anybody at all would actually read the book.

He had known authors during his life. Some had been very successful, but some had no luck in getting published at all. There was one author in particular that he remembered, a young man that he thought was talented, but as far as he knew that fellow never got anything published other than his technical writing. His name was Larry, and he worked as a technical writer in the old man's communications group at Gould. Larry had let him read one of his manuscripts. It started with the discovery of a small child's skeleton under the floorboards in the attic of an old house. The old man thought it was going to be a really terrific book, a best seller, but it never came to pass. That book never got published.

Of course, these days one could always self-publish, what with all the modern technology and self-publishing retailers, such as Amazon, Barnes & Noble, Smashwords, and others. There was no shortage of authors who were using this route to get their work published. There were issues to consider in using that approach, however, like plagiarism. Well, he guessed he would cross that bridge when he came to it, as his mother would say. After all, he wasn't writing a romance novel or an action-thriller. Those were the popular books, the books that people actually bought, and plagiarized. For now, he was just trying to document his story. He thought he could at least get his family to read it, with a little coaxing.

Suddenly, his cell phone rang. He could tell from the custom ring tone that it was his wife. That was odd, he thought. Wasn't she down at the barn?

"Hello," he answered.

"Hi," Chase said. "Can you come down to the barn to help me? I'm having trouble getting Jerry Lee back in the stall."

"Ok," he said simply. "Be right down," and hung up.

He got up immediately and headed down the stairs. He knew better than to keep her waiting. Chase had recently adopted two donkeys, ostensibly to keep her horse, Scout, company. The horse in fact, didn't seem to like the donkeys at all and often charged at them with his ears pinned back. The old man decided that he should not try to dissuade her from getting the animals, since she seemed to have her heart set on them. Besides, they appeared to give her a renewed enthusiasm for getting involved in ranch activities. She named them Elvis and Jerry Lee. Elvis was practically a lap dog, but Jerry Lee was kind of wild. The old man thought that they were both basically useless, but noticed that visitors seemed to think that they were a great attraction.

After they got the donkeys back in their stall, Chase commenced with cleaning up manure. On the other side of the stall, the old man fussed quietly to himself over having to clean donkey, horse, and cow shit off his shoes. It was winter, which meant that the vineyards were dormant and the winery work was minimal. There was always work to be done on the ranch, but this time of year was slower than during other seasons. He headed back up to the house.

He stopped halfway up. That sound, he suddenly noticed it again. It really hadn't just started, he realized, but rather he had just started to notice it. Yes, it had been there all along, but it just now wormed its way into his consciousness. How odd it was, he thought. On an impulse he began walking toward the north side of the canyon, in a direction that he sensed the sound might be coming from. He had not explored this part of the canyon the last time he tried to determine something more about the source. In fact, he had almost forgotten about it.

He wondered if his neighbor might see him walking across the property. The neighbor's house was built up at the top of the small mountain that punctuated the middle of the canyon between Starlight Mountain and Blackhorse Mountain. If the neighbor was near a window, it would be hard to miss anybody walking around below. The old man decided to just go for it.

On the south side of the neighbor's mountain, the side that faced toward the old man's ranch, was a gigantic, bare-faced granite rock. It looked to be the equivalent of four or five stories from the base to the top. The top of the mountain is where the neighbor's house stood as a sentinel tower keeping watch over the entire valley and all its inhabitants. The old man headed for the western side of the rock face, which was the opposite side from where the neighbor's driveway made its way up and around the mountain.

As he drew nearer to the base of the rock face, he could swear that the sound grew more intense, not especially louder, but more insistent. At the far left of the huge rock face, he noticed that the mountain began to break up, looking more like giant, house-sized boulders than solid, bare rock. At the point where the bare rock appeared to end, he saw what looked like a large crack. As he drew near, he could see that this crack was a place where a massive piece of the rock had split apart from the main rock face. He judged it to be ten or twelve feet high and maybe three feet wide at the bottom. The top of the split narrowed to a point where it became a hairline crack in the mountain.

He walked up closer to the crack and stood there for a moment. The sound still did not seem to have a directional aspect to it, but it was definitely more intense right there in front of the crack. Well, well, he thought. He had toyed with a hypothesis that the sound might be coming from the earth itself. Given the geology of the surrounding area, predominately decomposing granite, and the probability of numerous faults and underground aquifers, he thought it was entirely possible that some phenomenon could create a vibration that manifested itself as a subsonic sound.

He was beginning to feel pretty good about this hypothesis, and actually had a smile on his face, when he suddenly realized that the space within the crack didn't look right. He inched a little closer and leaned forward to get a closer look. The space looked, artificial. It reminded him of how the old TV screens looked when you were on a channel that didn't have anything broadcasting on it, kind of like a million black and white bugs buzzing wildly around each other. This space, however, was much, much darker. Maybe fuzzy was a good way to describe it. How odd, he thought.

He impulsively picked up a small stone and tossed it into the crack to see what there was to see. Nothing in particular happened, but he noticed that the rock just sort of disappeared. He didn't see it go back into the space or hit the ground. He had only tossed it in what should have been a foot or so. It was like the shadows beyond the crack swallowed up the light. Yes, very odd indeed, he thought.

He stood there thinking about what, if anything he should do next. Maybe it was time to talk to somebody else about this. He looked around to see if there was anything else that seemed peculiar about this area, but everything looked normal as far as he could tell. He walked a few feet away and broke off a branch from a Buckwheat Sage bush. He broke off all the smaller branches until he had a bare stick with just the end of the dark green foliage still intact. He wanted to see what would happen if he stuck this stick into the space while still holding it.

He slowly walked back to the crack, his apprehension building as he formulated his little experiment. He was just making this up as he went, his impulsive curiosity now in control. Without further contemplation of potential consequences, he slowly pushed the end of the stick into the space in the crack. There was no sound, no visible change, but he could feel movement on his end of the stick, as though the other end was being gently agitated by a light breeze. He pushed the stick further in until his hand was only an inch or so from the edge of the fuzzy, dark space. There was no change. He pushed further still, slowly, ready to pull back quickly if necessary. There was still no change in the stick, but his hand felt slightly cooler and he could sense the slightest, nearly imperceptible vibration. But it was definitely there.

He pulled his hand and the stick out and examined both. There was no change that he could see. His curiosity was now on overload. He wondered what the heck this was. Why couldn't he see beyond the opening? He was contemplating yet another tenuous experiment, possibly sticking his head in to see if there was anything to see. He thought that maybe he should go get some rope and tie one end around a rock and the other around his waist. He wasn't sure why this might be a reasonable thing to do or if the rope would actually do any good, but he didn't want to just charge in where angels might fear to tread. He was sure his mother would have had a saying for this occasion.

Just then, however, a small rock came out of the space and rolled to a stop just next to his feet. He picked it up and examined it. He was pretty sure it was the same rock he threw into the space a few moments before. The hair on the back of his neck and arms prickled up. What the hell? He turned around and headed back toward his house.

He went back up to his desk and sat down in front of his laptop. He ought to continue writing his book, but he just sat there staring at the screen. He needed to process what had happened, trying to decide what to do next. He thought he might try doing some research on Google, but research on what? Because he didn't know what else to do, he typed in "dark spaces between a crack in the earth". Although he knew that you could type in just about anything and get some kind of information back, he was a little surprised to find an article entitled "The Crack in Space", on Wikipedia. Good old Wikipedia always has something, he thought.

The article summarized a 1966 science fiction novel that described a transport machine that developed a defect creating a portal that led to an alternate, parallel world. It was actually an interesting article, but he doubted that it had anything to do with his crack in the earth. The rock coming back out of the space within the crack really blew his mind. Did somebody or something throw it back out to him? Could there be a parallel world like the one described in the article?

What the hell was he thinking, shaking his head and rubbing his face? There had to be some real scientific explanation for this phenomenon, but he thought that he should do a little more empirical research of his own before calling in the, well whoever one calls in for such things. He thought that maybe he should go back to the site when the sound went away. That did happen occasionally. If the space disappeared or changed when the sound was absent, that would at least connect the two things once and for all.

He decided to get his mind off this craziness and focus back on his book. He was getting to the part that he thought he would enjoy the most. After moving to California, things had really changed for him in a very positive way. He felt that he had finally "grown up" as he and Chase settled into their new life here. Yet, there had still been many adventures that had taken them to places that neither of them had ever thought they might end up.

This is the part of his book that would ultimately take him to the present. In some ways it felt a little like the end of the line, but he knew that he had many years left, at least he hoped so. He and Chase had just retired, and he was looking forward to enjoying the retirement years. After all that had happened in his life, he wondered what could possibly be ahead that could be as interesting and adventurous as his past. Maybe a trip to a parallel world, he thought sarcastically, laughing out loud.

He was about to start writing, when one of his dogs, a Doberman Pinscher named Pepper Potts, came down the hall and up to his desk. Her little bobbed tail was wagging enthusiastically, and she gave him a wet kiss. He greeted her affectionately. It must be dinner time, he thought, and looked at the time. His other Dobie, Rayne, also made an appearance. It was feeding time at the ranch and nobody around here ever missed a meal. He thought he also heard the steers bellowing and the donkeys braying. Good Grief! He supposed that it was only moments before Chase would be asking him if he'd given any thought to dinner.

"Honey," she called up from downstairs just then, "did you take anything out for dinner?"

He smiled. He loved that girl. He would get back to the book tomorrow. Right now, it was time to feed and have a glass of wine.

# Chapter 72

Our new home was very close to one of the community's equestrian centers. We were both curious to see what the facility had to offer, so we took a walk to see what there was to see. This facility was called the Western Equestrian Center, and it provided a large number of indoor and outdoor horse stalls, training and exercise rings, and storage for things like hay, feed, and tack. The other equestrian facility, we soon discovered, was called the International Equestrian Center, and it catered to so-called English style riding. That center also included a full race track, and an honest to God bull fighting ring.

The whole community was connected by a labyrinth of riding trails, and there was an open space preserve, maintained by San Diego's Parks and Recreation, which was accessible by horseback from the Estates' trails. All of this was set in a beautiful, mountainous setting that seemed to beg you go get on a horse and explore it.

We got the horse bug to be sure, and it was not long before we acquired a couple of horses. We initially kept them at the Western Equestrian Center, but soon had a small barn built in back of our house, complete with two 12 x 24 foot stalls. As we went through the process of acquiring all the necessary tack and associated accoutrements that come with owning horses, it became obvious that this was an expensive hobby, along the lines of owning a sailboat for example. Not only did we dive into the substantial investment of horse stuff, we started going cowboy.

Partly to get to know people in the local community and partly to get to know people who actually knew something about horses, we got involved as volunteers with the Ramona Rodeo. In order to look the part, we bought cowboy clothes, hats, and boots. As part of this familiarization process, we got to know the wrangler at the Western Equestrian Center who managed a horse rental outfit for the nearby time share Resort. People called him Wrangler Dan.

Wrangler Dan was the great grandson of Augustus Barnett, one of the founders of Ramona, who, in 1894, built and donated the Town Hall to what was then the town of Nuevo. Dan was a bit of a local character, but a hell of a nice guy, and he knew just about everything there was to know about horses. He taught us a lot about riding and caring for our horses. He was definitely into the cowboy thing, and through him we met a number of other cowboys and cowboy wannabe's.

Even with the advantage of retrospect, it is difficult to explain how our lives transformed so dramatically during this time. Having horses and being a cowboy had never entered my mind prior to moving to Ramona. I think that we just got caught up in the spirit of the West or something. It didn't happen overnight. It was a relatively slow process that seemed totally natural as it evolved. The only way that I became aware that our new lifestyle might be considered unusual was when professional colleagues started making comments about the way we dressed when we were not in our "day job" clothes. The transition was fun, and we just kept getting further and further into it.

After a couple of years of riding and getting to know our little group of cowboys, we started an unofficial gang, called the Moonlight Riders. Wrangler Dan was our de facto leader, and he would take us up to Blackhorse Mountain, also known as Mount Gower, just about every month on or about the full moon. Yes, we rode up into the mountains at night using just the light of the moon to make our way. We all dressed in cowboy gear, including batwing chaps, dusters, kerchiefs, boots and spurs, the works. Most of us had saddlebags as part of our tack, and these were all filled with as much beer as they could hold. A couple guys would also bring flasks of whisky.

Chase was the only female member of this notorious gang. Her horse, Pearl, was a mare that seemed to be in perpetual heat, which made the damn thing ornery as hell. Despite being mounted on this horse from hell, the rough-around-the-edges nature of several of the male members, the copious drinking, and the inherently treacherous nature of the terrain, Chase was all-in and never missed a ride. She was a good sport, and the guys loved her.

# Chapter 73

Chase eventually got a full-time teaching position at the local high school. I lost my job.

Things at my company, the company that we had managed to turn around, were actually going quite well, but Jack's wife got the offer of a lifetime back in Virginia, and he decided to give up his position as CEO. I didn't want to be a CEO, so I worked with the board of directors to find a replacement for Jack. We hired a man who had enjoyed tremendous success in a former venture and seemed to be one of those "golden boys" of business. Unfortunately, he was swayed to the dark side by the two dinosaurs that Jack and I hadn't gotten rid of during the transition to the new product focus.

These two guys didn't like me, at all. They fought me tooth and nail ever since I had taken over the development and operations of the company. They wanted to stay firmly ensconced in the past with their very profitable old products. The new CEO didn't seem to catch on to the necessity of driving toward the future vision thing, and he fired me. I was incredulous. I essentially hired this bozo and he fires me. If there could be a bright side to this experience, it was the day I got to exercise my "I told you so" rights a year later. The company shut down. What a waste.

I was able to land on my feet. Jack offered me another position at a consulting group that he was working with. This venture didn't last long for either of us. It was another case of an unenlightened CEO, ill-equipped to manage growth through innovation. My computer career thus far had exposed me to the disappointing reality that many, far too many senior executives have achieved what is known as the "Peter Principal", which is to say that they have been promoted to their level of incompetence. Even those who seem to have enjoyed exceptional results in the past, are often little more than lucky, one-hit wonders. It was not very motivating, but I tried to take away whatever lessons I could from these experiences.

Jack found another opportunity very quickly, and brought me on to help with this one as well to help. Good ol' Jack. The only drawback was that my new job and my office were in Fairfax, Virginia, near Washington DC. This all happened about the same time that Chase and I decided to purchase land in the back country of San Diego County and build a ranch, from scratch. I was not about to move to Virginia, so it was agreed that I would commute.

One day, while Chase and I were riding our horses in the Mount Gower Preserve, we came upon a small trail cutting off of the main park trail. These are called "pioneer trails" and are created by people going someplace that they're not supposed be going. Being rebels without a clue, we did not hesitate to follow this little side trail to see where it would take us. Within a short distance we came upon a barbed wire fence that had been cut. The trail continued past the fence.

We were a little reluctant to proceed since this was obviously private property, but our curiosity got the best of us and we ventured forth. The trail took us to a riparian forest that ran along an occasional stream. Over tens, maybe hundreds of thousands of years, this stream had formed what was known as the Schwartz Canyon. This canyon and the forest were part of the open preserve and continued down into the Country Estates, where we lived, but the park trail and the community trails did not traverse the woods. Those trails kept above the creek, crossing only a couple of times.

The woods had a strong allure, so we kept following the trail. It took us across the creek in a most precarious manner, down a steep embankment and very close to, and under a huge overhanging branch of one of the giant old oaks that dominate these riparian woods. We had to duck under the branch such that we were lying on top of our horses to keep from being scraped off. The horses were skittish about dealing with this passage and we hoped out loud that they didn't decide to do anything stupid. The trail continued back up the other side of the creek, but unlike the other trails that simply crossed, this trail made a hard left and continued down the length of the forest.

It was like a whole different world under the grand old oaks. The canopy of the trees created a unique ecological environment that was a sharp contrast to the surrounding chaparral. The flora was entirely different, the air was cooler and smelled very unlike the sage scented air of the chaparral. The place was alive with birds and other creatures. The trail looked well used, so others had clearly already discovered this little wonderland. We traveled a mile or so through this forest when the trail suddenly crossed back over the creek and continued up a very steep mountain path. We decided to turn back.

"This place is beautiful," Chase said.

"Yes, it is," I agreed. "I'd love to live here. I wonder who owns this land."

"There seems to be no way to get here other than by horse and through the park," she said.

"Well, it's like a place out of a fairy tale," was all I could say in response.

We asked others about the "secret trail" to the woods. Many people knew about it and told us that it belonged to a guy who used the property as a mining operation. Some told us that the guy who owned it had died recently and that he was very old when he died. We could see for ourselves that the upper part of the canyon, past the park, didn't look like anybody was doing anything there anymore.

# Chapter 74

I had arrived at a point in my cowboy transition where I was daydreaming about starting a ranch. I even put a business plan together for a dude ranch operation to channel my cowboy inclinations. Chase was not as enthusiastic about this kind of an endeavor as I was, but she tolerated my planning. I often thought that she was probably treating me and my plan much like she would if one of her students told her he was going to be the next Rembrandt. Well, I've never been one to be dissuaded by common sense.

We had become decent horsemen by this time. I had traded my initial horse to Wrangler Dan for one with more spirit. He needed horses that were less spirited for trail riding, and my old horse, Tacoma, fit the bill. The horse I traded for, Gus, was a thoroughbred from a local breeding farm. He was trained for the track and apparently didn't make the grade, but he still had as much spunk as I could handle.

Chase had gone through a number of horses, trying to find one that suited her. She gave up on the mare from hell, and got an appaloosa gelding that was even worse. That damned horse eventually put me in the hospital after catapulting me off his back. We got rid of him and she found her dream horse, Wolf. That was his name when we bought him. Now we had two Wolves in the family. He was a gray, nearly all-white, gelding of mixed breed, and he was sweet and steady on the trail. Unfortunately, he didn't last long. He developed stomach stones, called enteroliths, which ultimately led to us having to put the poor thing down. Chase was devastated. She always grows so close to her animals.

Finally, she found a healthy horse that was a good fit for her. She named him Scout. He was a paint-bred horse, but was a "solid", meaning that he was only one color, a light chestnut. He had one blue eye and one brown eye, which is not unusual for paint horses.

We tried our hand at team penning, but our horses were not trained for such duty. They did alright though, and this encouraged me to daydream a little more about having cattle on my daydream ranch. I tried to learn how to use a lariat, but that typically resulted in humorous entertainment to anyone who might be watching my efforts. Still I practiced until I could almost do it right. My horse, Gus, tolerated the activity even when I managed to lasso him rather than the target. Sometimes I would catch him looking back at me as I was re-coiling my lariat with an expression that I'm pretty sure amounted to "you gotta be kidding me."

Our adventures on the mountain with the Moonlight Riders continued and increased in derring-do. One evening we decided to go on a ride even though there was a dense fog obscuring the full moon. The rationale was that we would ultimately be above the fog once we were on top of the mountain. Chase's horse was out of commission that night, so Wrangler Dan let her borrow one of the string horses, a gaited mare. Chase was not enthusiastic about riding another mare, but didn't want to miss the ride.

We got to the top of the mountain and it was still foggy. We had a difficult time keeping track of the trail, which was small and obscure even in the best conditions. Something spooked the mare that Chase was riding and it bolted away from the rest of us, yanking the reigns out of her hands in the process. Off they galloped, into the fog and out of sight. Chase could be heard trying to get the horse to stop, as her voice faded off into the distance. I was frantic because this part of the mountain was rife with gullies and other hazards. There was not much we could do immediately, however, since dashing off to save her would put everybody in the same possibility of running off a cliff.

I called after her, and it was not long before she hailed back that she had the horse under control. I kept calling to her so that she could home in on my voice to find us. Eventually, she appeared out of the fog with a scowl on her face, but apparently no worse for the wear. I recommended to the others that they best keep their comments about the incident to themselves.

We did eventually emerge from the fog into a beautiful moonlit night. As was typical, there was an enthusiastic consumption of beer during the ride. At a late hour we headed back down into the fog and toward the Western Equestrian Center.

We were, as usual, all dressed in full cowboy gear. In consideration of the foggy conditions, most of us were wearing canvas dusters. A couple of us, including me, were carrying rifles in scabbards attached to our saddles. This was more for effect than out of necessity. We had been drinking and we were all tired, including the horses.

We clambered down the mountain trail and onto a paved street, in a single file, heads hung down. One after the other we emerged from the fog and into the dim light of a nearby street lamp, giving us what must have been an incredulous and ghostly appearance. Parked right there, on the other side of the street, was a sheriff's cruiser with two deputies inside. We all saw them, but everybody was too tired and hungover to show any reaction at all. We just kept moving, passing right in front of the cruiser, just a couple of feet from the front of the vehicle, and then disappeared again down onto a wooded trail that led back to the equestrian center.

The deputies just sat there, staring at us, not making a move. A few days later, several of us met at the barn and talked about how we must have looked that night, appearing and then disappearing, with the effects of the street light and fog. We figured that the deputies might not have believed what they were seeing. Maybe they thought we were ghosts of old cowboys. We wondered what they were doing there, since that place was essentially the end of the road. Beyond that point was wilderness. I would have loved to hear the exchange between the deputies after we passed by.

"Hey Bob, did you see that? What the hell was that?"

"I didn't see nothing, George. I didn't see nothing at all."

# Chapter 75

Soon after that ride, I talked Chase into looking at property in the area, just to see what was available and how much ranch property might cost. No harm in looking. I contacted the real estate person who helped us find our house in the Country Estates, and asked him to see if he could find a few properties for us to look at. He called us a few weeks later and asked us if we were ready to go out and take a look at what he had found. I told him that it would have to be on the weekend because I was in Virginia during the week.

He had five properties for us to see. The first one was interesting, and it got our ranch daydream juices going, or at least it did mine. The second one was quite a surprise. We traveled up a private paved road that ended about a half mile from the main road, where we met the agent who was representing the property. We were told that we would have to all go in his four wheel drive vehicle because the rest of the way was pretty rough.

We traveled through a high meadow on a dirt road and up to the crest of a mountain pass. At the top of the crest was an amazing view of a canyon with Mount Gower towering above it. Chase and I looked at each other.

"Is this Schwartz Canyon?" I asked.

"Yes," came the reply. "Are you familiar with it?"

"Wow," we both said at the same time. "What part is for sale?" I asked.

"The whole canyon," the agent said. "We've divided it up into five parcels."

"Is the part down by the park with the woods one of the parcels?" I asked hopefully.

"Yes," he said simply.

"Let's go see it," Chase said.

The rest of the road, down into the canyon, could barely be called a road. It was a steep drop and the trail was full of ruts. I had never seen this canyon from this vantage point. It was amazing. It was a wide canyon, almost like a valley, bordered on one side by Starlight Mountain and the other by Mount Gower. These mountains met about a mile or so east of the road to form a box canyon. We were told that the entire area was around 450 acres.

When we got all the way down to the bottom of the canyon, we stopped at a place that looked like it had been carved out by a large dozer. In fact, there was a monstrous old Caterpillar D9 sitting off to one side of this large, flat space. We got out of the car and Chase and I immediately walked to the edge of the flat pad and looked down into the riparian forest. It stretched from the east end of the box canyon all the way down through the mountains until you couldn't see it anymore.

"So, that's the Estates, right over there somewhere?" I asked. "And this land over there would be the Mount Gower Park?"

"Yes," both agents said.

"Wow," was all I could say. I grabbed Chase's hand. I wasn't sure how she was feeling, but I was ecstatic. After several moments of looking at it all, "What's the price?"

It didn't sound like a lot to me, but I wasn't really thinking about everything that would need to be done to make the property viable.

"Okay," I said. Chase was giving me one of her looks, the kind of look that says, "Hold on there, big fella."

"So," I said quietly, "Well, let's just get some more details and talk about this at home." She sighed and looked back out over this incredibly beautiful land.

"We've got three more properties to look at," our agent said.

"No, we don't need to see any more," I said. "If we buy ranch property, this will be it."

At home, Chase and I discussed the possibilities of purchasing the property. I didn't really have to convince her about the desirability of the land. She thought it was as cool as I did. Even the money was not that challenging, given our current employment and financial situation. I was always ready to jump in with both feet at anything that I thought was worth doing, and this was my daydream in cinemascope and technicolor. I was in passion mode. Careful analysis had never been my strong suit when I wanted to do something, and my impulsive nature was in full control regarding this possible adventure. Chase, on the other hand, was not that easily convinced.

"I don't know if I want to do a dude ranch," she said.

"Well, we don't have to do that," I said. "That was just one idea. We could sell our house and build another one out there and just make it our ranch to start with. We can decide what we want to do with it as we go. You like it out there don't you?"

"Yes, of course, but there's a lot of details that we don't know anything about yet," she said sensibly.

"You're right," I said. "Well, how about this. Let's write down all of our questions and all of the things that would have to happen to do this deal. We can get the real estate guys to work on getting answers to those questions. We can make a list of all the things that would have to be done in order to make this happen."

"Here," I said and grabbed a tablet of paper and a couple of pens. "Let's start making a list. Road, we can't realistically live back there unless there was a paved road. Electric, how does that happen? Water, there's already a couple of wells on the property, but what else is needed to deal with having water?"

"Selling our house," Chase said. "We would have to sell this house to have the finances to do this thing."

"Right," I said, "and then what arrangements do we need to make for a place to live while a new house is being built?"

"It just seems impossibly complicated, Honey," she said.

"I know it does right now," I said, "but that's because we don't have any of the answers yet. Let's just make our lists and see how it comes together, or not. If it's not meant to be, then I'll let it drop. I promise. What do you say?"

I poured her another glass of wine. "You're beautiful." She gave me one of her you're-full-of-shit looks. I was going to have to pull out all the stops, but she was beautiful, and I was hyper-excited.

Over the next several weeks, we slowly put together the semblance of a plan, including all the caveats and deals and deal killers. It took a long time because I was out of town all week, every week, and of course, we both had our jobs to focus on during the week.

There were fifteen parcels on the land that the developer was trying to sell, and nobody was buying. The property that we were interested in was the very last parcel in what they were calling Starlight Mountain Estates. We were showing genuine interest, which put us in a pretty good negotiating position. We wanted to build a house on the flat area that we had originally stood on when we looked at the property. It overlooked the entire canyon. That land, however, was not included in the parcel that we wanted. To make a deal they would have to add ten acres to that parcel, increasing the size of the property to nearly fifty acres.

We needed a paved road and electricity. The selling agent worked out a deal with a local paving company to do the road in exchange for two of the properties at the top of Starlight Mountain. The electric and telephone would be put in at the seller's expense, and those costs added to the cost of the remaining properties. The assumption was that if we bought and started building, others would buy.

We discovered that the housing market in our community was hot and we could sell our current house pretty easily for a profit. We looked into putting a "Park Model" manufactured home on the property to live in while a larger house was being built up on our pad. We went to the manufacturer to look at models and really liked one in particular. We got information on converting a land loan to a construction loan. All the pieces were falling into place.

Chase was into it enough to start planning the main house with me. We originally wanted to build a log home, but discovered that, for reasons that were never quite clear, we could not get a loan for it. We switched gears to designing a pueblo style home, like the ones I remembered from my time in Albuquerque and Santa Fe. The architecture was not entirely unknown to the area, but still pretty rare. Our architectural skills were limited, but we were eventually able to get down on paper the main concepts we wanted.

Within a month or so we found ourselves looking at a situation where everything seemed to line up. The project was actually doable. At that point, we just continued to follow the bouncing ball, as they say. We finalized the transaction for the property and the land was ours. It almost seemed like we woke up one day and it was done. I'm not sure who was more surprised, Chase or me.

We bought the "Park Model", which looked like a little cabin, and decided to put it down in the woods to live in while we built "the big house" up above. The cabin was ideal there among the ancient oaks, with its cedar wood siding, green metal roof, loft, and open-beam ceiling. This manufactured cabin was just under 400 square feet, making it an ideal temporary home for us. Even with our two Doberman Pinschers it was enough room for us all to be comfortable.

Before we could get the cabin done and all hooked up, we spent several weekends camping in the woods. The very first

363

thing we constructed on the property was a campfire ring. It was simply a ring of stones placed in the middle of a clearing that we had made for our campsite. Our friend, Darrel, who was one of the Moonlight Riders and a farrier, made a tripod for us to place over the campfire to facilitate making coffee or a batch of Buzzard's Breath Chili. The second thing we built was a little outhouse that featured a flushing toilet, the kind you find in a camper or a boat.

We put up corrals for our horses and built a shed for keeping our tack, hay and feed. These basic necessities allowed us to have the Moonlight Riders ride over Mount Gower to the ranch and spend the night rather than go back to the equestrian center. Over the years these campouts grew in frequency and size.

One of the great advantages to belonging to the Moonlight Riders was that the members of the gang seemed quite willing to help build the ranch in exchange for beer. I often tried to buy them upscale beer, but they complained, saying they preferred Old Milwaukee Lite. I aim to please, so that's what I kept on hand, in large quantities. I think all of these guys enjoyed the opportunity to build the ranch with me because it fulfilled some basic guy thing relating to the allure of being a cowboy.

Another aspect of how this all worked out is that we all used the building of the ranch as an opportunity to create this little community of like-minded people, all focused on building a kind of Western life-style dream. To those who have not experienced this, I realize that it must sound corny, but it created a comradery that was similar to what I experienced during my military life. It's definitely a guy thing. Whatever the reason, it would have been almost impossible to build the ranch from scratch without these guys, and we had some great times doing it.

Together we strung miles of barbed wire fence, cleared acres of land, built a barn and established a herd of Hereford cattle. We dug a septic system in the woods that resulted in everybody getting the worst case of Poison Oak imaginable. We put in additional horse facilities so that all the guys could put their horses up when visiting.

One of the coolest things about the ranch, at least in my mind, was that a lot of people who visited did so on horseback. That made it seem like the old days in some way. While nobody ever made a big deal out of it, I know that everybody loved saddling up at their house in the Country Estates and riding over to the ranch to spend two or three days, and of course drink a lot of cheap beer. I am pretty sure that it felt like going from the civilized, stressed out world that most of us live in, to a kind of fantasy environment where guys got to pretend they were cowboys.

I have to say that Chase was incredible during all of this transformation to a Western life style. She was definitely the rose among the thorns. Some of these guys were pretty rough around the edges, but they always had the utmost respect for Chase and treated her like she was Barbara Stanwyck in *The Big Valley* TV show. In other words, she was the queen bee of the ranch. Despite the fact that she was a sophisticated cosmopolitan girl, she threw herself into the project of creating a ranch. I was so impressed with her grit, and she was always a source of rational guidance for me along this journey.

# Chapter 76

We had to come up with a name for the ranch. I wanted to register a brand with the California Bureau of Livestock Identification. Not that this was particularly necessary, since we did not intend to sell our cattle to a stockyard, but I just thought it would be cool. However, to devise a brand we needed to have a name.

Before we bought the property that was to become our ranch, Chase and I would ride our horses nearly every weekend. She would almost always ask me where we were going to ride to that day, and I would reply, trying to be funny, that we would probably end up in some Hell and gone place. It became a sort of ritual. When we decided that we should pick a name for the ranch, not wanting to let a tired old joke die, I said that maybe we should name it Hellangone Ranch.

"I always told you that we were going to end up in some Hell and gone place, and here we are," I said lightly. "We found it."

After a few days of knocking around a couple dozen alternative names, we both thought that maybe Hellangone Ranch was a pretty good name after all. The place was kind of in the middle of nowhere and not easy to get to. We shared our thoughts on this with a few of our cowboy friends, who thought it was a great name for a ranch. A couple of them even suggested some brand designs, which we kicked around until we decided on one that was a capital "H" and a stylized capital "G" stuck together, with the H and G sharing a single vertical line down the middle. One day shortly thereafter, Darrel, our friend and farrier, presented us with an HG branding iron that he made in his forge. That settled it. We were now the Hellangone Ranch.

I bought an old 1955 Ford 600 series tractor for the ranch. That was a big day for me. When I was a little kid, I had a toy tractor that I would ride around our yard, making tractor sounds and pretending that I was doing farm work. I have always been fascinated by tractors, and I can still vividly remember my first opportunity to drive a 1940 John Deere B. I was probably only 9 or 10 years old at the time, and I thought I was on top of the world driving that old Johnny Popper. Later, I got to drive the 1939 Olivier Model 70 that my grandpa used on the family farm. I would even agree to work the old converted horse drawn field equipment, which involved eating a lot of dust, so that I could be part of the tractor operation. I loved tractors. I loved driving a tractor.

I spent $2000 for that old Ford, which is exactly what that tractor sold for when it was brand new back in 1955. Over the years, I probably invested another $10,000 in that damn thing, but it runs like the day it rolled off the assembly line. Somebody told me recently that it's still worth around $2000, but I don't care. It's worth a lot more than that to me.

After we got the tractor we started planting barely every year. I used the barley for pasture, never actually harvesting the grain. I used the manure from the cattle and horses to fertilize the field. I bought an old manure spreader that resembled a World War One tank. There were no replacement parts for that old beast, but fortunately one of my Moonlight Rider gang members, Gail, was a heavy equipment repair guy, and he could fabricate parts for it when something broke. That's what I always thought ranching was all about, being resourceful and making things happen. Of course, having friends who actually had the talents to do that sort of thing was extremely lucky. My lack of mechanical skills was legendary among my friends.

We acquired a couple of cows with calves to get our herd started, but we needed a bull. We eventually found a little bull calf for sale in our local area and went to pick him up in our truck. He was just a little fellow, but we really hadn't thought about how we could transport him back to the ranch. We realized that we couldn't just throw him in the back of the pickup, so I drove while my friend Darrel held the little guy on his lap in the bed of the truck. That worked pretty well, except for the fact that Darrel's lap was covered in cow shit by the time we reached the ranch.

We named the little bull calf Beauregard, and Chase immediately made a pet out of him. Over time he grew, and grew, and grew. Like most things that I do, I didn't know much about raising beef cattle. One thing that we came to eventually understand was that bulls are big, and even if they are friendly and like pets, they can be dangerous just by virtue of their size. We learned that when any of the cows were in estrus, Beauregard got bully, and you did not want to get in his way when he was bully. It gave a whole new meaning to the term.

We eventually figured out a lot about raising cattle. Some of the knowledge came from reading reference books that we acquired, some came from advice from others more experienced, but perhaps most of it came the hard way. I knew, for example, that it was not uncommon to have to assist a heifer, a young cow, deliver her first calf. I read about it. I studied the diagrams. Nothing quite prepares you, though, for the moment when you realize that you have to stick your arm up there and grab a calf. That's pretty intense.

It was difficult when we lost animals. During one difficult calf delivery, the poor heifer died giving birth and we found ourselves having to figure out how to deal with an orphaned newborn calf. I knew about the importance of newborns nursing right away to get the colostrum needed to assure the calf's health. Unfortunately, I wasn't prepared for the possibility of the mother dying. In previous experiences, we had to help a newborn calf get dry and standing so that it could nurse. In other cases, we had to get a heifer to allow the newborn calf to nurse, as these first-time mothers sometimes rejected their calves. In those cases, the source of colostrum was the cow.

Chase and I worked on getting this little bull calf dry and standing up using towels and a hair dryer. I called my neighbor, Wayne, who happened to own a feed and livery store, to see if he had a source of colostrum. He didn't, but told me he would call one of the large dairy operations in our area. He told me they almost always had some on hand. I read that a calf should have this colostrum within six hours or less, so I was anxious about getting it in a timely manner. My neighbor called me back quickly and told me I could get what I needed from the Van Tol Dairy, located on the other end of Ramona. I left immediately.

We were ultimately successful in saving the little guy. He had been born on Valentine's Day, so Chase named him Rudolf Valentino, Rudy for short. I could see right away by her affection and bonding with him that this calf was not going to be allowed to be turned into a steer for market. We decided that he would be raised as one of our herd bulls. He was a very handsome bovine and loved all the attention he got from us, especially from Chase, who treated him like one of our dogs. She fashioned a little halter for him so that she could take him for walks on a leash. She cracked me up sometimes.

Meanwhile, I had to dispose of the dead mother. The County requires large dead animals be disposed of using a disposal service. I felt like it should be done in a more natural manner, so I dragged the poor animal with my tractor back to a remote area of our woods to let nature take its course. That was not an easy task, and I did not relish having to drag the dead animal, but there are many things that one has to do as part of ranching that are not necessarily pleasant.

Rudy, meanwhile, was enjoying the life of Riley. Chase had kept him in his own little stall inside our barn, away from the rest of the herd. His only companions were humans and the dogs. I don't think that he ever actually saw another bovine until the day that Chase decided to introduce him to the rest of the herd.

It was a beautiful day and the cattle were mostly clustered out in the western-most pasture. There was one steer that was grazing in the east pasture, but on the other side of a hill that stood between it and the barn. Chase had Rudy rigged up in his custom halter, which was attached to a lead rope. Together with our dog, Spike, they headed out from the barn to the pasture. When Chase detached the lead rope, Rudy at first just stuck to her side, following her everywhere she went. It took some coaxing to get him to do a little exploring, with Spike helping by trying to get Rudy to play.

Suddenly, Rudy seemed to discover the world of freedom in a rush. He began running around in a zigzag, jumping high in the air every few yards. He would bounce up off all four legs like he had springs attached to his feet. Spike was running next to him playfully, barking when Rudy made his little calf grunts of excitement. Then Rudy caught sight of the nearest steer, which was about fifty yards or so away. He suddenly stopped and stared at this new thing, then cautiously began moving toward it. Spike stood off to the side wondering why Rudy had stopped playing.

Chase caught up with them just as Rudy reached the steer. He was very curious, trying to figure out what this thing was. The steer looked bewildered and nervous, at least that's how I would describe it. Rudy instinctively went back to where an utter would be, if in fact this steer was a cow. The steer looked back at the calf, as if to say "what the hell are you doing", and then looked at Chase who was now next to both of them. It was a funny sight. The steer just stood there wondering what was going on. Spike was barking at Rudy, trying to get his attention, and I was laughing my ass off.

Then Rudy spotted the rest of the herd on the other side of the fence that separated the east pasture from the west pasture. He immediately headed off in that direction. Chase hollered at him to wait, worried about the barbed wire fence, but Rudy just passed through it like it didn't exist. A couple of the older calves came over to check Rudy out, but he didn't seem much interested in them. He went up to each cow and tried to nurse on her, but they would have none of it. It was kind of sad, I thought. A poor little orphan and nobody wanted him. He was figuring out that these things were like him, but they weren't giving him a very warm reception.

Then Rudy spotted Beauregard, who, by this time was a fully-grown, 1,500 pound bull, and made a beeline for him. Chase's foster motherly instincts kicked in and she headed over to keep Beau from hurting little Rudy. Rudy attempted a little nose-to-nose greeting while Beau just stood there, and then he went right to the back end to see if there was any milk. He started nosing Beau's substantial scrotum trying to figure out how that thing worked. Chase was yelling at Rudy to get away, while Beau looked at Chase as if to say "Who is this guy and what the hell is he trying to do?" I was laughing my ass off again, but Beau quickly lost patience with the whole scene and jerked his head around to get Rudy away from him. Rudy was still focused on figuring out what that thing hanging down in the back was. *It kind of looks like an utter*, he must have been thinking.

"Be careful," I warned Chase. "Beau is acting bully. Don't go near his head."

"I don't want him to get hurt," she called back. She was on a mission, so I decided that I better move closer just in case I had to play rodeo clown and distract Beau from running over both of them.

Beau finally moved and turned around to confront Rudy. Chase moved in, trying to get hold of Rudy's halter.

"I don't think that he'll hurt Rudy," I said. "This is probably an important lesson and we should just let it happen. I'm more concerned about you right now than Rudy."

That day ended well, and Rudy's first introduction to the herd was considered a success. We decided to keep him in the barn, apart from the herd for a while longer to make sure that he could fend for himself as a member of the herd. We did not foresee that this decision would have a tragic consequence. Rudy managed to squeeze through a section of his stall one night and found the bin where grain was kept for the steers. He gorged himself on the grain, resulting in a bowel obstruction. A veterinarian was called in and several methods were used to resolve the problem, but to no avail. Poor little Rudy died a couple days later.

# Chapter 77

In those early years, we lost other animals. It was always sad and distressing, and Chase was ready to throw in the towel a few times, but we kept at it. We managed to save some of them and that seemed to balance things out. One morning I found a new calf that had lost its hoof. It probably got stepped on shortly after it was born, and the hoof material was stripped away at the coronet. I called a vet and asked if there was anything I could do for the little calf. I was afraid that I would have to put it down, but the vet suggested that I cut a block of wood in the approximate shape of a hoof and duct tape it on the foot.

"Really?" I asked incredulously. "You can do that?"

"Yes," he said. "The hoof will grow back eventually."

"Put it on with duct tape?" I asked. I thought maybe he was pulling my leg.

"Yep," he said.

So I did, and it worked. Within a couple of months the calf had a new hoof, good as new. Duct tape, how did mankind survive before it was invented? Over the first couple of years, out of necessity, we learned how to care for our cattle. Eventually, there wasn't much we couldn't do. We did all the immunizations, helped birth calves, dealt with infections, and learned to cope with the losses.

One of the fun things about having cattle was driving them from the front pastures to the back pasture, which we did each summer. We thought of these events as "the big cattle drive". Truth be told, we never had more than two dozen head, and the distance between the pastures was maybe 300 yards, but at the ranch the roundup was a big event.

On the appointed day of the roundup, all our cowboys and wannabe cowboys congregated at our place. Some were on horseback, some on motorized quads, and some on foot. They brought their wives and children and dogs. We loaded up all the kids on an old horse drawn hay wagon that I had bought and converted for pulling with my Ford tractor. The people, horses and vehicles used in the roundup outnumbered the cattle significantly, and while that might seem like an unfair advantage, the process of getting the cattle from point A to point B was anything but smooth. The primary objective, however, was to have fun.

On one memorable roundup, the cattle were being less than cooperative in leaving the front pasture to enter what we called "the shoots". The shoot was a dirt road that led from the front pasture to the back pasture and it was fenced in to ensure that the cattle didn't stray off. All we had to do was get the herd into the shoots and push them to the other end, which led to the back pasture. There was a small opening at the beginning of the shoots, where the road branched off in another direction. We blocked this opening with the tractor and the hay wagon. The kids, we thought, would make an effective discouragement to any cattle trying to go in that direction.

A few of the cattle were finally driven into the shoots, and we thought that would convince the rest to follow. Beau, however, decided to balk and went around behind a big oak tree that was close by the gate. This caused a couple of the cows to follow him rather than the others already in the shoots. A display of some fairly good horsemanship by a couple of the cowboys coaxed him out, but that resulted in separating one of the cows from her calf. In fact, that cow was the matriarch of the herd, Abigale. She was a Holstein, unlike the rest of the herd, which were Hereford or mixed breed if they came from her. She was the only bovine in the herd with horns, and she was bossy. Bossy meant she'd kick your ass if you pissed her off.

The whole herd was eventually wrangled into the shoots, but Abigale's calf was bringing up the rear and was scared. It started bawling and Abigale began to try to get back to it, which caused the others in the herd to try to follow her. After all, she was the actual leader of the herd, not Beau. It was turning into a train wreck, so I started hollering orders to keep them all moving down the shoots. But the calf managed to go under the hay wagon, into the brush, and right down into a narrow gully, which was not something I had anticipated. I pulled my horse up and went around the hay wagon to make sure none of the cows tried to follow the calf. Darrel pulled back with me and jumped off his horse, handing the reins to one of the wives on the wagon with the kids. Darrel dove into the gully to fetch the calf, which resulted in getting Darrel all cut up from the frantic thrashing of the animal.

Both Darrel's horse and my horse, Gus, were getting all worked up because the rest of the horses and the cattle were heading down the shoots, leaving them behind. Gus reared up on his back legs, calling out loudly to the departing herd. His front hooves were pawing wildly over the hay wagon full of children. I tried to keep from falling off his back, simultaneously trying to keep him from falling over backwards with me still on him, and also trying to keep him from bashing some kid's brains out with his hooves. I finally got Gus under control, and went over to grab the reins of Darrel's horse, Cado, before he pulled away and tried to run over the wagon and through the barbed wire fence to catch up with the other horses.

One of the guys on foot ran over to give Darrel a hand out of the gully. He emerged bloody but with the calf in his arms. They got the calf on the wagon and a couple of the boys helped to keep it down and quiet. We checked to make sure Darrel was not going to bleed to death right away. He and I then made our way around the hay wagon to see how the operation was going up ahead.

As we headed down that part of the shoots that crossed the creek, I saw Abigale coming back toward us.

"Oh shit!" I said. What else could one say in this situation? "Darrel, help me drive her back. I don't want anybody on the ground getting gored."

We spurred our more than willing horses into a gallop, whooping and hollering. Abigale decided that we were more than she wanted to encounter and turned around, heading to the back pasture. All the cattle were in the back pasture now except for the calf. I sent my brother, Tiger, to drive the hay wagon to the back pasture so that we could reunite Abigale with her calf.

When the tractor, pulling the wagon was inside the gate, we all regrouped and headed toward the middle of the pasture. I heard Abigale bellowing for her calf, and it responded with a frightened bawl. I warned everybody on foot to get behind the wagon as she burst out of the woods. Darrel was putting the calf on the ground as she ran up to the wagon, and he backed away to let them reunite.

Everybody was now gathered around the hay wagon in the back pasture. I rode Gus around the group in triumph. He was all jacked up and prancing like a show horse. I'm sure we looked good.

"Well now," I said smiling, "that wasn't so hard now, was it?" Everybody laughed.

It was time to retire to the woods, unsaddle and brush the horses, and begin the best part of the big roundup. Bring out the cold beer and heat up the Buzzard's Breath Chili.

I loved the ranch and I loved pretending to be a cowboy. I was in my fifties, but I had no problem pretending, as if I was a kid again. The difference between my childhood fantasies and my adult fantasy was that I could afford to do it with all the bells and whistles.

One of the unexpected issues that we had to deal with the first few years on the ranch were trespassers. Locals had become used to wandering over from the park onto the land that was now our ranch. There were two problems with this. One was that some of these people had no compunctions about cutting our fences to get onto the property. Since we had cattle, this was a serious problem. Second, we discovered that our insurance company considered our property an "attractive nuisance". This apparently meant that if somebody, specifically "youths", came on our property and got themselves injured, they could sue us if the injury was caused by an object on the land that attracted them. I thought it was some kind of joke, but the insurance company wasn't laughing.

One day I was riding my horse, Gus, around the ranch. I was playing cowboy and checking the fence line, just like I'd seen in the old cowboy movies. I was decked out in full regalia, from my $300 felt hat, to the red kerchief around my neck, western shirt, Wrangler jeans, wide belt held together with a large silver buckle, custom made bat-wing chaps, bull hide packer boots, and spurs. I had a lariat draped over my saddle horn, and I was wearing a .38 caliber Smith and Weston at my hip. The gun was in case I encountered any rattlesnakes, which are numerous on the ranch.

I had put up "No Trespassing" signs all around the borders of the ranch, but that did not stop people from coming over. We were just too damned attractive, I guess. As I rode the perimeter that day, I heard some voices in the distance. I urged Gus into a gallop and came up to a sharp rise that overlooked a section of our fence bordering the park just twenty feet away. There I saw a very startled young man on the fence, straddling the barbed wire. Another young man, an Asian, standing a few yards away in the park, quickly ducked behind a bush. It was a scene that I found humorous due to the looks on their faces, the precarious position of the man on the fence, and the ridiculous attempt of the Asian guy to hide behind that little bush.

I turned Gus so that he stood sideways from these two would be trespassers, allowing them to see my sidearm. Gus was snorting and pawing with the excitement of the run and the unexpected encounter with these people. I touched the brim of my hat and said, "Howdy boys". That's what cowboys do, of course, and I was in full cowboy mode at that moment.

"You know that you can damage fences when you climb over 'em like that," I said with a slightly affected draw.

"We didn't mean to damage anything, sir," the one on the fence said. He hadn't moved so much as a muscle. The guy behind the bush was still crouching as if I didn't see him. I just sat there looking at them, not saying a word.

"My friend is visiting from Japan and I'm showing him around San Diego County," the man on the fence said. The guy behind the bush finally stood up. I shook my head and absent mindedly rested my hand on the butt of my gun. The Japanese man quickly ducked behind the bush again. I had to force myself not to laugh out loud.

"Well, I'd appreciate it if you boys would stay on that side of the fence, in the park," I finally said.

"Yes, sir. Yes, sir," the man on the fence started to get down, not taking his eyes off me. He joined this friend behind the bush, who stood up again. They backed away and hurriedly headed back down toward the trailhead.

I moseyed on down the fence line, because that's what cowboys do, mosey. Gus and I both felt pretty good about ourselves after that. Later, the volunteer park caretaker called me to tell me that two very excited young men had run into the park station to tell him that some crazy cowboy on a big horse was up there in the sage brush and that they thought he was going to shoot them. He said he told them they were lucky. He knew about that crazy cowboy and that he often shot trespassers. Apparently, they left the park feeling lucky that they were both still alive. I figured the guy from Japan would tell that story back home for the rest of his life.

Yippee ki-yay ki-yo.

# Chapter 78

In the early days of the ranch, we spent a lot of time down in the woods. The area where we built the campfire ring and the outhouse was also where the cabin was located. This spot became a gathering place for lots of parties. We would go there after moonlight rides and the gang would camp overnight. We hosted campouts with other friends that included lots of time around the campfire and copious amounts of beer.

One of these events turned out to be special. My brother, Tiger, visited us from his home in Arizona for a Labor Day, three- day weekend campout. Many of our friends were there, including the usual gang of cowboys. Tiger brought a couple of his friends with him, and one of these guys, along with Tiger, played guitar. In addition to the guitars they brought with them, Tiger had thrown a snare drum and a high-hat cymbal in the car as well.

My friend, Gerry, also one of the Moonlight Riders, zeroed in on that drum and cymbal. Every time the boys played their guitars, Gerry would be on the snare drum and high-hat. I had a harmonica at that time, a single harmonic in the key of G. I don't remember why I had such a thing, but I did, so I brought it down to the campfire and tried to play along. I'd try to get Tiger and his friend to play everything in the key of G, otherwise I would be left out. For Gerry and me, it was a humbling experience, but a musical spark had been ignited.

A couple of years later my brother and his wife got a divorce and he seemed pretty down in the dumps. I invited him to come stay with us for a while. Chase and I had moved up to the big house, so the cabin was vacant. I needed help in building and maintaining the ranch. I was still commuting to Virginia in those days, so I only had the weekends to try to do everything that needed to get done. I thought that the change would be good for him and help take his mind off the breakup. He accepted the invitation and moved to Hellangone Ranch.

Tiger was a huge help and I felt better about having him there close to Chase while I was so far away every week. He was no cowboy, however, and didn't particularly like horses. But he played the part on his own terms. The arrangement also allowed me to get to know my little brother much better. We were six years apart and had not spent much time together since I had left home for the military.

When we were little kids, Violet, Bear, and I thought he was too young to play with us, but my mother insisted we include him. We had a make-believe game that we always played, called Joan Puppy. We were all different animals and I was Joan Puppy, the leader of the pack. Since we had to let Tiger play, we told him he had to be the worm, and that worms didn't talk and mostly just had to lay around. It seemed to placate him, but as adults we wondered if maybe this ruse had resulted in his very quiet personality. Tiger is a man of few words. Daisy was a baby at that time, too young to play our games with us, so she escaped being relegated to being something lower than a worm.

Now that Tiger was living at the ranch, I would go down to the cabin and sit on the porch to visit with him. I had to remind him occasionally that he didn't have to play the worm any longer, and that it was okay to talk to me. Sometimes I would bring down a harmonica and we would play a couple of songs together. My brother was actually a bass player and had played with a rock band for several years. He was pretty good on an acoustic guitar, but really good on the bass guitar.

Gerry bought himself a drum set, and I bought an inexpensive Casio 61 key electric keyboard. I hadn't played piano since I was a little kid, but discovered that I still had the ability to play something if I knew the tune in my head. It took time to learn a song because I was not familiar with most of the stuff that the others wanted to play. I'd have to find a recording and listen to it until I had it memorized. Gerry practiced all the time in a little shed outside his house, and he started to get pretty good.

We got hooked up with a local guitar player, Duke, who was very good. He was impressed with my brother's ability on the bass guitar, but probably didn't think too much of Gerry and me, especially me, since I didn't have much time to practice early on. However, we started getting together to practice as a group on a relatively regular basis. By this time I was no longer working in Virginia, and I told the guys that we should treat band practice night like other guys do bowling night, and we ultimately decided that Thursday nights were the best.

Sometimes we'd practice up at the big house, sometimes we'd set up in the cabin, and sometimes over at Gerry's shed. I liked playing harmonica, and Duke would suggest old rock and blues songs that were a good match for the old juice harp. In the early days, we called ourselves the G-Tones because I only had the G harmonica. I eventually started buying them in other keys so that I could join in on other songs.

Within a couple of years the Labor Day campouts grew into a happening, and we started referring to the event as the Labor Day Camp-o-Rama. This three or four-day campout would draw fifty or sixty people and, with the introduction of music, became a little micro-Woodstock of sorts. I brought in other bands to play on a makeshift stage that we built for the occasion. Our own nascent band also played at this function. After a couple of years, our band was the only band that played, although we did invite guest musicians to join us. In between the music, we prepared food and consumed heroic levels of alcohol. Truth be told, there were also mood-altering drugs involved as well. I sometimes wondered if my pirate days might be returning, but fortunately that never happened.

During this same period, my career was in the process of moving in a whole new direction. My boss and friend, Jack, eventually took control of a company producing predictive products for the merchant banking industry, applying artificial intelligence technology. The products focused on predictive analysis and reactive work controls for credit card usage. It was a very interesting field of computer science. I took on the same role as in the previous two ventures, providing executive oversight to the development, delivery, and support of the technology products.

The company was in the midst of a growth through merger and acquisition strategy, and soon after coming on board, we negotiated a merger with larger company, located in Texas, that was involved in payment processing solutions. After that merger, another acquisition of a credit card processing company, located in Arizona, ended the merger activity. This experience was a big opportunity for me to grow as a manager and learn some of the harsh realities of rapid growth. It also stretched me to the limit of my sanity. I had to rotate my time between offices in Virginia, Texas, and Arizona, and of course try to keep one foot in California.

In my opinion, the merger arrangements with all the former founders and senior executives created too many chiefs, making critical strategic planning difficult to hammer out. I was getting increasingly frustrated with the challenges of making relatively straightforward management decisions. It felt like each group of left over executives from the merged companies were loath to let any other executive provide strategic leadership. I complained to Jack, who was still the CEO in title, and he confessed to his own frustration. I grew less and less confident that this company was going to continue to be the right place for my career to flourish.

One day, as I was returning from town, I found a man on a bicycle on the other side of our security gate. I stopped my pickup truck next to him and asked who he was and why he was there. I pointed out that he was on private property. He introduced himself as a neighbor, and we exchanged some information about ourselves. He owned a large ranch just up the road from us, as well as a dotcom business in San Diego. I told him of my computer background and who I was currently working with. He told me that he was looking for a senior manager to help him in his efforts to build a new payment processing capability.

*Well, what do you know*, I thought? We exchanged business cards. I eventually signed up to join that company as Chief Technical Officer and got involved with some very impressive people there. The venture's goal was to create a brand new payment processing center, using the latest in dotcom technology. It was right up my alley and the start-from-scratch aspect of the project was very appealing.

In the very early days at this company, I was introduced to a young man and asked to interview him. When I asked what position this person might be looking at, I was told to just talk to him and see what I thought. The company owner was a pilot and this young man was also a pilot, and that was apparently the connection that ultimately brought him to my office. His name, I was told, was Tyrone.

When he walked into my office and introduced himself, I could not help but smile. He was a kid. I figured that he couldn't be more than high school age. I asked him to sit down and pointed to a couch at one end of the room. My office was inordinately large, as if it was meant to be a conference room, and the only furniture in it was this couch at one end and my desk at the other end. There was a credenza behind the desk as well. So the result of somebody sitting on the couch and me sitting behind my desk was this grossly exaggerated distance between us. I regarded this young kid, sitting off in the distance from my desk, for what I assumed must have been his first interview, and I couldn't help but laugh. He smiled broadly back at me.

"Well, I presume that you know something about this company and our project since you are friends with the owner," I said.

Tyrone proceeded to tell me he knew that we were going to build a payment processing capability using new technology, but that he didn't know any technical details.

I laughed again, and said, "That's most likely because there aren't many technical details yet. We need to design it first. I'll give you a brief description of the proposed architecture, but first tell me a little about yourself. What would you bring to that table?"

He told me that he was the founder of a website design firm that developed an early shopping cart technique, employing some impressive technology in the process. He told me that he was the CTO of a company that produced real-time video streams over the web, and revealed that his product was being used at the San Diego Zoo. As he described what he had done, I was surprised that one so young looking could have accomplished so much. I thought he must be one of those people who look much younger than they actually are. Either that, or he was full of shit.

"Excuse me Tyrone', I interrupted. "Have you graduated from college?"

"No," he said. "I just graduated from high school. I don't want to go to college right now. I think I can learn more by working with smart people."

I sat there nodding my head slowly, not sure what to say next. I didn't have any particular reason to believe that he was trying to bullshit me with his experience, but it seemed so unlikely. He did come across as quite earnest, however.

"So, what is it that you see yourself doing here at this company?" I asked.

"I can work on design and programming," he said. "I just need to understand what it is that you are trying to accomplish."

I was incredulous, but knew that I had to at least go through the motions of an interview. I gave him a quick overview of my experiences in developing specific industry solutions over the years and of my ideas on the architecture that I wanted to use. I explained why I thought this architectural approach would be superior. To my amazement, he got up off the couch, walked over to the large white board hanging on the wall between the couch and my desk, and proceeded to produce an abstract architectural drawing of what I had just described. In doing so, he clearly demonstrated that he knew exactly what I was talking about, even though what I revealed was relatively vague. I was impressed, but I didn't have a position to fill.

As the new CTO, I was also responsible for the technology support of the older, ongoing billing business, and we were having a specific problem at that time that nobody was able to fix. I told him about the problem, but confessed that I did not have any personal experience with the programming language used for that application, Cold Fusion, or the existing technology environment. I happened to have a Cold Fusion book at my desk, anticipating the need to figure out how it worked so that I could personally address the problem. I impulsively told him that if he could fix the problem we'd see about a full-time position, and handed him the Cold Fusion book so he could go learn it. We shook hands and I thought that might be the last I would see of him.

He came back to my office a few hours later to tell me that he had fixed the problem. I figured I'd better hire him.

The billing company didn't last long. Within a few months of my joining, the big dotcom bubble burst happened and the owner decided to pull out. We all came to work one day to find the doors locked. The senior managers met to talk about what we all might do. Five of us decided to take a chance and start our own company. Levi, a Wharton graduate, had been the CEO of the billing company and told us he was in. Octavius was a contractor who had been working with us on contract development and finance. He was a former CEO and a good business man, and he told us that he was in. Jim had signed on as a director of sales in the billing company and he said that he was in. I said that I was in.

Although Tyrone was not an executive, I was smart enough to know that he was the kind of guy we would need to get any new technology off the ground. I recommended to the others that we bring him in if he was willing to join, and it was agreed. He said that he was in.

I had never tried my hand as an entrepreneur, at least not since I had worked as a budding artist in Florida, painting murals on garage doors. I had always been a company man, but I had clearly started to wonder if I could tolerate the way things always seemed to work out in a large company environment. J. Paul Getty may have said what was on my mind in those days. "Going to work for a large company is like getting on a train. Are you going sixty miles an hour or is the train going sixty miles an hour and you're just sitting still?"

All my new partners were much younger than me and all of them had been involved in various entrepreneurial pursuits during their careers. I was out of my element, but felt that these guys would make a good team. Besides, I was tired of other people who had apparently reached their level of incompetency directing my professional destiny. I was ready to forge my own path. It was to be an expensive and stressful decision.

Without the substantial executive salary that I had become accustomed to, I began to live off my retirement funds and Chase's salary as a teacher. Keeping the ranch operating became a challenge, although the ranch was still one of the main things in my life that kept me feeling fulfilled. All the partners were in the same boat of course, so the individual stresses of keeping body and soul together, combined with the stresses of defining, building, and selling a new product from scratch, were considerable. There were many times when we all had to sit down, look each other in the eye, and assure the others that we were not going to leave, at least not that particular week.

Then in May of 2003, my daughter was involved in a life-threatening accident down in Mexico. Arrangements were made to return her to the U.S. and get her into a trauma center hospital in Phoenix. She had delivered my first grandchild five months earlier, and the family was in crisis. I dropped everything and headed to Arizona. My brother and Chase assured me that they would take of things at the ranch, and my business partners told me that I had to go and that they would cover for me.

Alexa's condition was not good. She had multiple broken bones, including her back, jaw, ribs and arm. Her arm was nearly severed from her body during the accident. She required several surgeries to piece her back together. I stayed with her every day to monitor what was going on at the hospital. I learned how important it is for somebody to be there at the hospital bedside when a loved one is there for an extended stay.

There were more things that could get screwed up than I would have ever imagined. As hospital staff changed from shift to shift, and from day to day, I was appalled at the inconsistency of care and attention. I made a point of not confronting the staff in a belligerent manner, but calmly kept track of what was going on and made a point of knowing what was supposed to be happening day to day. After a few weeks, I had to suggest that the doctors reduce the amount of morphine they were administering to her. She was hallucinating and trying to get out of her bed to the point that they eventually had to strap her in. I did a little research and discovered that these were potential side effects of prolonged administration of morphine.

I took care of the baby in the evenings so that her husband, Ely, could be with her at that time. I picked up my grandson at the nursery where he was kept during the day so that Ely could continue to work. I tried to help whenever and wherever I could. It was an incredibly stressful time for everybody, but we all made it through.

Alexa's recovery was slow and painful, but she is a strong woman and slugged through the protracted process of healing. During the experience, I realized how much she and her family meant to me. My mother had passed away the year before, and I was at a point in my life where I was feeling very introspective. My time in Arizona at Alexa's hospital bedside, helped to transform my thinking about the importance of my family, as well as how fickle life can be. My mother had been wise when she frequently reminded me that we should live for today, for tomorrow we may die.

After that close call, life got back to the new normal. We continued to work on making the company successful. Work on building the ranch and maintaining what we already had, consumed most of any free time I had. My brother now lived in another part of town with his fiancé, so the only time I saw him was when he and I played in our new rock band. We continued to try to meet every Thursday night to practice. I actually got a little better at playing the piano. We hosted another Labor Day Camp-o-Rama. Life was kind of crazy, but pretty good.

All normal life, however, came to a halt in October, 2003. That was when the historic Cedar Fire, fueled by howling Santa Ana winds, burned 280,000 acres of San Diego County, including most of Hellangone Ranch. Nearly 3000 homes were lost and 16 people were killed as a result of this wildfire.

# Chapter 79

We were in our hot tub when we noticed that there was a fire over in the direction of a place called Cedar Creek. It was just before sunset so there was enough light for us to see the smoke column off in the distance. As darkness fell, we could see a red glow off to the south, beyond the Mount Gower range. I was the president of the board of directors for our local Intermountain Volunteer Fire Department at that time, so I called in to see if I could get more information. Our team was supposed to join a strike force and were awaiting further direction.

We went to bed that night but didn't get much sleep. We could see out our window that the fire was growing. The wind was also howling so hard that it made our house creak, and the dogs were restless. By the next morning the situation was getting critical. Chase kept the news on to see if we could get a better idea of what was happening, and I checked in with the fire department. Our team was sent to another area. I started contacting our neighbors to make sure everybody was aware that the fire was getting big and that evacuations might be ordered.

Later in the afternoon, we got the word from the Sheriff's Department that we should evacuate the canyon. We loaded up our truck with all the things we thought would be essential, but in that kind of situation it's hard to think straight. We made sure that all of our important papers were gathered up, and then collected the things we considered valuable, like photos, some clothes, artwork, and the wine collection. The truck was full, but there was so much left. We headed up to the top of Starlight Mountain and arranged to stay with one of our neighbors who lived up there. From their house we could look down into the canyon and see our place.

Night fell and it became apparent just how huge this wildfire was. It was a terrifying sight. From our vantage point it looked like the San Diego Country Estates was being engulfed. The electricity went out and the whole area where the Estates was located plunged into darkness. The only light was from the vast fire which now seemed to be everywhere south and west of the ranch. We started hearing explosions and guessed they might be propane tanks or gasoline tanks blowing up. Then we saw the fire edge over the top of Mount Gower. The fire line was now only about a quarter mile above our ranch and that meant that it was capable of consuming our place.

We got no sleep that night. We all stayed up and kept vigil. The neighbors we were staying with began packing up their valuables. Down in the canyon we could see lights from vehicles down in the canyon, which we assumed were firefighters, but it was too dark to determine what was going on. Where we physically were that night seemed to be out of immediate danger, but we expected that dawn would reveal bad news.

As daylight began to break in the east, we saw that the fire hadn't reached our place, although the fire line was still burning on the north side of Mount Gower. The wind was blowing from east to west, so the fire line was not roaring down the mountain, into the canyon and onto our place. I got the feeling, though, that it was hovering, waiting for us to think we got lucky. The disaster felt personal, and even years later, when I'd meet people who had been through that awful, life altering fire storm, it was clear that we all felt that it was personal.

We could see several fire trucks in our driveway. I decided to go down and talk to the firemen to see if I could get some information. As part of our volunteer fire organization I carried an official identification card that allowed me to get through road blocks, but all of those were located on main roads. We were too far back in the boonies for authorities to bother setting up road blocks.

When I arrived at our house, I found several firemen spread out on our front yard, catching some sleep. I located the strike force commander and got an update. He told me the fire was heading west and our immediate area seemed to be out of danger. He warned that we were not out of the woods yet, but if the wind cooperated we might dodge the bullet. Chase offered to make coffee for everybody, for which they seemed to be very grateful. I asked if it would be okay for me to go down to the cabin in the woods to retrieve some things, and he approved. He told me that his strike force had been told to pack up and move to a more volatile area. I interpreted that as hopeful sign. Maybe we would be okay after all, I thought.

I called my brother, who was with fiancé, Molly, at her house on the other side of town. Chase had introduced Tiger to Molly, a friend from the high school where they both worked. Tiger and Molly had hit it off and planned to be married on the ranch in a couple of weeks. I told him that we had evacuated, but that we were back for now and planned to go down to the cabin to get some things out. He told me he'd be right over to help.

While Chase was getting coffee, I went on down to the cabin and started checking things out. I could not remember what we had left down here. I grabbed a couple of appliances, and some things from the loft that I felt had sentimental value. Tiger quickly arrived with Molly, and we started collecting things that he indicated that he wanted. Chase joined us shortly thereafter, and we were just beginning to take stuff out to put in the cars when I heard something that sounded like a jet engine or a locomotive close by.

As the others came out of the cabin, I asked, "Do you hear that?" They all stopped to listen.

"What is it?" somebody asked.

"I don't know, but it can't be good," I said. "Let's get back up to the big house and see what's going on. We need to go now."

We all jumped into our cars and headed up the hill to the house. It became immediately apparent what was generating the sound. The next few minutes were a mixture of awe, panic, and confusion. A wall of flame, at least one hundred feet high was coming down the canyon from the east. It stretched from one side of the canyon to the other. The wind had apparently shifted enough for the fire to jump into our canyon and was now consuming everything in its path. The fire was so intense that it was consuming all of the oxygen in front of it, causing it to travel up toward the sky. The wind caught burning material that had been lifted to the top of the flames and tossed it in front of the wall of fire like catapulted fireballs. It looked like scene from a science fiction movie.

Firemen were scurrying everywhere, totally ignoring us. I could see the panic in their eyes. We had all gotten out of our cars and my brother, who was standing next to me, asked if I thought we should evacuate.

"Oh my God," I exclaimed, finding it difficult to tear my eyes from the inferno. "Hell yes, let's get out of here. We'll have to escape through the park."

The fire was blocking the main road we would normally use to leave the canyon. The only other way out was through the park on a dirt road. I knew there was a gate on that road that was usually locked, but I assumed that it had been unlocked and opened to provide access and regress by firefighters.

We jumped back into the cars and headed for the park, past our new barn. The barn had just recently been filled with a tractor trailer load of hay. The thought flashed through my mind that we would never see that barn or the hay again. As we reached the gate, which was, thankfully, already open, several U.S. Forest Service fire trucks rushed past us, causing us to pull over momentarily to let them through. We drove pell-mell down to the park entrance and stopped to look back. It was not a sight that anybody would ever want to see. It was bad, and it gave every appearance that it was going to keep coming. We weren't out of the woods yet.

We got back into the cars and drove down to a little commercial area at the entrance to the Country Estates. That was the spot where evacuees were supposed to congregate for further instructions. Chase was sobbing.

"We've lost everything," she cried. "The horses!" She jumped back into our car on the driver's side. I opened the passenger door.

"Where the hell are you going," I yelled.

"I can't just sit here," she sobbed. "I'm going back. I'm going to go up to the top of Starlight Mountain."

"You can't," I said. "That may all be on fire now too."

"I don't care," she howled. "I can't just sit here and do nothing."

I knew that there was going to be no reasoning with her in that state of mind so I got into the car. She took off, and Tiger and Molly followed. Chase was driving fast through the residential section. A couple of residents yelled at her to slow down. She was fixated on getting to the top of Starlight Mountain.

When we approached our destination, it became apparent that side of the mountain was not engulfed in flames. She pulled over at the crest of the road, and we both got out. We walked over the crest until we could see down into the canyon. It was a sight I will never, ever forget. It looked as if we were peering down into the depths of Hell itself. There was black and gray smoke mixed with towering red flames covering the entire canyon floor. The howling wind made it all whip and boil like some insane maelstrom from a nightmare. The noise was deafening. It was impossible to see any sign of houses or buildings or fire engines.

I felt sure none of the houses or other buildings would escape this inferno. I wondered if my neighbors had time to get out. Our horses and cattle were down there, so they would perish as well. All our stuff was gone. We were all crying. It felt so utterly devastating.

I looked to the west, the direction the firestorm was heading, and was amazed to see firemen on the side of the mountain we were standing on, hundreds of them. There were also fixed-wing air tankers and helicopters dumping tons of pink retardant on the mountain side. It reminded me of a movie war scene. I looked back down into the canyon and thought of the firemen we had left behind at our house. There was no way all those guys could have survived, I thought.

There was nothing we could do but wait until it was over and then assess the damage. We all drove over to Gerry's house. They were getting ready to evacuate. There were now wild fires burning everywhere in the backcountry, and it was all heading toward the heavily populated areas to the west. The Santa Anna winds could last for days, and the canyons of the back country made the wind do crazy things. It would take another full week to get the fire under control, so meanwhile, nobody was safe.

We helped get stuff loaded into Gerry's vehicles, which temporarily distracted us from our own problems. We wondered about other friends and their safety. Contacting anybody was increasingly difficult as land lines poles and cell towers were burning up, and what cell service there was got so jammed with call overload that it was impossible to complete a call. When we had loaded all the stuff we could possibly cram into Gerry's cars, we all sat around and drank.

At 5:00 that evening, I told Chase that I wanted to go back over to Starlight Mountain where we had looked down into the canyon earlier that day to see what was going on. She readily agreed and we hopped in the car and headed that direction. We had to go through the eastern edge of Ramona to get to the road to our place, and what we saw there was nothing short of amazing. The town had been transformed into a regional staging center for firefighting assets. The middle of Main Street as far as we could see was filled with fire trucks of every description. The streets were full of people, mostly firefighters, and there were makeshift tents and shelters lining the sidewalks.

"My God," I said to Chase, "this is like the end of the world. It's like a war zone."

As we pulled up to our destination on Starlight Mountain, it became obvious that the fire storm had passed because there was no longer heavy dark smoke in the air around the place. The intense winds had blown it all toward the ocean. We walked over the crest expecting to see the worst. To our utter amazement, I could count all five houses that populated the canyon floor. I couldn't see any evidence that any of them had burned at all from that vantage point. The whole place looked like the surface of the moon though, and it was so surreal.

"I'm going down," I said. Chase made no objection. We didn't see any fire engines or other vehicles in the canyon. Apparently, everybody fighting the fires had followed the firestorm as it ravaged its way west. I felt certain that there was nobody around to stop us from going in. In fact, the canyon was deserted, no firefighters, no neighbors, no living thing in evidence. It was creepy.

As we drove past the first neighbor's place I couldn't see any obvious damage to the house. Everything around it was burnt to a crisp, but the house was intact. I drove up our driveway and could see that our house also looked okay. We got out and walked in the front door. The place had some dirt and mud from what looked like the firemen being inside, but no damage. I quickly noticed that some of the back porch pergola was scorched, but it was still standing. All the landscaping was scorched, and I could see evidence of what was once our porch furniture transformed into black mounds on our now ash gray yard.

I walked out to the east side of the house where our swimming pool was located to find a macabre sight. The pool water was ink black and was filled with what looked to be scores of dead animals floating in it. I could identify rabbits, squirrels, mice, rats, birds, a skunk, and a raccoon. They must have dived in to escape the fire and drown.

I came back around and saw that the barn was completely gone, as if it was never there, including the $4000 worth of hay we had just put in it. I looked down into what had once been our beautiful woods. It reminded me of what the place might look like if a nuclear bomb had exploded nearby. The cabin was gone, replaced by a heap of gray ash and some twisted metal.

The air stank of burnt things and smoke. There was a lot of ash in the air, making it almost look like it was snowing. Occasionally, glowing embers could be seen flying by in the howling wind. Almost immediately, our eyes were burning and we were coughing. I realized I'd have to get a couple respirators.

There was no electricity. The poles were still burning outside, so I knew that we would have no electricity for perhaps weeks. The generator we kept for emergencies had been stored in the barn. I walked out to where the barn used to be and found the generator's charred remains. Finding a new one would have to be one of our top priorities. Without electricity, we had no water. Although we had a 10,000 gallon reserve tank, the strike team had emptied all of its contents in fighting the fire. We would need to pump water from the well to refill it. We also had two freezers full of meat that would be ruined if I couldn't get electricity to them within the next several hours.

Our field gate terminals were made of railroad ties, and they were all either burned into oblivion or still in the process of burning. As a consequence, all of our gates were lying on the ground. Most of the cattle could be accounted for, but I could see that some of them had burns on their feet. Our horses were nowhere to be found and I feared the worse. I would have to quickly get the cattle into an area that I could fence off and find them food and water.

Despite the depressing aftermath, we felt oddly giddy with relief. Our house and all its belongings had survived. It seemed impossible based on what we had seen with our own eyes, yet there it was. I managed to get a call through to my brother and Gerry on my cell phone to update them on the status of the ranch. I told them that we planned to spend the night, and in fact would stay there until things got back to some semblance of normal in an attempt to thwart any possible at looting.

I eventually got through to my business partners to tell them our status and that I would not be able to come to work for a while. They asked if they could help in any way. I asked them to try to find and purchase a generator and bring it up to the ranch, if they could get through the blockades. Hours later they called back to tell me that every generator in the county seemed to have already been sold that day, but that they did find one, probably the last one available. They promised to bring it up as soon as they could.

People started calling Chase and me on our cell phones to find out if we were okay. Cell service was spotty, but people could eventually get through. One of the Moonlight Riders had an extra generator and said that he'd bring it over right away. A couple of other local friends came over to help with the cattle and the search for our horses. My old boss and friend, Gerald, called from Cincinnati. He had heard about the disaster on the national news. He committed to come help us with the recovery as soon as he could get a flight. Since the fire was national news, all of our friends and relatives from all over the United States were trying to reach us to see how we had fared.

We got the first generator a little after dark that first night, allowing us to have light and keep our refrigerated and frozen food from spoiling. We also managed to get the cattle rounded up and fenced in before dark, but there was no time to look for the horses. We had the second generator early the next day, and several people arrived to help us assess the damage and take the first steps at cleanup. We contacted our insurance company and were given instructions on how to get prepared for the paperwork, basically making lists of things damaged or destroyed.

Later the second day, as we were sifting through the debris of the cabin, somebody noticed a strange animal wandering nearby.

"What the heck it that?" he asked. We all looked.

"It's a buffalo, I mean bison," I said. "The ranch just over that mountain there kept a small herd."

Just then a few more made their way into our view. Everybody stopped what they were doing and stared. Within a few minutes, there were a dozen of these bison milling around us. It made the surreal surroundings even more surreal.

"I'm sure these animals come from the neighbor's ranch," I said finally. "We should probably try to head them back over the mountain. Maybe we can get them back into their corral so that they can get access to hay and water."

It sounded like a great idea to everybody and seemed to lift their spirits. A buffalo roundup, now that would be something to talk about. It turned out to be easier said than done. The infamous difficulty of herding cats has nothing over the challenge of herding bison. By the time we gave up, the bison were scattered over all points of the compass. A couple of days later I managed to contact the neighbor who I knew owned the animals and discovered that the bison had all eventually gone back to where they belonged, probably to get water.

It took many months to recover from the big fire. Recovery usually came in small steps. We found our horses a couple weeks after the fire. I was visiting a neighbor, whose farrier happened to be there. We were comparing experiences with the fire, and I mentioned that we lost our horses.

"Oh, I'm sorry to hear that," they both sympathized.

"No," I said, "I mean we lost them, as in we can't find them. I couldn't find any evidence that they perished, so I'm holding out hope that they escaped and are either roaming around here somewhere or somebody picked them up. I couldn't get them in the trailer when we had to evacuate, but our gates were all open or down when we returned."

"What do they look like?" the farrier asked.

"Well, Gus is a bay thoroughbred, with a while blaze on this forehead and three white socks. Scout is a one color, light chestnut paint with one blue eye and one brown eye."

"I think they are at my place," he said. "I found two horses running around on Old Julian Highway after the fire, so I got them rounded up and took them to my place. Found several others as well."

"Oh, my Gosh!" I exclaimed. "Can we go take a look?"

We did, and they were our horses. Our horse trailer had burned into a twisted metal hulk, so I had to prevail on this Good Samaritan to transport them back to our place. Chase was very glad to see them alive and well. It lifted her spirits in the early days of the aftermath.

To our amazement the big oaks that were not burned to the ground actually recovered after a year. In the two years following the fire, much of the forest and the surrounding chaparral had recovered. There was still plenty of evidence that it had all been charred, but the landscape was greening up again. We built a new barn, repaired all the fences, and disposed of the remains of our old barn and the cabin.

We decided not to replace the cabin. To our dismay we discovered that we had been under insured. The barn was not insured and it was a total loss. We needed a barn, so we used the insurance money from the cabin to build a new one. There was a lot of cleanup that had to be done. Two sides of the house were turned pink from the fire retardant that the attack planes dropped. It was very difficult to remove. We had to replace all of our ranching tools, shovels, rakes, wheel barrows, and the like. There was soot in every crook and cranny.

We came to realize how precious our friends were during these difficult months. I don't know how we would have gotten through the trauma and aftermath without their help. My brother and his fiancé were supposed to be married in a big cowboy wedding on the ranch, but the place was no longer suitable for the event. So our friend, Gerry, volunteered his place. We all gathered there a few weeks after the fire, everybody in full cowboy regalia, and got them married in a good old fashion, mock shotgun wedding.

One of the long-term consequences of the fire was the health of our cattle. I'm pretty sure that the ash on the ground and in the air created several catastrophic problems for nearly all the individuals in the herd. It started several months after the fire when the herd matriarch, Abigale, died trying to give birth. She had delivered several calves over the time we had her, with no problems at all. So when I saw that she was ready one evening I didn't think anything of it and expected to find her with a new calf the next morning. Instead, I found her dead. I felt terrible and chastised myself for not staying with her to help.

A month later a second cow died calving, as did the calf. This one was named Ruby and she also had been through several successful births. Other cows got sick, and Beau developed cancer around one of his eyes. Within three years our herd was gone, and while I don't have any hard evidence that this was related to the fire, I don't have any other explanation.

There were other consequences of the fire. We never went on another moonlight ride after the Cedar Fire, and we never had another Labor Day Camp-o-Rama. Most of the old gang move away or moved on, so the "good old days" slowly came to an end. It was a difficult time.

Life continued though. I redoubled my efforts to bring our volunteer fire department up to a level where it could provide adequate service to the vast back country area it served. The County ofSan Diego did not provide any funding for this critical first responder service, so I had to figure out how to raise money, a shit-load of money. In going around the back country begging for donations, I got to know a lot of people. I spent a lot of time trying to convince all these folks the volunteer department was all that we had if there was an emergency. Most people just didn't believe their taxes didn't include first responder services.

Thanks to the dedicated efforts of a handful of people, we eventually quadrupled the size of the volunteer team, created a grass roots fire academy, built a fire station, acquired new fire engines and equipment, and badgered the county into getting more involved in back country services. I got very tired of trying to raise money by begging, so I applied for grants and won some of them. I also initiated an auxiliary citizen group to focus on fund raising. They called themselves the Hot Spots and they were very effective at putting together big fund-raising events which generated an impressive amount of cash.

# Chapter 80

I was now very focused on growing our company. We struggled mightily in the early days, but finally got a client who underwrote the early development of our healthcare revenue management applications. We did not set out to get into the healthcare industry, to be sure. In retrospect, I think it was an unfortunate path, but at the time we were quite happy to be generating revenue from any source.

We were essentially trying to build a general technology platform that would be ideal for creating any business application. We used a generic approach for automating the fundamental components of business that are typically needed for any industry. It was all to be developed using the wonderful new technologies that had emerged in the 1980s and 90s, before the notorious dotcom bubble burst. We set out to be one of the first, if not the first company to create an application development platform that was entirely Web based. Up to that point, technology focus had been on Web enabling existing applications.

This approach is what is often referred to as "bleeding edge", a somewhat cynical allusion to the term "leading edge", and we found that there was little appetite within the investment community at that time for betting on new technology products. In other words, it was not an ideal time to start up a company whose intention was to build a new technology product. I felt we were a solution in search of a problem.

My partners and I tried to break into a number of different industries, but by pure serendipity we landed in healthcare. By that time, we were in dire straits financially, and it seemed that we might be at the end of our rope in keeping our nascent company afloat. In a previous company I had been involved in, we had used a business tactic whereby we saved a struggling company by feigning interest in purchasing another company. No matter that we did not have the wherewithal to acquire another company. The goal was to get other companies to take a close look at us. The gamble was that there was a company out there who would see us as a potential strategic partner and would discuss a merger.

We thought it was worth a try since we had little to lose. We started with healthcare billing. There were lots of little medical billing companies around, and we knew the mechanics of billing, if not actually anything about medical billing. We ultimately found a privately-owned company in Los Angeles willing to discuss a potential purchase.

We met with the owner and began the discussion with a review of her business. It was great because we knew that this kind of operation was very manual, with tons of opportunity to automate the business functions. It was relatively easy to match our theoretical technology platform with her operation, inferring that her business would be an ideal application for the technology and would enable us to grow the business as well as make it more profitable.

She decided that she didn't really want to sell, but revealed that she had just been awarded a large contract from a federally funded community health center, and that she was struggling to keep up with the volume. We told her we were sure that our platform could take care of her problem. We offered to provide a demonstration if she would agree to provide us with all the information we needed. She agreed, and Tyrone and I stayed on to begin the process of automating the billing process.

There was a catch, of course. Neither one of us knew the first thing about Medicaid billing, nor did we actually have the applications that would be needed to implement the solution. Mere details, we told each other. We spent the next four days frantically figuring out processes, data formats, and Medi-Cal rules. Tyrone did all the coding. I did research, talked to staff and tried to act like we knew what we were doing. We didn't sleep much those four days, and I knew that Tyrone was near the end of his rope when he finally put it all together so we could demonstrate how we could reduce the manual processing significantly.

The company owner was impressed, and over the next few weeks we returned to fine tune the automated processes until we finally had things figured out enough to realize that an alarming number of the claims were being rejected. We reported this to the owner and she admitted that her client was in receivership and on the brink of bankruptcy. A consulting group had been called in to try to salvage the healthcare center because the federal government did not want this facility to close.

We called the people at Medi-Cal up in Sacramento to see if we could get some help. When they heard who the client was, they were very accommodating. We quickly realized that the staff at the medical center were submitting claims with several very fundamental mistakes, which resulted in automatic rejections in the adjudication process. We put together some fundamental business rules that were designed to catch the problems before submitting the claim, errors the billing company staff could correct. This process had a dramatic impact on the results and the health center's revenue situation began to significantly improve.

As we learned more about the many healthcare programs under Medi-Cal, Tyrone came up with ingenious methods for analyzing data to determine the root causes for problems that the healthcare center was generating. In one visit to the clinic, we discovered a large cache of paper claims that had never been submitted because the staff didn't know what to do with them.

They were all dated past the time they could have been officially submitted for reimbursement. We contacted our resources in Sacramento, described the situation, and received permission to submit them electronically. The result was a few million dollars of revenue recovery.

All this "sudden goodness" eventually caught the attention of the national consulting firm that was working to save the healthcare center. "Who are these guys", was the question we were hoping to hear. Just in the nick of time, these guys discovered us and expressed interest in having us work with them. We would survive.

Working with a consulting company was a mixed blessing. They paid us to develop revenue cycle management applications, but getting the applications defined was a painful process. Now, I had always believed that consultants were people who made a living telling everybody else, at least those who could afford them, how to do something just the right way. After working with this healthcare team for a few months, however, I came to understand that a consultant is like a person who takes the watch off your wrist and tells you the time. They clearly knew about the mechanics of the revenue cycle, but they struggled mightily with defining how to create automated processes.

Once I figured out the work processes these consultants were struggling to articulate, I found myself doing most of the consulting. I was dispatched to Tampa, Florida to meet with a couple dozen of these consultants. The goal was to define specific applications, which the consulting company would pay our company to develop. After three intense days in Tampa, and several weeks of post meeting effort on documentation, we received an encyclopedic set of specifications that were essentially unusable.

While trying to distill all the consulting group's boiler plate documentation into a usable set of requirements, we were redirected to build an analytic application as soon as possible. We were told the consultants could sell something like that "all day long", ostensibly, for a large price. So, of course, we shifted gears to create this goose that would lay golden eggs. As it turned out, they couldn't actually sell it, but they did find it useful for closing consulting engagements.

The other thing about working with consultants which became apparent over time is that if you convince one consultant what you bring to the table is important, and a breakthrough capability, you have only convinced one consultant. Despite the fact that many consultants work for the same consulting firm, and that the consulting company is supposedly promoting the use of a particular, consistent approach, each consultant tends to have her own ideas about how things should be done and who she wants to work with. This made our lives very difficult, and over time it became evident that our relationship with the consulting company was not going to be a long term, successful strategy.

By the time we all started to agree on the notion that we needed to find other sources of funding so we could get back on our original track of building a more general platform, Tyrone was the president of our company. Although he was by far the youngest member of the partnership, and although there were some heated debates about who should lead the company, Tyrone was the one who emerged as the corporate leader.

I still find it amazing that the partners never sued each other, or tried to murder each other through the years, but that didn't happen. There were, however, some battles royale. Tyrone, while brilliant and energetic to the extreme, could be difficult to work with. He had strong opinions about nearly everything, and these caused many a debate and intense back room politicking. I decided early on to hitch my wagon to his star because I believed that his vision would eventually result in a successful future. My approach to working with Tyrone was to mentor him in terms of helping him develop an effective management and leadership style. I tried to try to understand his vision so I could distill it into manageable product development planning.

The world came apart again beginning in 2007, with yet another wildfire. We were all told that the previous Cedar Fire had been a one in a hundred years event, yet here we were, four years later, battling the Witch Creek Fire which caused even more damage than the first one. Witch Creek is just east of Hellangone Ranch so we were directly in the firestorm's path.

The Witch Creek Fire ultimately resulted in the largest mass evacuation in U.S. history, with over half a million people all trying to get out and away at the same time. The first problem was that the roads could not accommodate such a large-scale evacuation, and so, in the back country where we lived, the roads became parking lots, exposing prople to the possibility of the firestorm catching them in their cars with nowhere to run. The second problem was that this fire spread very quickly and seemed to be everywhere at the same time, burning all the way to the ocean in several locations. Eventually, there was no place to evacuate to.

My father was visiting from Ohio at that time. We loaded up our truck again, this time including my dad. Chase was hosing down the house in an attempt to make it less likely to burn. We were told to leave, but found that, due to the gridlock on the roads, we couldn't get past the edge of town. We made our way on back streets to my brother's place, right on the edge of town. We decided that we should hunker down there since there was really no place we could go.

The fire seemed to be everywhere. My friend and neighbor, Will, had recently retired from the City of San Diego Fire Department, where he served as Assistant Chief. Will had also helped me as a director on the Intermountain Volunteer Fire Department board of directors. I knew that he planned to stay behind to ensure that his house didn't burn down, which would have been too risky for most people, but Will knew what he was doing. I called him on my cell phone and was surprised to hear him answer.

"Hey Will," I said. "What's your status out there? You guys okay?"

"Yeah," he said. "The actual firestorm just pasted, but there are still lots of hot cinders blowing around out here. That might be the most likely time for a home to catch fire."

"Do you think we could make it back to our place now?" I asked. "I'm worried about my barn. There's no strike team there this time."

"Yeah, I think you could," he replied. "The wind is blowing something terrible, so there's still a lot of hot cinders and a lot of fires still burning, but I think you could get through."

"Ok, thanks," I said. "Chase and I are going to try to come back to keep anything we can from burning. I'll call you again after we get there to let you know we made it and give you our status. Do you need me to stop at your place?"

"No, thanks," he said. "I think we're going to be okay. Be careful."

"Roger that," I replied.

I told my dad and my brother that we were going to head back to the ranch. Gerry and his family had joined us at my brothers. He and everybody else decided to stay put. We unloaded the stuff out of our truck and headed back into the firestorm. I thought we would encounter a roadblock, but we didn't see any on the back roads. In fact, it was eerily desolate.

When we got to Old Julian Highway and started heading toward our place, I could not believe what I was seeing. Once again I was reminded of a scene from a war movie. There were fires everywhere, houses, trees, cars on the side of the road. Just as we passed Bill's place we saw a Super Duty pickup truck with a large horse trailer still hooked up to it, on its side, off the road and all black from burning. It was still smoking.

"Oh my God!" Chase said, her hand to her mouth. "Do you think anybody is in there? Should we stop to see?"

"We can't," I said. "Look at all the burning cinders flying around. The air is full of them. We'll get injured for sure. If there is anybody in there, it's too late to do anything for them."

I slowed down just in case somebody was in the truck and able to leap out to ours, but I saw no signs of life. I kept going. The truck was getting pummeled by the wind and bits of burning material. Several days later I learned that wind gusts of 100 mph were being recorded around the county. I started to smell burning rubber and plastic. I worried about what this was doing to our truck. If it stalled we would be toast, literally. I kept going, as fast as I could, but the smoke was making it hard to see.

We pulled into the road that led to our place. Unlike in the Cedar Fire, that side of the mountain had been hit hard by the Witch Creek fire. Every bush was on fire and the smoke was more intense up here. It also looked like the homes on that side of the mountain were burning. I felt sick. We passed through the upper valley and, as we crested over the top of Starlight Mountain Road, I could see that it wasn't as bad on the other side, our side. I stopped long enough to take advantage of the bird's eye view to determine the situation below. It looked like the fire on our side of the mountain was contained to the woods.

We continued to our house to find everything there was untouched. I saw fires burning down in the woods, though, and one very large fire was burning precariously close to our barn. I ran down the hill to check the situation more closely. The fire nearby was intensely hot. I had to be careful not to get close enough for it to burn me. Two of the fence terminals near the barn were burning, and the layer of fine cow manure that had accumulated and surrounded the barn was burning like a bunt, moving steadily toward the barn wall.

I checked one of the hoses next to the barn and found it working just fine. The power poles had burned down again, so we had no electricity, but, since there had been no firemen to use the 10,000 gallons of water in our storage tank, we could use that water to fight the fire. The difference of elevation from the tank down to the barn was considerable, so there was also plenty of water pressure. I started hosing down the ground between the advancing line of embers and the barn. Chase soon joined me and I gave her the hose so I could use a rake to scrape the burnable material away from the barn.

For the most part, we escaped any serious damage from this fire. Some fence posts burned and the woods, was once again, pretty charred, but not as bad as in the Cedar Fire. Unfortunately, some our neighbors were not so lucky. A total of six homes up on Starlight Mountain burned to the ground. The electric poles burned down again, so there was no electricity for several weeks. We had generators this time, so there was very little interruption in our ability to keep things running.

One of the big concerns I had about the Witch Creek Fire was the potential damage that it might cause to the new vineyard I had recently planted. Planting a vineyard was never in my plan. Hell, it was never in my wildest dreams, but now I had one, and it had been a huge investment. Fortunately, it escaped the ravages of the fire.

# Chapter 81

One day, out of the clear blue, somebody who knew somebody else told Chase and me that there was a winery in town and that the owners were going to be harvesting one weekend. If we were interested, we were welcome to come join a group of volunteers to help pick grapes. That was something that I had never done, but it sounded interesting enough to go give it a whirl.

I discovered that picking grapes is an activity that begins at daybreak. We dutifully arrived at the crack of dawn to find a large number of people ready to help out. These people were all volunteers, apparently willing to work in the vineyard for the joy of the experience. There were so many people that the owner asked me to work with him in the winery rather than in the vineyard.

My job was primarily emptying lugs of grapes into the crusher-destemmer as they came in from the vineyard. I was also tasked with much of the cleaning which was apparently a big part of winemaking. In between the spells of hard labor, I asked the owner about the winemaking process. He obliged me with a great amount of detailed information and some demonstrations. He also treated me to tastings of the previous year's wines from their barrels. This was a new experience, and I found it very delightful. The wine was quite good, and I offer him my considered opinion about each wine that I tasted. I was surprised to discover that he did not drink, at all.

"How do you know how your wine is doing," I asked.

"I usually find somebody who knows what they're doing and get their assessments and input," he said. "Just like the way you commented on the wine now, I keep notes on that kind of input."

Being a very sensory oriented person, I could not imagine how this guy could make good wine without tasting it. He explained that much of winemaking was just following a process and paying attention to the details. Based on what I knew and felt, I thought that there had to be more to it, but his wine was quite satisfactory.

That experience was enough to pique my interest in learning more about wine grapes and to find out more about what was going on in the local area relative to the production of wine. I discovered that there was a local, nascent wine grape association comprised of a couple of dozen members. These people were working on reviving the wine industry in the Ramona Valley. I impulsively decided to join the group. The association leadership put together a viticulture seminar that was targeted to newcomers who were thinking about installing a vineyard. Although, at that moment I had no intentions to plant a vineyard, I decided to attend it. Following the seminar, I decided to plant some vines, just a small number, to get more hands-on experience.

Later that year, the vineyard association managed to get the federal Alcohol and Tobacco Tax and Trade Bureau, the TTB, to designate the Ramona Valley as an American Viticultural Area, or AVA. That, I realized, was a big deal and meant there was a ground floor opportunity to create something pretty special. I decided to expand our vineyard. That is the typical pattern of how things happen in my life. I wasn't really thinking about any grand plan. I was just moving forward on yet another thing that seemed worth doing.

The couple, who owned the vineyard where I had helped out a year and a half before, got divorced. I was contacted by the ex-wife and she asked me to help make the winery's wine that year.

"Um, well, I don't actually know how to make wine," I said. "That is, I've never actually made any before."

She didn't seem to think that this was a particularly strong argument for not helping out.

"Ok, I will work with you this season, but on the condition that you agree that this is on your nickel and if the wine isn't any good, well I told you that I am not an experienced winemaker." She agreed.

That's how I started down the road to becoming a winemaker. Since I didn't know anything about wine making, I threw myself into the effort of learning. I discovered that the process is perhaps one of the most difficult things one could possibly do. I mean, you can distill the process down into a few steps which are not difficult to get your arms around, but the devil is in the details.

I was extremely lucky to have connected with a wonderful mentor during my initial years as a winemaker. A man named Lum Eisenman, who was active in the local winemaking industry and very generous with his time, readily shared his extensive experience and abilities with others. I attended an event the local association sponsored where Lum was providing training on various types of chemical testing associated with making wine. I introduced myself and asked for his ongoing help, which he agreed to provide.

I read all the material I could get my hands on regarding viticulture and winemaking. I took classes in enology and vineyard management. I attended seminars that discussed topics like irrigation, canopy management, pest management, diseases, chemistry, wine faults, fermentation, aging, and barrel management. In typical fashion, I became very involved in the local vineyard association and soon found myself serving as the president.

While I felt completely inadequate for that responsibility, it turned out to be a tremendous opportunity for accelerating my growing knowledge of the winemaking industry. I received calls from new members asking for help, which I felt obliged to give. To be sure I was giving them accurate information and advice, I plunged into even more research on the myriad aspects of viticulture and winemaking. I also learned what not to do in my own vineyard and winery by working on other people's mistakes. I was often asked to help resolve these problems, and this was especially useful in my wine making endeavors.

My latent philosophy is that anything worth doing is worth doing well. Having said that, I have rarely been very good at doing things well, which is to say that I'm not particularly talented in most areas. The winemaking endeavor, however, really fired up my imagination, and I developed a passion for making good wine. I wasn't always successful. I made mistakes, and the results were sometimes not particularly good. The difference in my case was that I knew when I didn't hit a mark that I had set for myself. When that occurred, that wine was not bottled and sold, or even given away. I was painfully aware that some of my colleagues in the trade gave in to the economic pressures associated with throwing away bad wine, or even worse, some didn't seem to know when their wine was crappy.

Chase and I obtained our Federal Permit and California State license in 2010 and started making wine that we could sell under the Hellangone Ranch business name. We created a logo that consisted of a black horse with a red eye, rearing up in the midst by flames, implying the survival of a journey through Hell. We began evolving our branding strategy around the theme of ranching, Western life, rigorous independence, and casual, but elegant, living.

I sometimes tell people that the rearing horse on our logo is my old horse, Gus, but the truth is that the black horse is a small recognition of the black stallion of local legend. The legend goes that in the early 19th century, there was a cunning black stallion that escaped one of the large ranchos in the local valleys. The stallion roamed the nearby mountain, occasionally coming down into the valley to steal mares from the ranchers' stock. The stallion became very successful at this, much to the ranchers' chagrin. The ranchers tried to catch him on several occasions and recover their lost horses, but the stallion was too clever and always eluded them.

One day, the ranchers got together and made a plan to capture the stallion and stop his thieving once and for all. They formed a group and headed up into the mountain, now known as Mount Gower. They chased him relentlessly, breaking up into smaller groups so that the stallion could never get any rest. Finally, the magnificent stallion collapsed and died of exhaustion. The ranchers recovered their stolen mares, but they recognized that their adversary was a very special animal and they ultimately lamented the outcome. Thereafter, they referred to the mountain as Black Horse Mountain in recognition of their worthy foe.

Building on our Western theme and the notion of "Hell and Gone", we decided to use a bison skull on the labels of wine that we made from locally purchased grapes, and the rearing horse logo for our estate wines. When I started making white wines, we settled on the Leonardo da Vinci sketch of a rearing horse. We called our rose', Purgatory Pink, and our super Tuscan, Devil's Due, all in keeping with the Hellangone theme.

In 2012 we opened our tasting patio and started actually earning revenue for the first time since founding the winery business in 2007. It took three more years before the winery income exceeded the cost of managing the vineyard and the making of the wine. The profits were not anything to crow about. It was clear that we would not get rich from owning a winery. There is, in fact, a running joke in the wine industry that if you want to make a small fortune with a winery, you must start out with a large fortune.

Chase was not enthusiastic about the winery vision and plan, but, as always, she stuck with me through this, yet another, hair-brained scheme. She toiled along my side in the vineyards, planting, training, pruning and harvesting. She was up to her elbows, literally, in grapes at the crush pad and became the undisputed "press queen" during that part of the operation. She did most of the paper work and managed the wine club. In short, she was a trooper. I always found it odd, though, that she rarely drank my wine. She preferred her chardonnay, and I don't make chardonnay, so I leave it at that.

One thing is for sure, owning a vineyard and winery is a lot of hard work. We were once interviewed by a magazine, and the topic was focused on the "romance of wine" for a Valentine's Day article. When the correspondent asked Chase what she felt was romantic about owning a winery, she answered wryly that the only romantic thing about a winery is the pointy end of the bottle. Everything else is just damn hard work. I contributed that the vast majority of winery activity involves cleaning, which is never romantic.

At the height of the growing season, when the weeds are under control, the vines are green and healthy, the canes are all tucked into their trellis wires, and the grapes are reaching full veraison, meaning that they've turned purple, the fruits of all our labor might indeed be viewed as a sort of victorious culmination of our passion for this endeavor. Growing something, and then crafting it into something else that is a reflection of our land and our fruit and our effort is something one might think of as romantic in the classic sense. Those moments are typically enhanced by frequent visits to the pointy end of the bottle.

Not unlike most of the personal undertakings of my life, the most gratifying aspect of all this work is when people compliment me and tell me how much they enjoy my wine. I discovered early on that if you are a decent winemaker, you are, in many circles, considered a "rock star". That's the kind of attention that feeds my fire, and I would be liar if I said that I didn't love that kind of recognition.

The ranch and winery would have been impossible to build and manage without the help of our many friends and my brothers. It would be difficult to calculate all the hours that others put in to help us make this dream happen. I'm sure that most people who know me think that I'm crazy, yet they are right there with me as I go over the next proverbial hill, charging after some cockamamie idea.

Chase and I retired from our "day jobs" and settled into the less stressful but no less difficult work of managing the ranch, the vineyard, and the winery business. Life is good. The ranch is a beautiful place to live and we feel very fortunate to be where we are at this stage of our lives. We have wonderful families and wonderful friends. We make our own wine and raise our own meat. There is not much else to want. I live every day like it may be the last, like every day is an adventure. So, I guess I can say, "We lived happily ever after."

# Chapter 82

While his story didn't have a dramatic ending, no final world disaster that had to be overcome, no big murder mystery solved, no bad guys destroyed, it did have a happy ending, and isn't that the best kind of ending? The old man decided that he was satisfied with it. Hell, he thought, that's just the way it ends, and that's that.

He was glad that he had finally finished the book. He still had that nagging feeling he had when he started the book. There should be more. After all, he wasn't dead yet. Toward the end of his writing efforts, however, he had found it more and more difficult to concentrate.

That weird sound and the crack in the mountain had been terribly distracting. A couple of weeks after he discovered the mysterious crack, the weird sound that seemed to emanate from it just stopped. It wasn't something he noticed right away, just as he wasn't always cognizant of when it was active. He was sitting at his desk writing when it happened. It was a particularly quiet afternoon. Chase was out shopping, the dogs were napping, and there weren't even any birds singing. The one sound that eventually drew his attention to the quietness was a fly, buzzing around in the room. It was an annoying sound, and the old man felt like the damn thing was going to drive him crazy, but then the fly landed somewhere. The old man lost his focus, now anticipating the fly to take off again at any moment, as flies tend to do, possibly landing on him. Then he realized that there was no sound at all. It dawned on him that the weird, subsonic sound was missing.

He sat there for several moments, trying to see if maybe he was just not letting the sound come into his consciousness, but there was nothing. He quickly got out of his chair and headed down the stairs. That is what he had been waiting for. He needed to go investigate the crack to see if it had changed. He walked through the house, his excitement growing. The dogs got up, wanting to go outside with him, but the old man told them to stay. He didn't want them to attract the attention of the neighbor, and besides, he didn't want them to dash into the abyss if the crack was still exhibiting its mysterious properties.

He walked across the neighbor's field, as nonchalantly as he could manage. As he approached the place where the crack was located, it was immediately apparent that it had changed. It was now just an ordinary crack in the rock. He could plainly see that the opening went back just three or four feet from the entrance and the odd fuzziness was gone. He had no hesitation about walking into the space. It was just an empty space between the rocks.

Wow, he thought. It seemed clear to him now that the sound and the transformation of the crack had some correlation. Still, not enough evidence to draw any conclusions, and if he talked to anybody about it now, they would just think he was nuts. He would have to wait until the sound came back and then check the crack again. If it exhibited the same characteristics as the first time he found it, he would be certain that this thing was associated with the sound. Then he would decide what to do next.

The sound didn't come back though. The old man got back to his book, reviewing what he had written. He also spent more time in the vineyard pruning. He became so absorbed with his daily life that he nearly forgot all about the crack and the sound. The phenomenon would occasionally invade his mind, and he wondered if maybe it was just a once-in-a-lifetime event, or if it really happen at all.

His mother had had Alzheimer's. Maybe he was starting to have symptoms of some kind of dementia. He thought of dementia as various forms of forgetting thing, not seeing things. No, he was certain what he saw and experienced was real. Then he remembered the rock. He should go back there and recover that rock, maybe take a closer look at it to see if there was anything peculiar about it. When he went back to the crack, however, the rock was gone.

He didn't remember seeing it on his last visit, when there was no sound, but he hadn't actually looked for it. He was sure it would be easy to spot. There weren't any other small stones in the immediate area. He recalled having to walk away from the crack a distance to find a suitable stone. There were no small stones just in front of the crack at all. This would drive him crazy, he thought.

One day, shortly after the old man had finished reviewing and editing his first draft, he was out in his vineyard, pruning. It was a glorious day, not too hot, a light breeze blowing, birds singing. He was by himself. His friend, Byron, who usually helped him with this effort, was down in San Diego visiting an old Navy buddy. He could hear a woodpecker tapping away in the forest below the vineyard. He thought of working in the vineyard as very therapeutic, almost Zen-like. Now that he was retired, keeping up with the management of the vineyard wasn't as stressful as it had been when he was running his business down the hill.

He was letting his mind drift when he suddenly realized the sound was back. He stopped what he was doing and stood there listening. Yes, it was definitely there, and now that he had become aware of it, the sound intensified. He wondered if it had been going on all along and he had just not noticed it.

He started back toward his house. He had not told anybody about his discovery, partly because he was sure everybody would think he was nuts and partly because he wanted to try to figure this thing out before talking to people about it. As he walked up to the house, the thought popped into his mind that he might be obsessing about it. No, he didn't think so. Lots of time had passed since the discovery and he had kept up with his daily life. He was sure that it was natural to be curious about such an odd thing.

He had given some thought to what he would do if and when the sound returned. He had stashed a coil of strong rope, a canteen of water, a flashlight, two pencils, and a small tablet in a rucksack up in his closet. He was already dressed in outdoor work cloths, and was carrying his Kershaw pocket knife. He also had his cell phone with him. He thought these things might be useful in a variety of situations he might find himself in if he decided to explore the space beyond the opening in the crack. Assuming, of course, that assumed that this thing, whatever it was, still manifested itself now that the sound was back.

Chase was sitting at her computer in her studio, just inside the back door. The old man decided he should tell here where he was going, just not why, or what he might do there.

"Honey," he said, "I'm going to go up to the neighbor's place, the bottom of the bald-faced rock, over on the far south side. There's something there I want to look at."

She looked up from her computer. "What is it?"

"Well, it's just something that looks funny. I don't know what it is. I'll let you know when I get back. I won't be gone long."

She returned her attention to what she was doing, not particularly interested in his mission. "Ok," was all she said.

The old man went upstairs to get his rucksack, and exited through the front door to avoid any questions from Chase about why he was taking such a thing. He walked up the road that separated his property from the neighbor's. It was just a matter of time before the neighbor spied him trekking across the field and inquired about his purpose. Perhaps he had been seen in the past, but so far, there had been no questions.

He arrived at the crack, and found that it was exhibiting the same opaque, slightly fuzzy quality at the entrance that it had the first time he discovered it. His excitement was palpable and he knew he needed to calm himself down so he could think clearly. Adding to the tension, the sound had intensified there at the crack.

He took a deep breath. He had thought about it quite a bit, so he would stick to his plan. A short distance away, he spotted a large boulder big enough to be immovable by any effort he could muster, but not so large as to make it difficult to get his rope around. Using a bowline and stopper knot, he tied one end of the rope around the boulder, and then walked back to the crack. He judged that, after he tied the other end around his waist, he had about fifteen feet of rope left to use beyond the entrance of the crack. That should be plenty of rope since, when there was no sound, the space beyond the entrance was only about three or four feet deep.

He allowed for the extra rope in the remote case that it was some kind of portal. He thought it more likely the space was just being distorted by a sonic disturbance, but just in case some aspect of this phenomenon became harmful, and he wanted to be able to pull himself out if it became difficult to walk back through whatever this was. Hell, he didn't know what this was, but he had to find out, and if it was a sci-fi situation, he wanted to be prepared.

He took out an envelope containing a note that explained everything he had discovered thus far and what he was about to do. On the front of the envelope was written "to Chase". He took a pencil out of his rucksack and wrote the date and time on the envelope and set it on the ground a few feet away from the crack's entrance, placing a rock on top of it to keep it from blowing away.

He was ready. He didn't feel fear, just mild apprehension. He had only felt true fear a few times in his life. He had always just gone ahead and done things that he thought might be worth doing, without dwelling too much on consequences while he was doing them. He had been afraid plenty of times in his life for sure, but he didn't think that that being afraid and fear were the same. He thought that fear is what kept people from doing things. Being afraid was how you felt when you were doing things. He was certainly afraid when he was getting shot at during the war. He was afraid when his canoe started filling up with spiders on the Turner River. He was afraid when he rushed to his daughter's hospital bed after her terrible accident down in Mexico.

He knew that he was lucky. He had often felt that he led a charmed life. He had never become rich or famous, not that kind of lucky, but he had had an extraordinary life, nevertheless. He had done a lot of things that he was sure could have killed or maimed him, or ruined him one way or another. But here he was, still kicking. Maybe the immediate adventure before him now was a bad choice, but nothing ventured, nothing gained. He was sure his mother would say something like that, although he was pretty sure she would not approve of what he was about to do. Nor would Chase, or just about anybody else he knew.

Well, life is kind of like jumping from an airplane. It's not something that you want to think about too much, you just do it. He had put his hand in the first time and nothing bad happened. Even the rock came back. He thought there was a pretty decent chance he might survive this. Of course, he also might get whisked away into another dimension, he thought lightly.

He approached the entrance and stuck out his hand as he had done before. He watched his hand disappear into the shroud of black static. After a moment, he pulled it back out and examined it closely. Nothing amiss as far as he could tell. He put his hand back in and then moved forward until his whole arm was enveloped beyond the entrance. Nothing unusual, other than the almost imperceptible tingle as before.

He stepped back and checked the figure eight knot holding the rope around his waist. He didn't think there would be much chance of going vertical, so he just looped the excess rope into a coil and put it over his shoulder. He walked back up to the entrance, took a deep breath and pushed his head in past the entrance.

There was just a gray darkness inside, nothing to see so far. He felt that slight tingling, but it wasn't uncomfortable. He pushed a little farther until he thought he must be all the way in. He held his arm out and shuffled carefully forward, thinking he would be able to touch the backside of the opening fairly quickly, but he felt nothing. He continued to inch forward until he began to see something lighter ahead. He moved his arm back and forth, but there was nothing solid. Another few inches forward and suddenly he was out in the open, past the darkness and fuzzy tingling. Before he could process what he was seeing, he turned around to see if the crack was there. It was, just inches from where he stood, and it looked pretty much just the way it looked when he entered. He was sure he hadn't turned around, yet the entrance was now behind him.

He turned back around and made a quick surveillance of the immediate area. It was definitely not where he had just been. It was a different place for sure. Everywhere around him there were lots of very large trees. The terrain gradually opened up onto a broad meadow a short distance ahead. At one end of the meadow was a building. It looked like it could be a house, but the style was like nothing he had ever seen before. It looked like it might be made of mud or clay, with three or four domes that appeared to be squished together. He could make out what had to be windows and a door.

He took a few more steps forward and turned around to examine the portal. The mountain he had passed through was gone, replaced by a large tree which had an opening in it that looked very much like the crack. It might have been a hollow in the tree, but now it exhibited the same opaque, black static as the crack in the rock. The rope was still around his waist and only a small amount had paid out to get through. He decided it would be a good idea to go back to make sure whatever it was went both ways.

This time he stepped through quickly and emerged on the other side, back where he started. He looked around to reassure himself that he was indeed back home. He saw his vineyard, his barn, the house, and the steers out in the pasture. He turned back around and went through to the other side. "Wow, this is a portal," he said aloud. He suddenly realized he could hear that weird, subsonic sound on both sides.

The old man tried to collect his thoughts. The air seemed okay, he was breathing and the temperature was similar to what it was on the other side of the portal. There was a blue sky. He wondered if he was in another time, or another dimension, or another world. It was really hard to get his mind around all of this. He decided he had accomplished what he had set out to do, so he should go back and figure out who to tell and how to tell it. It suddenly occurred to him that he should take some pictures, or else he would have no proof that he'd been to this place. If the portal closed up forever, anybody who heard his story would reasonably consider him insane.

He pulled out his cell phone. How did people survive before these things were invented? He wondered if it would work there. He assumed all the functions that relied on the communication infrastructure from the other side would be useless, but the camera should still work. He took a picture of the tree and its opening. Seemed to work. He took some pictures of the odd house, then the trees.

He decided he would video his crossing from this "new" world back to his. He turned around to go back through and saw the most unbelievable sight imaginable. There, standing next to the big tree, not more than three feet from where he himself stood, was another person. Well, not exactly a person.

"Whoa," he exclaimed, jumping back in surprise. He was looking at a humanoid-being that looked a lot like the "typical" alien many people have described over the years, but not quite so exaggerated.

"Hello," the old man said. He held up his hand in what he hoped was a universal gesture of friendly greeting. The being returned the gesture, but made no sound. Good Grief, he thought. Now what the hell was he supposed to do. He loved fantasy and science fiction, and had watched scores of movies and read lots of books in that genre over the years. His mind raced through some of the scenarios of initial greetings he could recall like this one, ones that didn't result in evaporation by an alien weapon or worse.

"I'm Wolf," he said, putting the fingers of both hands on his chest. He took off his rucksack and pulled out his small paper tablet and a pencil. The being watched as he wrote his name in large letters on a page. He turned the page toward the being and pointed to the word. "Wolf," he repeated, then touched his chest again and said, "Wolf."

The being looked at the paper then at the old man. It then looked at the open space in the tree and looked at the rope leading out of the opening and up to the old man's waist.

"Tick," the being seemed to say. "Tick," it repeated in a high-pitched, nasal tone, making the same gesture that the old man had made on its chest.

"Tick," the old man tried to say as close to what he heard as he could manage, and smiled. The being didn't change its expression. He wondered if it could make facial expressions

The creature was tall, at least as tall as the old man. It had a large head with a somewhat pointed chin, a small, thin-lipped mouth, small nose and large dark eyes, which made it look like what you might expect an alien to look like. It had very small ears that were more like folds in its skin. The old man made mental notes of as many features of the being as he could. It wore a light grayish garment that had a V-neck collar. Its skin didn't look that much different from his but was perhaps more leathery looking. It had very thin short hair on the top of its head.

The being pointed to the opening in the tree, then pointed to the old man, who grabbed the rope attached to his waist and made gesture that he hoped was interpreted as coming through from the other side. The being spoke, but it was nothing the old man could make out. He had an idea. He was holding his camera, so he thought he should show this being a couple of pictures from the other side.

He looked through his sparsely populated picture gallery and found a picture of his house. Now that he looked at it, it didn't really seem that different than the house in the distance. He held up the phone so that the being could see the picture. The being looked at it intently. Then the old man found a picture of his barn with cattle nearby grazing on the barley fields that he had planted. The picture included the mountains in the background. He showed this picture to the being, who again looked at it with what seemed like a great deal of interest.

When the creature looked up, the old man gestured first to the phone then to the opening. The being cocked its head slightly, and then pointed to the building in the meadow. The old man nodded his head to express understanding. He felt like they were communicating on a very basic level. He then showed Tick a picture of himself posing with Chase, pointing to his image and then pointing to himself. Tick looked from the picture to the old man, and cocked its head again.

The old man wondered what would happen if he tried to take a picture of this being. He guessed that he should start thinking of it as "Tick". One way to find out, he thought. He selected the camera icon, held the phone up, and quickly snapped a picture. Tick didn't move, so he put his phone away. The old man realized it must be getting late. He looked at this wrist watch. Chase would be wondering what had happened to him. He had better go back.

He wanted to give this guy something. Was it a guy? He didn't have much with him that he thought would make an appropriate gift. He didn't want to give it his knife. He decided that his watch might be just the thing, so he took it off and held it out to his new acquaintance. Tick reached out its hand to take the offering. Its fingers were long and slender. It had an opposing thumb but only three fingers. It took the watch and put it in its other hand to examine it. Tick then put it on its wrist, having obviously noticed how the old man wore it.

He wasn't sure how to say goodbye or to indicate that he was going to leave. He assumed that Tick would not probably not understand what an outstretched hand would mean, so he simply raised his hand as he had when he greeted the being and turned to walk back through the portal. Tick reached out and touched the old man's arm. The old man stopped abruptly and turned back to look at him a little apprehensively. Tick then reached into its tunic and pulled out a small metallic box. It held the box in one hand and stroked it with a finger from its other hand, then slowly handed it to the old man. He took the box, not sure what it was, but then he assumed that Tick had no idea what the watch was either.

"Thank you," the old man said, making a slight bow with his head. Then he turned and walked back through the portal.

The old man passed through without incident. He looked around to make sure all was as he had left it. He untied the rope from his waist and then from the rock. He picked up the envelope from where he had left it on the ground. He took one more look at the portal, half expecting Tick to emerge, but that didn't happen. As he walked back toward his house he wondered if these portals had opened up in other places on earth in the past. That might help to explain why this creature looked so familiar. Other people might have run into them. Maybe these beings had crossed over into our world, and met other humans. He recalled that others who had tried to convince people that they had encountered aliens were all considered kooks. He had to think about how he was going to deal with this.

He dropped the rope in back of the winery bottle house. He went back into his house through the front door so he could stow his rucksack undetected. He went into his wife's studio where he found her still at the computer. She looked up at him.

"Where have you been?" she asked.

"Oh, just out looking around at stuff," he said casually. "Has it been so long?"

"I was starting to wonder where you were," she said.

"I'd like to talk to you about something, Honey," he said. She had already refocused on whatever it was that she was doing on her computer. "I'd like for you to come into the living room to talk to me."

She looked up again, with a concerned look on her face. "What's wrong?" she asked.

"Nothing is wrong, but I need to discuss something with you. It's important," he said.

They headed toward the center of the house, where the large living room was located. The dogs followed, as well as their cat, Rocky. He gestured for her to have a seat in the big recliner, and he sat in the middle of the leather couch. The dogs took up their customary positions on either side of the old man and lay down. Rocky jumped up on the arm of the recliner. That was how they all assembled when retiring to the living room. Everybody had their own positions. It was earlier than they customarily assembled, so the pets were a little restless.

"What is it?" Chase asked pensively.

"I have something extraordinary to tell you," he began. "So, I want you to just hear me out, and then you can give me your reaction and advice." He took his cell phone out of his pocket and selected the gallery icon, looking to see if the pictures of the alien world were still there. They were. He retrieved the little metallic box that Tick had given to him and placed in on the coffee table.

"You recall the weird subsonic sound that we've been hearing?" he began.

"Yes," Chase replied. She seemed to be giving him all her attention.

"Well, over the past several weeks, maybe two months now, I've been trying to see if I could find the source of the sound," he said. "I've walked all over this valley to see if I could detect any variation in the sound. I eventually found the source." He hesitated for effect. Chase just looked at him as if he were about to tell her something silly.

"I found the source," he continued, "and it is quite extraordinary. It's up at the bottom of the big rock face on the neighbor's property, over on the south side. There's a big crack in the rock face and that's where this sound is coming from."

"Really?" she said. He could tell she was already losing interest.

"Ok," he said very seriously, "this crack turns out to be a portal to some other place. I don't know what it is exactly, but it's definitely not here in this valley. I went there today for the purpose of going through the portal. I took several precautions, but I'll explain them later. The bottom line is that I went into this crack, which is actually a portal, and came out in this other place. Look at this picture."

He showed her the picture of the tree with the opening that was the other side of the portal. She looked at it. "What is this?" she asked.

"It's the other side of the portal," he explained. "On this side, the portal is that crack in the mountain. On the other side, it's this big hollow part of that tree. Go to the next picture."

She did so, and was looking at the scene of the meadow framed by huge trees, and the odd dome-looking building in the distance.

"That is a picture of what it looks like on the other side," he said.

"I don't understand," she said. "Where is this?"

"It's just up there," he pointed towards the neighbor's place. "That's what is on the other side of this portal, or whatever it is."

She looked at him with some concern, "That doesn't make any sense. Where are these pictures from?"

"They are from the other side of some kind of portal to another world, or time, or dimension, Sweetheart. I know it's hard to believe, but I have just been there. Look at the next picture."

She swiped the phone screen. "Oh my God," she said. "What is that?"

"Its name is Tick," he said. "At least I think that's what it said. It was standing there by the portal. I tried to communicate with it, but I don't think I got very far. It seemed to be friendly. I told him my name and he told me his. I don't actually know if it's a male or female."

Chase looked at him as if stricken. "Honey, why are you telling me these things? Is this a joke?"

"No, no," he said emphatically. "This really happened. As I was leaving I decided to give it something, so I gave it my wrist watch, and it gave me this." He handed the object to her.

"What is this?" she asked.

"I don't know," he said, "but I think it was something Tick valued by the way he gave it to me. I haven't had time to examine it carefully. I doubt that he, it, knew what my watch was. Look, if you think I'm making this up, I can take you up there right now and we can both go over to the other side."

She just looked at him, then looked at the pictures on the phone again, and fingered the metallic object. "I don't know what to say or think about this." She continued toying with the object, then suddenly seemed to focus on it. "I think this is a box. I think it's hollow. Did you notice that it has faint markings on one side? They look kind of like glyphs or something."

The old man shifted his attention to the object as well. "I didn't notice the markings," he said. "Can you find any kind of latch?"

"I think this end of the box is some kind of mechanism, but I can't figure out how it works," she said. He moved closer to see if he could determine anything about its nature. He knew better than to take it from her. Once she got locked in on working something he just had to let her keep at it until she figured it out or gave up.

Suddenly, she flipped up one whole side of the box. "That's it!" she exclaimed. They both looked at the end more closely. It didn't appear to do anything obvious, but there was another side to the box just under the one she had flipped up.

"I think that's is some kind of release," the old man said. "See if anything else will move now that the side is loose."

She fiddled with it a couple more moments and found that one of the large sides of the box flipped up, exposing what looked like some sort of button inside.

"That's it," the old man said enthusiastically. "What the heck is that?"

Inside the little metallic box was a small, oval button-like thing that had the color and translucent quality of an opal. It had an opalescent quality that seemed to almost pulsate.

Chase closed that box again. "This thing you saw gave this to you?" she asked.

"Yes. His name is Tick," he responded.

"I thought you didn't know if it was a guy," she said.

"Ok, its name is Tick," he said in a more exasperated tone. "Let me take you up to the portal. I want you to see it. Maybe we could see Tick again and try to figure out what this is."

She looked reluctant. "I don't think it's safe, if this thing actually exists."

"Well, why don't you just take a look at it," the old man pleaded. "I don't want to spend the rest of my life having you think I'm crazy."

She finally agreed, and they headed up to the crack together. The old man desperately hoped that the neighbor didn't see them. Both of them tramping around his property would definitely arouse curiosity and bring him down to investigate. The old man didn't want any interference.

They reached the portal. Chase immediately saw that it was indeed something unusual, and they both recognized the increase in intensity of the sound.

"Let's both go in and take a quick look," he suggested.

"I don't want to go in there," she said. "What happens if we can't get back?"

"I've already been there and back," he said coaxingly. "I really think you should take a quick look. It's quite amazing." He reached for her hand, which she took after a few moment's hesitation. They turned toward the opening and Chase reached up with her other hand and grabbed his arm, drawing close to him. She was going to do this. She was a brave girl, he thought. She had always gone along with his crazy ideas and adventures.

He was about to take her through, when, suddenly, two figures emerged from the other side, and stood there in front of them. Chase let out a small shout of alarm and moved behind the old man, still clinging on to his hand and arm. The smaller of the two beings took a small step back as well. At first glance, the two beings looked nearly the same, but the old man could see the smaller one was probably either a female or an adolescent. It had rounder features, and bit more of the thin hair on its head. It also looked, well, more delicate.

They all stood there for a few moments looking at each other. Finally, what the old man assumed was Tick raised his hand in the greeting that he had used in their earlier meeting. The old man did the same and asked Chase to do likewise. She moved out from behind the old man and raised her hand, which was then repeated by the smaller of the two beings. Tick then held out his arm, displaying the watch he had been given.

"Sweetheart', the old man said, "this is Tick." He gestured with his hand toward Tick. He then pointed to Chase. "Tick, this is Chase. Chase, Chase," he repeated pointing accordingly. Tick cocked his head in a way the old man assumed meant some form of acknowledgement or maybe the equivalent of "yes".

Tick looked at his companion the said something that came out as "Oof," pointing to the old man. The old man realized that Tick was trying to pronounce his name, "Wolf." That was followed by what he assumed was his companion's name, "Sen," as he pointed toward the other being.

"Oh my god," Chase breathed. "They're real. Oh my god."

Tick once again held up his arm sporting the watch and pointed to it. The old man wasn't sure what Tick was trying to communicate. Maybe he was trying to figure out what the thing was used for. The old man looked at the time on the watch, then looked at the position of the sun. He pointed to the sun, and bent down to the ground to draw a picture with his finger. He drew a straight line and made gestures that he hoped would communicate that the line represented the earth. Then he drew a circle in approximately the current position of the sun relative to the line. He pointed to the watch on Tick's arm and drew a separate circle in the dirt, making twelve hash marks to represent the hours. He pointed to the fourth hash from the top. Having finished, he then stood up and gestured to see the watch. Tick apparently knew what he was trying to do, and so he lifted his arm.

The old man pointed to the numeral 4 on the watch, then the facsimile of the clock on the ground, then to the sun. He made another gesture of the sun getting lower in the sky, and then pointed to the fifth position of the dirt clock, followed by pointing to the numeral 5 on Tick's new watch. Tick cocked its head several times. He got it. He was now looking at the watch with what seemed like renewed interest.

"Honey," the old man said. "Did you bring the metal box with you?"

"Yes," she said.

"May I please have it?" he said. She withdrew the little box from the pocket of her jeans and handed it to him. This brought a decided reaction from Sen, who took hold of Tick's arm and spoke in a quiet, but seemingly insistent tone. They looked at each other, and after a moment, Sen dropped Tick's arm.

The old man opened the box, held it in his open palm and pointed to the opalescent button. Tick gently took the box from the old man and looked at him in what appeared to be a solemn manner. He pointed to the opening of the portal and then put his finger on the button. The intense subsonic sound ceased immediately and the portal was gone. Now there was just that small space between the rocks. Tick looked back at the old man, who nodded his head slowly in apprehension.

"This is a key," he said mostly to Chase. "They are giving us a key to the other world, to their world." He looked at his wife, watching her stare at the now ordinary space. She looked up at him in wonder.

"What does all this mean?" she said.

"I don't know," was all he could say. "I guess they trust us, or at least Tick does, but beyond that, I just don't know."

Tick pushed the button again and the sound began again, followed by the reappearance of the portal. He then offered the box back to the old man.

"You have to go take a look, Sweet P'," he said. She was still holding on to him for dear life. He made a gesture to communicate that they were going in. Tick cocked his head, and the old man ushered his wife through the portal.

They emerged to find the same scene the old man had looked upon earlier. Tick and Sen followed them through the portal and stood quietly to one side. Chase was taking it all in. She ventured further out than he had earlier.

"These trees are gigantic, like the ones we saw at Sequoia National Park. That house over there is amazing. It's so different. Do you think that's where they live?" She was obviously as overwhelmed by all of this as the old man had been when he first discovered everything.

"I think we are being invited, although to where or what I'm not sure," he said. "It's not like being invited over to the next-door neighbor's house for tea. I think this is something much more profound. I can't tell if these beings are as surprised and amazed as we are or if this is something they do on a more frequent, more structured basis. They obviously have the technology to control the portal. That's what that little box does.

"The only reason that I can think of for them to offer this key to us is that they want us to come here. But for what purpose? To learn about us, to study us, to keep us for some purpose? I don't know what to make of it. Did you notice how Sen reacted when we revealed we had the box? It looked to me like she was surprised or maybe upset that Tick had given it to us. It's clearly a powerful thing. For all they know, we could use it to invade their world."

The old man reflected several moments more. "I don't know if giving us the box was a gesture of trust or an enticement. I think we better go back now. I need to think about this some more."

Chase went back to where the old man was standing. He made a motion to indicate they were going to go back, then raised his hand to indicate "goodbye" like he had done earlier. Chase mimicked his motion. Sen walked over and touched Chase's arm, and Tick did the same to the old man. He and Chase awkwardly returned the gesture, and then they turned toward the portal and walked through.

"My God!" Chase said breathlessly, "My heart is pounding a mile a minute. I just don't know what to think about it all."

"I don't either," the old man said. "This is truly an amazing thing, but I can't help but wonder if I've opened up Pandora's Box."

When they got back to the house they opened a bottle of wine. They talked about the possibilities and the considerations as they shared the wine. The unknown is a difficult thing to contemplate. The old man thought that if he was younger he would probably do what he always had done and just jump in with both feet and see where the portal might take him. He wouldn't have thought too much about consequences ahead of time. But, he wasn't that young anymore, and, of course, there was Chase.

Chase was excited, and the wine was adding to her enthusiasm to find out more about the other world and those people, but he knew that any adversity that went along with the experience would be less tolerable to her than it would be to him. They had a life there at the ranch that was engrained into their very fibers. Anything they might attempt regarding this other world would almost certainly be very disruptive.

Over the months the old man had been writing his book he had been wondering if there would ever be any more adventures, or if he had reached a point in his life where adventure was done. He had struggled with the notion of retirement, but came to realize that there were so many things to do, things he wanted to do outside the hectic business world. Now, there was this amazing opportunity for an adventure that was literally out of this world, and at this time of his life for crying out loud.

Neither of them got much sleep that night. The plethora of possibilities in trying to engage the other world and the other beings was mind boggling. What about all the responsibilities and activities that came with the ranch? So much to think about.

The next morning, after all the usual chores, the old man asked his wife to sit with him and discuss what they were going to do. He poured them each a cup of coffee, and they sat at their kitchen table which looked out over their ranch.

Chase started before the old man could say what he intended to say. "I have to tell you that I can't go off on some exploration of another world. I think that it could be incredibly exciting and interesting, but I don't have the constitution for that sort of thing and I don't want to give up my life here at the ranch. I know how you are and that you probably want to go do this. This sort of thing is right up your alley. I won't try to stop you if you decide to do something with these other creatures, but I will tell you that I will be very worried."

The old man smiled affectionately at his wife. She had been a trooper and a good sport their whole lives together. He knew that she had gone along with many things that he wanted to do even though she probably thought most of them were hair-brained. Even the ranch and the winery would not have been her choice of life changing things to invest in. Yes, he was very lucky to have her as his partner in life.

"I have also decided that I don't want to pursue this invitation," he said. "I want to believe that it was offered with good intentions and it would be an amazing adventure, but I am content with where I am now in my life. I have been concerned since I retired that the end of my life was going to be dull and boring compared with all the things I've done over the years, but now I have come to realize that the life I have right now is still an ongoing adventure. My life is an adventure that never stops."

"This invitation to another world is a very exciting prospect, and I'm sure that I would relish whatever it might bring, but I love what I have here and now. In the old days, I would abandon what I had and go do the next thing that caught my interest and that I thought was worth doing. I admit it was exciting, and much of that reckless behavior resulted in some very positive outcomes for me. On looking back over my life, however, I realize that I have regrets about some of the wreckage I left behind."

"I am content with our life together, with our ranch, and the animals, the vineyard, the winery, and our friends. I have lots of ideas for making what we have even better, and my love for you has transformed into something that is very precious to me. I don't think I need to look further than right here for my next adventure. I mean that very sincerely."

"As long as you don't object, I think I should go back to the portal, go to the other side and leave the key there. I want to communicate our gratitude in some way, but I don't know how to do that. If their intentions were not peaceful, that might trigger an inter-dimensional war or something, but I have the feeling that they were just trying to be friendly, but then I tend to be over optimistic"

"I thought I might leave a couple of bottles of our wine." The old man laughed heartily. "Who knows, they may keep coming back and become one of our best customers. I'm sure they would be a big hit at the wine club pick-up parties."

"You're amazing," Chase said. "I love you very much."

"I was hoping you'd say that, that I was amazing, I mean," he said. She smacked him on the arm.

"When are you going back," she asked.

"I thought I'd go now," he said. "I was hoping you would come with me. I'd like for you to take some video, just in case we need to explain what is going on. You know, in case there is an invasion."

They proceeded once again across the neighbor's property to the portal. The old man had his wife video him explaining what this space was and how it worked, showing the metallic box as he explained. She started another video segment as they walked through the portal.

On the other side, he spread out a linen cloth on the ground nearby and set the two bottles of wine on the cloth along with the metallic box, the portal key. He hoped they would not be offended. Then he walked back through the portal, and they headed home.

A couple of hours later the neighbor came knocking at their door.

"Hello," the old man said. "What's up?"

"I saw you walking around on the west side of our property a couple of times, including this morning," he said. The old man smiled. Of course he'd seen me.

"I kept seeing what I thought was a coyote up there in that area, and I was just poking around to see if maybe there was a den up there," the old man had rehearsed an excuse ahead of time. "I'm glad you didn't shoot me."

"No, I only shoot people I don't know or like," the neighbor joked back.

"I found something up there in the general area that you were in and I thought it might belong to you," he continued. Chase had come to the door to join them. They looked at each other quickly.

"What is it?" the old man asked.

"Well, it's a little metal box and an old-looking bottle," he said. "They were on the ground sitting next to each other like they had been left there." The old man could plainly see that the neighbor expected an explanation.

"Good Grief," the old man finally said, taking the items. "That bottle is an old antique that I've had for ages. I keep water in it when I go for walkabouts. That box is a trinket that I picked up at a flea market years ago. It's kind of a lucky charm. It must have dropped out of my pocket when I laid the bottle on the ground. Did you find it close by a big split in the rock face?"

"Yeah, that's where I found it," the neighbor said. "Is that where you thought the coyote den might be?"

"Yes," he said. "I was scouting around that immediate area but didn't find anything. Did you see anything unusual?"

"No, nothing but those things," the neighbor said, pointing to the box and bottle still in the old man's hands.

"Well, I apologize for not telling you that I was poking around over there," said the old man.

"Oh, no problem at all," he replied. "Say did you notice that the strange noise stopped this morning?"

"No, well, now that you mention it, you're right. I don't hear it at all," the old man said. Chase agreed that it was indeed gone.

When the neighbor left, the old man and his wife walked back into their house. He set the unique bottle down on the kitchen counter. They both examined it. It was cobalt blue with markings that seemed to be engraved into the bottle. They thought it might be ceramic, but it had a metallic quality to it that made it seem very exotic.

"What do you suppose it is?" Chase asked.

"I don't know, but it seems clear they were reciprocating our little gift," the old man replied. "Apparently, they want us to keep the portal key. Do you suppose it would be safe to open that bottle and try whatever is in it?"

"I don't know," she said. "Maybe we could try it with dinner. Did you take anything out of the freezer yet?"

# Epilogue

*Now I've done more things*
*Than the average guy*
*I don't know why*
*Things just seem worth doing*

He emerged into the bright Southern California sunlight, squinting and hooding his eyes with one hand. He breathed in the warm air, familiar with the scent of sage and rock. He was a Traveler, with a capital "T", and he was just returning from a journey few others ever take. The title was less a position than an honorific given to him by the Overseer, the being who managed travel through the portal.

Once his eyes had adjusted to the change in the light, he surveyed the immediate area to assure himself that he was indeed back home and that no one was close by to see him. He reached into his rucksack to pull out the timepiece given to him by the Overseer. This device was used to determine how much time had elapsed at home since he had been traveling. Time, he had discovered, was not measured in the same way in every alternate universe.

"Good", he thought, "only a few minutes have gone by here". He never traveled without telling his wife, despite the fact that it might only seem like he had been gone a few moments. He always made sure that he did not go to a place that caused a reverse time difference. Who knows what might happen if he thought he was only gone a day or so, and came back to find that many weeks or even years had passed?

He put the valuable timepiece back into his rucksack, and found the portal key in his pocket. He opened the small metallic box to expose the simple control, and shut down the portal. The key was actually a stone embedded inside the box that, when covered by his thumb, caused the portal to open or close. The box had a clever locking mechanism which prevented a casual, mistaken access by somebody who might come across it accidently and wonder what it was.

He headed toward his house, which was about a quarter mile away. He felt young and alive, much younger than his actual age. He couldn't wait to tell Chase about his latest journey. It was his fourth, and each one was remarkable. He was learning the language of the Overseer, and enjoyed visits with him and his mate. There was so much to discover, so much to learn, on both sides of the portal.

He had assured his wife that he would not cross the portal again, but she knew that he would not be able to resist the temptation to explore and experience the new worlds that lay beyond. For his part, he had originally been determined to avoid going back, content to live the life that he had created for his retirement years. As time passed, however, he kept thinking about what else there was to discover beyond that amazing portal.

Eventually, he approached his wife with the question of how she might feel about him taking another peek at the other side. She just looked at him with her "I knew you wouldn't be able to resist" looks. He was prepared to drop it then and there, but ironically her reaction was something he had not expected.

"I think you should go back," she said. "I know how you are, and I know that this will drive you crazy if you don't go, despite the obvious perfidy of your knowledge about such things,"

"I'll have to look up the word 'perfidy', but I presume that you mean that I don't know what I'm getting myself into," he replied. "I don't want to go if it will result in any unhappiness for you,"

"No, I've actually thought quite a lot about this because I knew that someday you would change your mind about going," she said. "I know that this is the kind of thing that you just can't resist, and frankly I think you are the perfect person to go to the other side. I will be worried when you go there, but I've reconciled myself to the eventual inevitability of you exploring this new path that's been laid before you,"

"Really?" he said. He looked intently into her eyes. They both knew each other pretty well after all the years they had been together. He wanted to be sure he wasn't making any heroic assumptions based on what he wanted to hear. In fact, he had assumed she would firmly object, and here she was sounding like she was giving him her blessing. This colored the whole notion going back through with a gravitas he was not prepared for. His decisions to do things were typically based on impulse. Now he would have to think about this idea in the uncomfortable light of objectivity

"Yes," she said, looking back at him with an expression that he could not quite read. "I love you, and I don't know how I would live without you, but I know you well enough to know this is the kind of thing that you were born to do. I can't think of a better person to represent our universe in the other worlds that are out there beyond the portal. I can't go with you. I'm not that kind of person, but I want you to go."

He stood there looking at her. She was an amazing woman, he thought. "I love you."

"I love you too," she said.

And that's how the next adventures began.